MUSIC
FOR SHELLEY'S
POETRY

MUSIC
FOR SHELLEY'S
POETRY

An Annotated Bibliography of
Musical Settings of Shelley's Poetry

by Burton R. Pollin

DA CAPO PRESS • NEW YORK • 1974

Library of Congress Cataloging in Publication Data

Pollin, Burton Ralph.
  Music for Shelley's poetry.

   1. Shelley, Percy Bysshe, 1792-1822—Musical
settings—Bibliography. I. Title.
ML80.S515P6   016.784'3   74-4446
ISBN 0-306-70640-7

Published by Da Capo Press, Inc.
A Subsidiary of Plenum Publishing Corporation
227 West 17th Street, New York, N.Y. 10011

TABLE OF CONTENTS

THE MUSIC COMPOSED FOR SHELLEY'S POETRY
INTRODUCTION

I.   SOURCES OF INSPIRATION

The many musical compositions based on Shelley's
poems, listed in the ensuing text, will give rise to a
number of questions needing a brief treatment in the
introduction. It is my hope that they will be more
fully investigated by students of music, musicology,
poetics, and esthetics after an examination of the
material provided by this book. I can try only to
suggest avenues which may be fruitful, on the basis of
my own experiences of several years in gathering the
data in the United States and Europe. Upon learning of
the number of entries, 1256, the reader may wonder
whether they do not prove Shelley to be the most
popular English poet for settings of music, aside from
Shakespeare. The dearth of compilations of this sort
makes it impossible to do more than hazard a guess,
based in part on the many non-Shelley compositions
which turned up in the British Museum music catalogue
while I was working on this list. Perhaps one might
find more pieces based on Byron and Tennyson than on
Shelley, since as early as 1815 Byron published his
HEBREW MELODIES for Braham's settings--models for
music. Later, during the whole Victorian period, the
vogue of Tennyson's honeyed verses argues the creation
of many musical settings in the style of "Sweet and
Low." It was not my task to collect these musical
settings of poets other than Shelley for the purposes
of comparison, but three published compilations of
settings of nineteenth century poetry may help us to
gauge the relative popularity of Shelley before
examining its causes. In 1939 May Garretson Evans
published her book on MUSIC AND EDGAR ALLAN POE,
listing 252 compositions--not all of them in print. To
these I was able to add almost 200 more, in a 1972
bibliography published in MUSIC AND LETTERS,
representing either omissions in her list or pieces
issued subsequently to 1939. Edgar Allan Poe (1809-
1849), slightly later in period than Shelley (1792-
1821) and with a markedly smaller corpus of poetry,
totals 450 settings. Longfellow, another American poet
of great nineteenth century popularity, has been
collected, I have been told, in the Bowdoin College
music library for many years; Richard Arnell, composer

of one of the Shelley pieces, has informed me that he
has found about 600 Longfellow selections for a list to
be published. Walt Whitman has inspired many musical
compositions. The tally of Bella Landauer is 244 in her
LEAVES OF MUSIC (1937); there are 309 in Henry
Saunders's WHITMAN MUSIC (last "edition" in 1950), and
about 500 in Kenneth Neilson's THE WORLD OF WALT
WHITMAN'S MUSIC (1963).

Two other nineteenth century poets provide a
standard of comparison: Robert Browning and his wife
Elizabeth. Musical settings of their works have been
painstakingly collected at Baylor University in Waco,
Texas, as we learn from the preface to the 1971
bibliography which has received preliminary
"publication" as a mimeographed typescript, before
final printing. This is properly an expansion of
rather than supplement to Broughton's list (see below).
There are 521 entries for Robert and 145 for Elizabeth,
although these figures are inflated through listing
separately each edition in a different key or at a date
later than the first printing. If I had followed a
similar pattern for the Shelley listings, the
equivalent number of entries would total more than
2000. A rough estimate, then, would lead to about 450
separate compositions for Robert Browning and 100 for
Elizabeth. My initial interest in compiling the Shelley
songs stemmed from seeing the much shorter list of
Leslie Nathan Broughton, Clark S. Northrup and Robert
Pearsall in ROBERT BROWNING: A BIBLIOGRAPHY (Ithaca,
1953) pp. 389-402 (a few over 400 entries) and from
soon becoming aware of the inadequacy of the only
existent Shelley list, the 108 entries in John P.
Anderson's bibliographic supplement 7 (pp. xix-xx) to
William Sharpe's 1887 LIFE OF SHELLEY. In Anderson's
list there were a few omissions of items published even
before the 1887 date, but almost all the 1100-odd
additional settings are of a later date. Afterwards I
shall discuss the nature of the specific inspiration
which led to this tremendous expansion of Anderson's
small list. How widespread and keen has been the
interest shown by approximately 1,000 composers in
setting Shelley texts to solo voice and mixed voices,
in songs, choruses, cantatas, operas, and tone poems,
employing in addition to English the languages of
Welsh, German, French, Spanish, Italian, Greek,
Russian, Danish, Finnish and Swedish!

Index II, "The Titles of the Shelley Poems Set by
Composers," gives an inkling of one reason for this

surprising popularity; these show that many deal with
music in their text and in this regard Shelley is
probably preeminent: "Music, when soft voices die,"
"To Music" and "Music." An even larger number implies
that the words are a text for a song to be composed
virtually calling for a composer's efforts: "Hymn of
Pan," "Hymn of Proserpine," "Hymn of Apollo," "Dirge,"
"Cythna's Lament," "Beatrice's Song" (from THE CENCI),
"Indian Serenade," "A Bridal Song," "Weave the Dance,"
"Chorus of Echoes," and "Spirit Song," "Storm Song,"
"Fragment: The Rude Wind Is Singing," "Song to the Men
of England," and "With a Guitar, to Jane." No English
poet, for a comparable body of work, has paid more
attention than has Shelley to the loveliness of music,
often associated with the human voice. This becomes
apparent, in the large number of his references to
music. Studies have shown the importance in Shelley's
work of the role of light, symbol of intellectual
development or enlightenment, and the role of music or
harmony, in a sense symbol of concord, peace and love.
See, for example, one of the few studies purely of
Shelley's poetry in relation to music: May de Rudder's
"La Musicalite de Shelley," in successive issues of the
GUIDE MUSICALE; REVUE INTERNATIONALE DE LA MUSIQUE, of
Bruxelles, in 1907, 53; 587-591, 603-607, 623-626, and
639-643. This double theme is adopted as two of the
conjoined elements in Andre Coeuroy's MUSIQUE ET
LITTERATURE (Paris, 1923), pp. 152-172, and throughout
Helene Le Maitre's interesting book: SHELLEY: POETE DES
ELEMENTS (Paris, 1962), passim and especially pp. 371-
377. Individual poems and especially PROMETHEUS
UNBOUND have been mentioned for their musical
references in the course of general discussions, e.g.
Carl Grabo, THE MAGIC PLANT (Chapel Hill, 1936) and
Newman Ivey White, SHELLEY (New York, 1940), 2.133-134,
which judges PROMETHEUS UNBOUND with its thirty-six
different verse forms to be more like an opera than a
drama. Incidental remarks have linked Shelley to
composers for his lyricism; e.g., see Edouard Schure
in PRECURSEURS ET REVOLTES (Paris, 1920), pp. 78-79,
for a chance comparison of Shelley to Beethoven--not
the most appropriate in my opinion. We should also note
the analysis of Shelley's poetry in terms of musical
elements, such as rhythm, theme, and variations,
embodied by Anna Marie Lichtenberg in her dissertation
(Marburg, 1935), DIE BEDEUTUNG DES MUSIKALISCHEN FUR
DIE AESTHETISCHE EINFUHLUNG IN P. B. SHELLEYS LYRIK.
One wonders why Koszul failed to fulfill his wish to

list all the compositions based on Shelley's texts in
the British Museum, as reported by Coeuroy (p. 153).
The only serious and scholarly treatment that I have
found, of the musical content in Shelley's texts, is
that of Jean de Palacio, in the MODERN LANGUAGE REVIEW
(1964), 59.345-59, "Music and Musical Themes in
Shelley's Poetry." In this well documented study the
author treats of Shelley's interest in music during the
periods before and after 1817 and his use of music as
the key to his concept of the world of spirit or, one
might almost say, universal love. He renders it
unnecessary for me to cite the texts themselves with
their references to the Aeolian harp, the beauty of
song, bird's voices, and the combined ecstasy of the
experience of love and of music-listening. It is clear
that despite the extraordinary euphony of his mature
verse and the great stress upon music in the texts
themselves, Shelley had to learn how to appreciate
music, and this was probably from Claire Clairmont in
1815 as well as from the circle of Leigh Hunt in 1817,
q.v. in "Music at Marlow", by Neville Rogers, KEATS-
SHELLEY MEMORIAL BULLETIN (1953), 5.20-25, and Leigh
Hunt, MUSICAL EVENINGS (Columbia, Mo., 1964). One can
follow the growth of Shelley's musical taste via his
attendance at operas, especially those of Mozart as
recorded in Mary Shelley's Journal. Biographers of
Shelley have not failed to point out that for Percy
Shelley learning to appreciate music was a continuing
process of listening to Constantia Stacey, Jane
Williams, and perhaps others, q.v. in Dowden, SHELLEY
(London, 1886), 2.111, 310, 467, 474.
      One factor in Shelley's early musical awareness
seems to be ignored by the few commentators on the
musicality of Shelley, namely, that his earliest poems
were intended by him to be set to music. Read his
letters to the young musician, Edward Fergus Graham,
who was patronized by Shelley's family (Frederick L.
Jones, LETTERS, 1.21-22, 76, 105-106, 112-113). Indeed
Shelley speaks about the eminent Joseph Woelfl (1773-
1812), Graham's teacher, as being also involved in the
settings (see the sketch in Blom's edition of GROVES'
DICTIONARY). The letters request Graham, as early as
1810 and 1811, to set to music two poems later
published in ST. IRVYNE and also Shelley's translation
of the "Marseillaise." It would appear that even though
the ST. IRVYNE poems contain no allusions to music or
song, Shelley thought of them as the paroles for a
song; he must therefore, have been mindful of their

phonic effects and may have labored to regularize the
meters and the stanzaic pattern accordingly.
Unfortunately, none of Graham's settings have survived,
although the letters prove his collaboration in these,
the earliest songs to Shelley texts, which are among
the few unlocated entries in my listing.

A few other poems obviously intended as songs as
well as the internal references to music show us that
Shelley was interested in the practical relationship
between a poetic text and the music that might ideally
be composed for it. "The Indian Serenade", for example,
was published by Shelley as "Song written for an
Indian Air" in the LIBERAL of 1822 and reprinted by
Mrs. Shelley as "Lines to an Indian Air." This would
represent another early collaboration, in a sense, by
Shelley himself with an unknown composer, who provided
the melody for the "Knautch girls," whom Shelley had
presumably heard in a concert. (For this matter see
"Knautch girls" in my list.) On the other hand, the
same poem was composed, according to another view, to
an aria from Mozart's LA CLEMENZA DI TITO, an effect of
Shelley's love of opera (see Mozart in my entries).
From 1817 on, Shelley's increasing awareness of the
enchantment of music and his many references to music
in his poems would not have guaranteed that composers
find his poems stimulating to their musical
imagination. It is true, as I have indicated above,
that more of his lyrics were directed toward music as
harmonizing agency, especially in the love
relationship, a theme that encourages a musical
setting; in addition there would have to be a division
into manageable stanzaic units, regularity of line
lengths, melodious language, and all the other elements
that enter into the complex problem of setting a poem
to music.

It was Thomas Moore's IRISH MELODIES and Byron's
HEBREW MELODIES that must have contributed not only to
popular awareness in the modern period of the implicit
connection between lyric poetry and song, but also to
Shelley's awareness, subtly shaping his poetic
conceptions. This collaboration of two arts is one of
the aesthetic contributions of the Romantic poets that
has been inadequately studied by students of poetry on
the one hand and musicologists on the other. There is
no lack of articles and books on Renaissance song; the
composer-poets themselves and the close collaborators,
such as Campion and Morley, suggest practices and
conventions in settings, through their works and their

statements. But the latter do nct always bear directly
on the esthetic merits of and the necessary approaches
to the semi-popular and the art song of the nineteenth
century. John Butts, in his POPE, DICKENS AND CTHERS
(1969), pp. 17-38, reminds us that every Elizabethan
lyric poet expected his words tc be set to music.
Philip Miller, in the introduction to THE RING OF WORDS
(1966) speaks of the "drift" of the English composers
into the art-song, an earlier development on the
Continent. One of the best of the recent discussions is
that of Edward T. Cone, "Words into Music: The
Composer's Approach to the Text" in SOUND AND POETRY
(1956), pp. 3-15, but he confines himself largely to a
comparison of the approaches and success of Zelter and
Schubert in setting Goethe lyrics. What is needed is a
thorough study of the increasing effcrts of English
song-writers of the nineteenth century to translate the
poetic essence of lyrics such as those of Shelley into
music; perhaps the organized list in this book along
with a fuller store of copies of the music in the New
York Public Library will lead to one.
     There was an early awareness amcng parlor-music
writers of the value of Shelley's texts for musicians,
as one can see from the items listed under John G.
Barnett, Henry Hugh Pearscn, James William Davidson,
Mrs. Townsend Stith, and Elton (nc. 382). It would be
difficult to maintain, however, that the calibre of the
Shelley music before the last quarter of the nineteenth
century was very high. The stress was upon a simple
ballad type of melodic accompaniment or the highly
decorated melodic line, with a flute obligato (see
Pearson, no. 923) perhaps derived frcm arias in Italian
operas. One should not expect the Shelley musical
compositions to rise above the pedestrian level of the
prevailing musical culture. The knowing and competent
composer, W. H. Hadow--represented by two Shelley
songs--declared that "at the very nadir" of musical
life in England, Sir Hubert Parry's "Scenes" from
PROMETHEUS UNBOUND, at the 1880 Gloucester Festival,
brought a rebirth, thanks to Shelley's drama: "its
flame cf imagery, its soaring verse, the sublimity of
its themes . . . turning passion itself to the service
cf pure beauty" (COLLECTED ESSAYS, Oxford, 1928, pp.
154-155). Whether or not Shelley was indeed responsible
for the new surge in musical awareness and upgrading of
musical standards, there is no question about a surge
in the interest in Shelley's works manifested by very
respectable and even outstanding composers. With a few

exceptions, a list of eminent names for these
compositions far outnumbers any like list that can be
drawn up for Poe, Browning, Whitman, Housman, or other
lyric poets. One need mention only a few: in England,
Elgar, Delius, Bantock, Tovey, Britten and Vaughan
Williams; in America, Macdowell, Barber, Ives, and
Antheil; and, abroad, Spohr, Gounod, Gliere, Arensky,
Myaskovsky, Rachmaninoff, Tcherepnin, Tanayev,
Respighi, Chavez, and Ginastera.

     One may wonder why the 1880's marked the beginning
of this new trend in Shelley settings. The factors
operative in changing "tides of taste" are so complex
that no specific causes can be assigned as
categorically major or minor in this shift. One can
credit, in part, the new, scholarly editions of
Shelley's work, under the aegis of D. G. Rossetti and
H. Buxton Forman (see his Shelley musical composition,
no. 443) and the biographical publications on Shelley
and his large "family," including the Godwins, that Sir
Percy Florence (one of "our" composers) and Lady Jane
sponsored. There were the books of Dowden, Mrs.
Marshall, and Kegan Paul. There was also the founding
of the influential Shelley Society, which distributed
its well-edited monographs and journal or NOTEBOOKS.
Reading through these, one can find many references to
its musical activities and those of English composers,
for example, the rendition by Alma Murray of Beatrice's
farewell song in the 1886 first performance of THE
CENCI at Islington, or the "musical evening", a concert
on 11 May 1887 of twenty (originally intended to be
thirty) Shelley songs. (The Pforzheimer Library copy of
the program added a few entries to my listing.)
Shelley, as eroticist, peeps through the Society's NOTE-
BOOK reference to Rev. Meares's revised version of
Ernest Ford's song, "Good-Night" (see both, as listed).
Certainly, after the turn of the century, it was no
longer the Shelley Society that spearheaded the use of
Shelley texts for music. There is no doubt that the
reputations of Keats and perhaps of Byron have risen
while that of Shelley has been in decline. Whether this
can be matched in the musical settings of his work is
an open question, to the solution of which this listing
may make a small contribution.

     Certainly, among the Victorians one can find a
greater enthusiasm for setting Shelley poems than among
later composers. For example, look at the many songs
composed by "Dolores" or Elizabeth Dickson, the six of
Ernest Ford, the nine of J. Cliffe Forrester, the seven

of Macfarren including two versions of the "Widow
Bird", Storer's "Impromtus" (sic), and Maude White's
four settings. There were early enthusiasts too, as
Pearson shows, and later ones, such as Reginald
Robbins, and Charles Wood, and Ralph Vaughan Williams
and the strangely productive Solomon Pimsleur.
Consider also two others who could not refrain from
setting the same poem twice: Clarence Lucas and J. G.
Williams. It may be surmised that settings as recent as
those of Voormolen in 1971 and cf Arthur Bliss in 1968
indicate that Shelley will continue to inspire
composers.

II. THE VARIED FORMS CF SETTINGS

The appeal of Shelley for composers may, in part,
be indicated by the variety of forms in which settings
can be found. In Newman Ivey White's remark about
PROMETHEUS UNBOUND as an opera, he means, presumably,
the alternation of "arias" and choruses, as in a
musical opera, along with the mythic theme and
fantastic setting, as in Mozart's MAGIC FLUTE. These
aspects have led directly to cantata settings of that
work by Parry and Larsson, with William Christian Selle
setting HELLAS as a cantata, Martin Roeder similarly
scoring PAN and APOLLO, and Arthur Goring Thomas
writing a cantata on "The Swan and the Skylark." THE
CENCI has engaged the interest cf several composers of
opera, such as Berthold Goldschmidt and, in a Spanish
version, Alberto Ginastera, whose work opened the
Kennedy Memorial Theatre in Washington, in September
1971. The two operas by Rota and Rozycki raise
questions of directness of inspiration and ambiguous
sources which have only been suggested in the
necessarily brief annotation for the entries. For
example, it may be that Rozycki knew of Shelley's
version of The Cenci only through the version of the
play by the gifted liberal Pole, Slowacki. I can not
tell whether the latter was writing his own version of
Shelley's CENCI, to be used as an implicitly
revolutionary statement about the rape of Beatrice,
i.e. Poland, by Father Cenci, i.e. Russia. Limited in
my sources, through lack of Polish and lack of books on
Slowacki in America, I could do no more than prove
through Slowacki's letters in French about Shelley that
he knew English literature and the facts of Shelley's
life and admired him as a man and a writer. The absence
of treatments of the theme before Shelley's work and,

save for a brief work by Stendhal, before Slowacki's
life, makes it likely that this was indeed based on
Shelley's CENCI, hence to be listed for Rozycki's
derived opera. A similar instance was that of Giuseppe
Rota's opera, based on a Cenci play, presumably
Shelley's since that was the only dramatic version of
the tale. I was led to ferreting out Rota's little
known work through an error in Woodberry's edition of
THE CENCI. In listing translations of Shelley's play,
he ascribed an opera to Niccolini, which I list as
decidedly questionable by reason of his dates. This was
probably a matter of Woodberry's confusion about the
Italian version of THE CENCI by G. B. Niccolini of
1844, all of which is briefly indicated in my listing.
     Before discussing other types of compositions in my
listings, I must pursue the matter of the stimulus
given composers by the play THE CENCI, with its clear
direction that Beatrice sing a song, "False Friend, and
Wilt Thou Smile" in Act V, scene iv. The write-up of
the earliest performance of the play led me to recover
the name of the composer if not his music, the score of
B. L. Mosely for the 1886 Grand Theatre Performance at
Islington. It then seemed necessary for me to follow
this lead by checking on all performances of the play
in English and other languages. The path led from the
first to the highly experimental and free French
version of 1935 by Antonin Artaud in Paris, with
striking and avant garde musical effects by Roger
Descrmiere. The next production with music was in 1940,
at Bellingham, Washington, with a song drawn by Donald
Bushell from Schumann's "Romance." In 1950 a production
at the Walt Whitman School in New York City required a
music score by a Mr. Reiz, according to a German-
language newspaper; no further information about the
production by a now defunct school was available,
despite my inquiries. Next, in 1958 came the University
of Chicago production under Norbert Hruby and Otto
Preminger, with the song composed by Dolores Hruby. The
next year saw an Old Vic production with music by John
Lambert. Finally, early in 1971, we note another
production, at Cafe La Mama, this time in English,
adapted or translated from Artaud's French version of
Shelley's English play, with music by David Walker.
Later in the year, comes Alberto Ginastera's Spanish
version, based on a script by Girri and Sands,
obviously drawn from Shelley although not acknowledged
in the libretto which Boosey and Hawkes was able to
send me. Perhaps it might be added that for most of

this research, the drama section of the New York Public
Library, with its well-catalogued clipping file and
playbills, was invaluable.
     Other large forms beside operas can be found
derived from Shelley's texts although the connection is
often not a literal setting of the text. Elgar, after
setting two poems, one as a song and the other as a
four-part choral piece, used "Rarely, Rarely, Comest
Thou, Spirit of Delight" as a motto for his second
symphony in 1911. Similarly, Gnessin's 1910 Symphonic
fragment prints a line from PROMETHEUS UNBOUND on the
cover. In 1906-09, Gustave Samazeuilh in the dramatic
poem for orchestra called LA NEF develops the myth of
Prometheus according to both Aeschylus and Shelley, as
his preliminary note explains. Compare these rather
vague connections with that shown by Hans Werner Henze
in his 1955 piece for violoncello and orchestra in five
sections which correspond to the five sections of "Ode
to the West Wind", which Henze prints as an
introduction to his score. The most purely allusive of
Shelley orchestral scores is that which Nikolai
Myaskovsky designates as ALASTOR: POEM FOR ORCHESTRA
without giving any further correspondence to the text.
This sort of thematic or onomastic connection is more
common among composers of short instrumental pieces;
for example, in 1888 Macdowell published a piano piece
with the "Widow Bird" as epigraph, long after W. H.
Grattann's 1850 piano suiteof "Musical Thoughts
Suggested by English Poets," one of which is based on
two lines of Shelley verse. In 1924 Harry Vibbard set
"Indian Serenade" for organ alone, with the solo part
carried by the English horn or clarinet stop, and the
words entirely missing from the text. More
impressionistically, in 1919 John Gerrard Williams
published "Three Miniatures on Poems by . . . Shelley"
for piano with a preliminary printed text but no
specified melodic line to correspond to that text.
Scarcely more literal is the "humming song" by Marcel
de Temmerman called "La Complainte de l'automne" in
which the total omission of words, whether in English
or French, makes it impossible even to be sure of what
text the composer had in mind. In general, of course,
this problem does not exist, since most of the items
are songs or choral pieces with Shelley's text printed
under the notes. The different combinations for which
composers have scored Shelley's text hold some
interest, and might lead to speculations about the
inherent nature of the stimulus to the musical

imagination provided by a poet's text. As an early
example of keyboard accompaniments of voice plus
another instrument, we note Pearson's 1836 "Hymn of
Proserpine" which is scored for piano and flute;
Macfarren's 1867 "Widow Bird," for piano and "clarionet
or harmonium"; Dudley Buck's 1905 chorus from
PROMETHEUS UNBOUND for piano, flute, and string
quartet; Respighi's beautiful quartet accompaniment for
"Il tramonto" ("The Sunset") of 1912; Karnavicius's
1924 "Music, When ..." for piano and viola; Arthur
Berdahl's 1936 "Dirge" for chorus and kettle drum; and
Elwyn Hughes's 1936 "Earth-Moon Dialogue" from
PROMETHEUS UNBOUND for electronic music." Alan
Hovhaness converts the melodic line of his "Lament"
into an alternate piece for trombone and piano.
Alexander voormolen enjoys the color of the celesta and
string orchestra for his 1971 setting of "The
Recollection," the last piece added to my list. Other
combinations beside varied types of choral versions, a
capella and with piano accompaniment, are almost too
numerous to mention. There is Selmer's 1890 set of
three songs for baritone and tenor plus orchestra,
influenced probably by arias in cantatas. As items of
"curiosa" I cite Max Schroeter's 1881 "Canzonetta: I
fear thy kisses" for the opera NAUSICAA and John S.
Crandell's 1910 duet for the "musical play" called THE
DEBUTANTE, with the lyrics combined from Shelley's
"Good-night" and verse by Thomas Moore. Finally,
mention might be made of Gnessin's "Declamation for
piano" of Beatrice's song from THE CENCI, a piece for
which I have searched in vain.
      Another broad category of unusual settings
circumscribes a set of pieces which Philip Miller once
described to me, graphically, as "shoe-horned" music;
this concerns the use by one composer of the melody of
another composer--often of fame--with adaptations for
the words of a poem. It produces such oddities in my
list as a 1684 item by Michael Wise used as a setting
for Shelley's "To Suffer Woes," arranged by Henry
Leland Clarke for a 1964 book of hymns. Both composers
must be listed in my bibliography. For this reason we
find Mozart, Gluck, Weber, and Rubinstein. Similarly,
two composers have gone rather far afield, in the area
of folk song: H. Elliot Button bases his 1910 choral
piece, "Swifter Far," upon a German folk song and
Charles Elliot in 1887 arranges words, without
specifying the Shelley source--probably "Matilda
Gathering Flowers"--for a chorus with music arranged

from a Peruvian dance." This melange, published by
Schmidt of Boston, turned up only in the East Berlin
music catalogue. Another type of matching of a set
melody to Shelley's words is the use of standard,
anonymous hymn tunes, as demonstrated by Patrick
Hadley. Perhaps Shelley himself would be more likely to
favor the use of his words for workers' songs, q. v.
under "anonymous," William Henry Bell, John Jones, and
Leonard Pearce. It may be assumed that there are more
of these than it has been possible to collect (see, for
example, F. E. L. Priestley, Godwin's ENQUIRY, 1946,
3.108, note 50).

Several of the names mentioned above, such as that
of Karnavicius, remind me of musical settings of poems
by other authors. A certain interest would attach to a
comparative study of the approaches to song settings
used by the same composer for the texts of different
lyric poets. My comparative "statistics" serve the
purpose also of showing their relative appeal and the
factors operating in musical culture. The lists of the
music for Edgar Allan Poe and for the two Brownings
enable me to point out which composers in my list have
been interested also in setting poems by the other
three poets. For Poe the names are given with the title
of the poem or tale musically set in parentheses
(details may be had from May G. Evans's book):
Creighton Allen (many Poe poems), F. C. Bornschein
("The Conqueror Worm"), Arthur Foote ("The Bells"),
Harvey Gaul ("Prayer"), Gnessin ("The Conqueror Worm"),
Stanley Hawley ("The Bells"), Cuthbert Harris ("The
Bells"), Bruno Huhn ("Eldorado" and "Israfel"),
Karnavicius (several), Ernest R. Kroeger ("Annabel
Lee"), Georg Liebling ("Annabel Lee"), Clarence Lucas
(four songs), Macdowell ("Eldorado", a fragment),
George Marston, who composed on a false Shelley text
("Eldorado"), Myaskovsky ("Silence"), Julian Mount
("Annabel Lee," not in M. G. Evans's list but included
in my supplement in MUSIC AND LETTERS, 1972),
Rachmaninoff ("The Bells"), Hugh Roberton ("Annabel
Lee" and "The Bells"), Martin Shaw ("Annabel Lee"),
Arthur Somervell ("Annabel Lee" and "Eldorado"), David
Stone, who set a false Shelley entry ("The Bells"),
Arthur Sullivan ("To One in Paradise"), Tcherepnin
("The Masque of the Red Death"), and Max Vogrich
("Annabel Lee").

A collation of Shelley-text composers with those in
Sally East's list for the two Brownings of 1971 (pp. 71-
80) yields the following names: for Robert Browning--

Granville Bantock, Alice Barnett, A. H. Behrend, Arthur Berdahl, Arthur Bergh, Alice Borton, Rutland Boughton, E. A. Bruguiere, Frederic Bullard, Noble Cain, Henry L. Clarke, Reginald Clarke, J. W. Clokey, Samuel Coleridge-Taylor, C. W. Coombs, H. W. Davies, Norman Demuth, Clarence Dickinson, Louis Drakeford, Roland Farley, J. Cliffe Forrester, E. V. Freer, H. K. Hadley, Julius Harrison, Henry Hudson, Bruno Huhn, J. P. Hullah, H. V. Jervis-Read, Ncel Johnson, Arthur Kramer, Liza Lehmann, Samuel Liddle, C. A. Lidgey, Frank Lynes, W. H. Neidlinger, Ethelbert Nevin, Juliet Raphael, George Rathbone, Arthur Somervell, C. V. Stanford, G. W. Stebbins, Ward Stephens, B. Treharne, Maude V. White, and R. Vaughan Williams (a total of forty-five). For Elizabeth Barrett Browning the "double-text" composers are F. N. Barbour, Alice Barnett, A. M. Beach, Noble Cain, Alfred J. Caldicott, R. C. Clarke, Samuel Coleridge-Taylor, Edward Elgar, E. E. Freer, Harvey Gaul, H. K. Hadley, C. B. Hawley, Lawrence Kellie, W. Metcalfe, Florian Pascal (i.e., Joseph Williams), Harold Rhodes, William Scharfenberg, Lindsey Sloper, D. S. Smith, C. V. Stanford, Mario Castelnuovo-Tedesco, B. Treharne, E. J. Troup, Kate Vannah, M. V. White, Healey Willey, and Charles Wood (a total of twenty-seven). One might note that the names of eminent composers who have set both Poe and Shelley include only Rachmaninoff and Arthur Sullivan, Tscherepnin, and Myaskovsky. The only other "eminence" on the Poe list who did not do any setting for Shelley was Debussy. On the Browning list the highest level of "fame" might be shown by Ethelbert Nevin, Arthur Somervell, Samuel Coleridge-Taylor, Henry Hadley, and Reginald de Koven (the last not on the Shelley list). Similarly, on the Elizabeth Barrett Browning list, only Edward Elgar and S. Coleridge-Taylor ring the bell of recognition for those who are not musical specialists.

It is interesting to observe the errors that composers have made in their handling of the texts and titles of so-called Shelley poems; the importance of Shelley's name, very early in the development of the setting of Shelley pieces, is one of the inferences that we can draw. For good reason these errors must be included in my listing. In 1833 the second earliest piece set in the United States, duly copyrighted and published, was that of Charles Zeuner, published by C. Bradlee of Boston and entitled "The Glories of Our Mortal State: A Sacred Song written by Shelly" (sic). Surely the ascription to Shelley of this famous work by

the Jacobean poet James Shirley so soon after Shelley's
death is proof of the broad flight of "The Skylark."
One wonders why D. Cyril Jenkins, composer of three
more Shelley songs, should have made the same error in
1925. And in what anthology printed abroad was "Annabel
Lee" misattributed to Shelley, causing Eduard Levy to
publish his song thus, in Berlin in the present
century? Are we to assume a similar anthology error for
Skeete's attributing to Shelley his Wordsworth text,
"She Dwelt among the Untrodden Ways," in 1878, and
likewise David Stone, composer of "To a Snow Drop"
(1960)? Could any collection of verse have misled H.
Shepherd into ascribing "Music, When Soft Voices Die"
to Keats (1915), or Ned Rorem in so attributing "Now I
Lay Me Down to Sleep" (1956)? At least two more sets of
paroles have no connection with Shelley, although one
can not even guess the source of the errors. The first
is C. W. Marston's "If I Had but Two Little Wings"
(Boston, 1868); in 1875 Marston published Shelley's
"Indian Serenade" as a song. Similarly one wonders
about the printed source of Harold Jervis-Read's London
publication in 1920 of "Shelley's Day Dream: While
Skies Are Blue." More ambiguous is a text said to be
adapted by Henry Hudson, "Night: How Beautiful Is
Night," which may have come from QUEEN MAB. One source
of misattribution, especially important because Delius
included it among his lovely Shelley settings, is "To
the Queen of My Heart," sometimes called "Shall We
Roam, My Love"; the story of this hoax by James
Augustus St. John, dating from the early 1830's, is
told in detail in Woodberry's Cambridge edition of
Shelley's poems (1901), p. 589. The poem appeared in
enough editions of the works and anthologies to mislead
many composers, as the index of titles in my book
quickly reveals.

My references to the Shelley settings by
Rachmaninoff, Ginastera, Respighi, and others raise the
question of the translation of the texts used by
composers. The popularity of particular poems dating
from a given period in a specific country may be
largely attributable to the appearance of a good
translation of the poet's works--a causative factor
that the mere statistical figures may not even suggest.
This is undoubtedly true of the emergence of Shelley
settings in Russia after the publication in two volumes
of Constantin Balmont's translations of various Shelley
poems (1894-95). Finding, in the Library of Congress,
these two rare books would enable me, I thought, to

puzzle out which poems of Shelley's had been set by
Arensky, Blumenfeld, Krejn, Tanayev, and Tcherepnin.
The aid of a few translator-friends had not helped me,
in every case, to determine the text, since the
original Russian translation was too free to make such
identification possible. Unfortunately Balmont did not
indicate in any way which of Shelley's poems he was
translating; hence there are about five Russian entries
that cannot be listed under the title of the original
poem. Eventually, all the included Italian songs, by
Ghedini, Fedeli, Gazzotti, or Respighi could be
identified. In this long process of tracking down the
originals, I have found F. S. Ellis's book LEXICAL
CONCORDANCE (1892) to Shelley's poems invaluable,
although occasionally faulty or misleading in terms of
more recent scholarship. In any event, the index of
foreign language translations may prove useful to
anyone doing work in the whole area of "Shelley
Abroad," for there exists no general compilation, to my
knowledge, of the poems as translated into various
foreign tongues. My list might add translations in the
following: Welsh, French, Spanish (a free adaptation
here, rather than translation), Italian, Greek,
Russian, Polish, Finnish, German, Dutch, Swedish, and
Danish. My effort to add Hungarian, Rumanian, and
Japanese to the languages of the songs through letters
to music libraries and resident scholars has met with
no success at all.

III.   CULLING THE DATA

It may be useful, as well as occasionally amusing,
for me to describe the exact process of search and
research which yielded this long list of Shelley
settings. Its inception lay in my attempt to supply the
music to Shelley texts by Henry Hugh Pearson indicated
in footnote references in Mary Shelley's letters (F.
L. Jones, ed., 1948) concerning Pearson, a friend of
her son Percy Florence, who was accompanying the two
Shelleys on a trip to Germany and Italy. I was
determined to trace Pearson's CHARACTERISTIC SONGS OF
SHELLEY, said to be unavailable. The details of that
partly successful search were described in my article
in MUSIC AND LETTERS (October 1965). Thereafter, I
began collecting notes for a full list of Shelley
pieces, in libraries here and abroad. Thus, in the
summer of 1967 a visit to Edinburgh enabled me to
consult the parolier catalogue of the National Library

there and add about eighty composers to my list. The
parolier catalogues, here and abroad, I eventually
discovered, were few indeed. Perhaps my designating
them may save time for researchers on other poets. In
America I know only of those in the New York Public
Library and the Library of Congress, both of which are
markedly incomplete. Correspondence with curators of
prominent collections in other cities and the major
universities of the United States added few entries to
my list, although visits to Yale and Harvard were
fruitful. In Europe I found that the Bibliotheque
Nationale Music Library of Paris, and Lausanne
Bibliotheque Cantonale et Universitaire had music under
the paroliers. That was about all. This method yielded
only about 400 titles to be added to the 106 listed in
Anderson's bibliographic supplement to the 1886 LIFE OF
... SHELLEY by William Sharpe, mentioned above. Next I
circulated a questionnaire in rexographed form, with
reply envelopes included, to composers listed as
holding posts in universities and colleges in the
United States. This requested the name, academic
affiliation and address, title of any Shelley setting
and of the original poem and first line, full
publication data if any, or performance data, plans if
any for publication, length and type of piece, and
availability of a copy either by purchase or some
method of duplication. This elicited about 150 more
items for my list, and also many copies of manuscript
compositions, graciously sent gratis for full recording
in my bibliography. I should explain that early in my
search, I had decided to seek a purchased copy or
duplicated copy (if not published) of all pieces, for
two purposes: 1. to study and compare the material in
the course of listing and describing the music; 2.
eventually to donate to the library a copy of every
piece not in the collection of the NYPL at Lincoln
Center. This would make it much easier for students of
Shelley's music to verify for themselves the texts and
the music, to make evaluative judgments about relative
merits and quality, and perhaps to copy the scores in
order to play the material at home or in concert. In
1969 The Pforzheimer Foundation graciously made
available to me the sum of $1,000, administered through
the NYPL, for the purchase and duplication of any music
materials encountered here and abroad. This was
entirely expended for printed, xeroxed, and microfilmed
copies of about 500 titles, which will go to the
Library and for which the ensuing book will serve as a

catalogue, by prearrangement.

Grants from the Research Foundation of the New York State University, of which my college is a member, have enabled me to make summer trips to European collections and visits to libraries in Boston and Washington, D. C. more than once. While I have not kept figures on successive discoveries in different places, it might be interesting for me to indicate a few facts and experiences. The Houghton Library of Harvard University proved to have a small parolier catalogue for items in its collection, and fortunately it was rich in Shelley music, especially of American provenance, for the end of the nineteenth century. About twenty-five "new" pieces were added from that source; the Boston Public Library also had about fifteen titles for which I had long searched in vain, even some published in England. The Bibliotheque Naticnale provided about forty largely French titles through its catalogue and files; the microfilms of the music eventually had to be converted into flo-print copies for the collection. The East Berlin Library-- access to which required going through "checkpoint Charlie" several times--listed about 100 Shelley pieces, although finding the songs themselves (and each had to be examined for length of piece and other data) was more difficult since the collection of music had been divided between the library on Unter den Linden and the West German Library in Dahlem, at the other end of Berlin. Some shuttling between the two collections consumed a solid and very warm week during the summer of 1969. Trips to the libraries at Milan, Florence, and Rome in 1971 added several Italian items to the Shelley list, as well as to the 1972 "Supplement to the Poe Music List" of May G. Evans. Canvassing the libraries of Barcelona and Madrid proved that the only Spanish item was indeed Ginastera's opera of 1911, based on THE CENCI. The national library in Vienna yielded one of the missing Pearson songs, after my searching for years, and a few other items including the 1894 American publication by Pease in a song journal, unfound in America, of "Indian Serenade." Correspondence with a kind official of the Glinka Museum of Moscow yielded a "new" song by Karnavicius and a copy of one already in my listing but not seen (Blom's version of GROVE'S DICTIONARY provided these "unseen" clues). But the largest and most important sources were the British Museum and the Library of Congress. Two separate summer-time visits to the first

provided me with at least 400 additional titles and
almost as many xeroxed copies of the music. The special
music catalogue, unfortunately not printed for
distribution abroad, lists music by composer and by
title. Hence by tracing "Music, When Soft Voices Die"
or "Good Night" or "Love's Philosophy, I found a wealth
of material hitherto undreamed of. Moreover, since
each of the songs, comprising the major portion of my
findings, was bound in with the music for that year, I
could sift through the rest of the album, and often
discover Shelley songs with non-Shelley titles. For
example, "Indian Serenade," often called "I Arise from
Dreams of Thee," might also appear under "From Dreams
of Thee" and "Dreams of Thee". (My forgetting to look
up "Of thee" may have caused the omission of some
worthy claimant for listing.) "My Soul Is an Enchanted
Boat" twice became "Enchanted Boat," and finding that
one Shelley poem was set as "Heart's Devotion" led me
to another by the same title. Unfortunately incomplete,
however, were the catalogue listings, since hundreds of
"Good-Nights" and "To Music" and "Music and Moonlight"
and "The Skylark" (for "To a Skylark") proved to have
non-Shelley texts. Yet the rewards justified the
effort, even for only one title out of twenty bound
volumes sifted and scanned. The unfailing courtesy and
aid of the British Museum staff, which I had frequently
drawn upon for earlier research projects, need to be
experienced to be believed. Occasionally items were
missing or absent from their collection. Supplementary
trips to the Royal College of Music and the British
Broadcasting Company music library were helpful for
finding these.
     One more repository of music needs discussion--the
Library of Congress catalogues and files both in
Washington, D. C. and across the river in Crystal City,
Virginia. It was a surprise to me to learn that to do
justice to the copyright materials, I would have to
spend many days in this Virginia enclave of government
buildings across the river ten or fifteen miles out of
the city. Only thus could I see the lists of
copyrighted materials from about 1890 to the present,
first cumulated from 1903 to 1915, as I recall, then
to 1923, and then for shorter intervals. For the last
twenty years, I believe, parolier references have been
filed in the published catalogue, so that Shelley
appeared therein for registered copyright entries that
would otherwise have been overlooked, save by the lucky
chance of my looking up a likely title, such as "Love's

Philosophy". But these volumes did not list "Shelley"
as a subject. I found that the catalogues for the
"assignment of rights" in Crystal City also yielded
items, especially when the original piece was composed
by someone in England so that it never received a
registration in this country. This was rare, since most
of the English publishers copyright their songs in the
United States as well. One major source of difficulty
was the inadequacy of the listings for copyrights,
which permitted songs such as "To the Moon" to be
registered with an attribution, "Shelley's words", but
with no statement of the exact text. Thus for a few
titles of unpublished music I could not verify the
exact poem being set, even though I checked through the
bound volumes of the original registration statements
in the basement archives of the Copyright Building in
Crystal City. Fortunately, a few of the registration
forms gave a little more information than the catalogue
cards themselves, so that the entries left unidentified
are few.

     There is little need to do more than mention some
of the other standard reference tools that pointed the
way to full data and, sometimes, to procurable copies
of the settings of Shelley. These are almost all listed
in the list of symbols, used for the fifth field or
section of my data, called "g" or general provenance
and other data; the tools include the Anderson
bibliography in Sharpe's biography of Shelley, the
British Broadcasting Company catalogues, the yearly
British Catalogue of Music, listing all copyrighted
works published in England, the Brown music catalogue
of the Boston Public Library, the UNITED STATES
INFORMATION SERVICE CATALOGUE OF PUBLISHED MUSIC BY
AMERICAN COMPOSERS (1964), SEARS'S CATALOGUE OF SONGS
and the SUPPLEMENT, GROVE'S DICTIONARY OF MUSIC AND
MUSICIANS (Eric Blom revision), DIE MUSIK IN GESCHICHTE
UND GEGENWART, Pazdirek's twenty-four volume set of
titles, the MUSICAL NEWS article on Shelley songs (16
Dec. 1922, p. 564), the catalogues and collections of
numerous universities here and abroad (Yale, Columbia,
Oxford), and the quarterly publication of the Donemus
music foundation of Amsterdam, SPECUIUM SONORIS.
Uniformly, publishers have been a source of information
and assistance, often sending copies of their work
gratis for listing and inclusion in the Shelley
collection; a few that I remember are Boosey and
Hawkes, Shawnee Press, Donemus, Novello, Joseph
Williams, Enoch and Sons, Curwen Music Co., Paterson's,

and Edwin Ashdown. I should also mention the happy
coincidence of finding that Mrs. Verona Clifford in the
sales department at Schirmer's Music Store in New York
City had an old handwritten notebook compiled by a
young employee, listing by authcr or parolier the vocal
pieces previously sold in Schirmer's. This alcne
provided a clue to about fifteen American songs on
Shelley texts that had disappeared from all places
(even Schirmer's) except the Library of Congress files,
although they had not, for some reason, appeared in the
Library of Congress catalogues. More to be expected,
but surprising to me, was discovering through a visit
to the Bodleian at Oxford University that some kind
curator had culled from its printed music all pieces on
Shelley texts for insertion intc its special Shelley
collection of documents. From this, I was able to
supply data for and texts of abcut five songs missing
from the British Museum collection and about ten that
had never been listed in it. Clearly, compiling this
list and accumulating the supplementary materials, that
is, the copies of many hundreds cf pieces, required
voluminous correspondence, a personal search through
countless volumes and pages and catalogues, graciously
provided by the staffs of many libraries, the funds
needed for almost yearly trips abroad in the summer and
short visits to Washingtcn and Eoston, and the full and
generous cooperation of my own college for the
computerizing aspect of the work--of which more later.
     It early appeared obviously necessary to have some
means cf organizing so much data, of indexing it, and
of printing it out with ncne of the errors that
typesetters of bibliographic material of an
unconventional style so often introduce into their
expensive labors. Having computerized the texts and
indices of two previous bcoks (GODWIN CRITICISM and
DICTIONARY OF NAMES AND TITLES IN POE'S CCLLECTED
WORKS), I soon decided to prepare the material as a
computerized listing via the computer, an IBM 360/30,
in the laboratory of my college, directed by Mr. Meyer
Shopkcw. I had splendid ccoperation in having my text
programmed, after securing some outside financial
assistance, chiefly for keypunching the whole text. I
found, as I had previously learned from my other two
printouts, that one can carry "much in little" via a
computer printout. Thus, when I went abroad, in 1969
and 1971, I took with me a printout text, successively
larger, of course, which was organized as follows. All
the data were planned for five separate fields, divided

by a keypunched slash plus a letter for each one. These
were free fields, following successively and
continuously on the keypunched cards, according to the
amount of data and filed, one after the other. A
separate entry-number field began each item. Then came
a slash plus a "c" followed by the composer's name
(last name first). This was followed by a slash plus a
"t" (for the title of the piece) and then came a slash
plus a "p" (for the data of publication, namely, city,
company, and date or, for reprints, dates). The next
field was designated by a slash plus a "d", that is,
roughly a description of the piece, such as the
scoring, number of pages, and sequence of appearance in
an album. Last came a slash plus a "g", for general
information, this being the provenance, especially for
rare works or ambiguous and unfound entries, which
might be listed in GROVE'S DICTIONARY, the language of
the original, and the collection where a copy might be
found. If a xeroxed copy was in my own collection,
eventually to be donated to the music library at
Lincoln Center, the symbol "x" for "xeroxed copy held"
is included, and actually appears in hundreds of
entries. For long the alphabetization of these entries
remained only approximate, since it was expected that
eventually the machine would realphabetize all the
entries and assign strict and accurate index numbers to
each. Hence, I could add new entries with subnumbers,
such as 32a, 106a and 106b, between the others or at
the end of the entries. While abroad, I usually wrote
new entries into my computerized printout with all the
data given as fully as possible. My expectation of
having a xerox copy following me by mail made this
procedure less hazardous in the long run. Eventually I
prepared a looseleaf notebook sheet for each entry, on
which I had space to record fuller data than was needed
even by my final listing save for special questions
that I found arising. Toward the rather tedious last
stage of the whole project, the programmer, Mr. Kenneth
Weisman, gave me new printouts of the text, showing
realphabetizations of the entries. Since the cards were
inserted at different periods according to only
approximate alphabetizations, and since the correction
of entries, an almost continuous process for three
years, sometimes changed the order of entries, I
finally had to have a whole new set of cards extracted
by the computer from the tape, reordering all of the
cards. One serious error which I made cost me many
hours over lost and misplaced cards; I neglected to

assign a record number to each card, in the assumption
that this would make the whole keypunching task easier.
In fact, ways could easily have been devised for
preventing this, such as using prepunched cards, in
successive arrangements. I could have saved,
ultimately, a few hundred hours spent in looking for
cards, inserted by my assistant keypunchers, out of
order or misplaced in the printcuts by laboratory
technicians handling the cards with less than perfect
care. Such errors are inevitable, and I was inviting
fate to add to the necessary tedium and difficulties of
a project like this.

Toward the end of the project, Mr. Weisman and I
consulted often on questions of formatting and
reorganization of data. For one thing, we had used a
free field method with open spaces within each field
when corrections required them. A program had to be
used for closing up spaces between words. Then another
was needed for printing only whole words at the end of
a line of printout, and another for examining each
field, printed out separately, such as the titles
field, so that I could determine the parameters to be
needed for the extraction, or the publication data, to
show the companies publishing Shelley music to enable
me to determine the accuracy of capitalization,
punctuation and spelling. For every field, I asked the
programmer to print out the "empty" or omitted field
entries so that I could determine the reason for the
omission. Gradually too, I was able to insert cross-
reference entries, when names could be found in two
forms: Godfery-Sommeren) or "Dolores" for "Dickson,
Elizabeth." The punctuation that I had decided upon
used minimal capitalization, in view of the nuisance
enjoined by the asterisks before each letter for a
capital. These were needed for ultimately triggering
the upper case letters on the print chain. Periods
would be regarded as dividers between separate pieces
of information in the same field. I closed up the space
between a number and "p." for "pages," such as "3p." on
the grounds that with a computerized text, this is more
immediately meaningful. For the titles I arbitrarily
cut capitals down to the first word only, including
"a," "an," and "the," to avoid "back-flapping"
procedures for the indexing, always a difficult
programming matter. In this way too, since I had no
italics to designate song books and long poems or
plays, such as THE CENCI, I differentiated between a
poem and a full work by capitalizing all the words in a

book title. Only a few words in the poem titles, such
as names of classical deities, were allowed to retain
their capitals in the text itself. A change in our
programming, after the text was finished, enabled me to
capitalize every letter of book titles in this
introduction. Hence, there is a discrepancy in this
respect between the sections. For other programming
reasons the capitalization of names like Macdowell
varies. The spelling of the original title was given in
the form authorized by the Oxford University Press
edition, Thomas Hutchinson, editor (1967 printing).
(Arbitrarily I changed "sate" to "sat" in "A Widow Bird
Sate Mourning.") The use of this popular, fairly
accurate, and inexpensive edition was intended to make
the poem set fully available to students. Although
there is, unfortunately, no alphabetized table for the
titles in the Oxford edition, the index of first lines,
makes it almost as easy to consult as the older, less
accurate Cambridge edition; early I anticipated the
need, in my book, to have indexes both of titles and
of first lines. In extracting or printing out a new set
of cards from the corrected computer tape, which had
alphabetized all the materials, I allowed the machine
to determine the alphabetization, even for "Mcalpin,"
which comes after "Matthews" in my listing. I have not
wished to frustrate the will of the friendly computer
in such minor points! In one type of instance I had to
circumvent the strict logic of the machine--titles that
were identical but had a different text and titles in
which the first word or phrase of the whole was a
complete title for the second, as in "Time" and "Time
Long Past." By inserting a multiple punch character
that does not print out any symbol but serves to
differentiate one title from the other for indexing
purposes. This factor also explains the way in which we
had to print out titles together with the first line
for such ambiguous items as "Lines." I finally assigned
record numbers to every single card, in "tens" to
enable me to make corrections and insertions. This was
a great help in the final stages of proofreading, but
it still led to difficulties when three new entries
suddenly appeared after the "final" cards had been
prepared or when a space was left before the comma in
"Smith, W.", thereby causing this "Smith" to appear
before all the other "Smiths." The "Smiths" could be
shuffled around, but the three new entries, in the
early part of the alphabet required a redisking and
renumbering of all the entries; fortunately, this

crisis occurred just before the final extraction of the
indexes which otherwise would have been all wrong in
the designated numbers. Only a few Shelley-composers
were found too late to be included in the text. I
record them here: "I Arise from Dreams Thee," by
Davivid Lee, a song for solo voice and piano, printed
in the weekly magazine THE SUNBEAM, published by J. W.
Southgate, Circulating Library, London, December 29,
1838, vol. 1, no. 48, pp. 379-380; in the New York
Public Library, main collection. More recently, Robert
Turner published "Prophetic Song," for treble chorus,
22 pages, Peer Music Publishers, 1971, a capella, using
as text the final chorus from HELLAS. Finally,
Professor Oksana Klymowycz, librarian at Bronx
Community College, has brought to my attention the
Shelley-music of the eminent Ukrainian composer Victor
Samokhvalov (1895-1968). The Shelley titles must be
inferred from the titles given only in Ukrainian and,
for the last, in Russian. They are as follows: No. 4 of
Five romances for bass and piano, opus 5, composed 1922
and published by MUSICAL UKRAINE, 1969 TWO ROMANCES FOR
HIGH VOICE WITH PIANO, opus 10, the first being "My
Dreams Fade when I Am Alone," and the second being "To
the Moon," composed in 1924 and published by the State
Music Publisng House in 1926; Four romances for middle
voice with piano, all to the texts of Shelley--
"Harmonious Songs do not Sound," "I Fear Thy Kisses,"
"Good-night" and "Time Long Past," the whole comprising
opus 14, composed in 1924 and published in 1968 by
MUSICAL UKRAINE; OZYMANDIAS, SONG FOR BASSO AND PIANO,
opus 15, composed 1924 and published 1968 by MUSICAL
UKRAINE; and a manuscript song of 1931, in Russian,
"Days Long Past." These eleven entries would raise the
total in the text to 320, of which about twenty-five
are cross reference items.

     In planning the indexes, I had to give about 200
keypunched parameters for extraction to Mr. Weisman,
which had their equivalents in the set titles
corresponding to the Oxford SHELLEY. Extractions had to
avoid duplicates, such as "To the Moon," for which
there are three separate Shelley poems. By
concentrating upon a unique phrase or giving a large
enough parameter to render duplication on the machine
impossible, we were able to make the extraction of
titles accurate. In planning the whole, I had not
completely envisioned the process to be used for
titles and first line extractions; therefore, there is
some unnecessary duplication in the titles of such

songs as "An Indian Serenade (fcr "Indian Serenade)"
where the parenthesis represents the Oxford edition
title rather than that given by the composer. Some
extractions were made in terms cf part of the first
line given in the title, largely because the composer's
title often was very different from Shelley's title.
For example, Shelley's "To Mary" becomes "Mary Dear";
hence, I extracted "Oh Mary dear". Since the computer
was given a set of equivalent parameters for the two
indices (nos. II and III), this produced the same
results as extraction from the given or from a
parenthetically inserted title, representing Shelley's
title. Thus, "The flower that smiles" would classify
Elizabeth Masson's song under bcth its full first line
and also under its title of "Mutability."

Before the final formatting of the text, Mr.
Weisman and I had to decide upon the style of rubric to
be finally used for differentiating cne field from
another. We also tried out one set of multiple
indentations for separate fields, and then thought our
arrangement was confusing and wasteful of space. We
decided upon the idea of enclosing the letters, "t,"
"p," "d" and "g" with hairpin brackets to remove them
from the province of meaningful letters in a text and
give them a set symbolism. The computer, of course, was
eventually intended to place the entry number in the
margin, to print all lines double-spaced eight to the
inch (that is, four lines of text per each vertical
inch). Another plan was to print it six lines to the
inch, single spaced, with a double space between
entries. This became our final choice of printing
format. We had to estimate the optimal length of line,
i.e. the number of characters, in terms of good
readability and also in terms of the desirable size of
the whcle text, both of the page and number of pages.
The system for guide letters and paging that I had
emplcyed for my Poe DICTIONARY seemed feasible and
useful also for the Shelley music listing.

IV.   THE ARRANGEMENT AND THE SYMBOLS

A few words of explanation of the indexes should be
furnished. I have spoken about the second and third
indexes, which give the titles and first lines of the
poems set to music. The first, devoted to an
alphabetical listing of all the compcsers with the
numbers of the entries is useful to show at a glance
whether specific composers are present, and how many

compositions are theirs. Although the alphabetization
of the text might make this index seem unnecessary, it
is as functional as any table of contents. This
appeared evident to me while writing the above pages of
the introduction without benefit of such a listing and
under the awkward necessity of thumbing through the
large, clumsy pages of the printout for verification of
names and other facts. The fourth index--of the
chronology of all entries--is the sort of listing that
is easily managed by a computer and is both tedious and
inaccurate at first when done by hand methods. Although
I had always intended to extract the dates for this
purpose, I mistakenly included the reprint dates in the
field for "description" or "d" for several entries;
these had to be traced and re-keypunched, so that even
though reprints were discussed in "d" they appeared
also in the "p" or publication field. Many therefore
required rewording of the "p" field to avoid confusion
for the reader. Finally, the languages of the text
having been inserted into all entries, in so far as
these were known to me through personal inspection, it
was relatively easy to give the machine the parameters
of each language for extraction and listing in index V.
Originally I had intended to cancel the printing of the
language at the end of the entries of the text, leaving
them solely in the index. However, this would deprive
the reader of interesting information, such as the
multilanguage translations of such a song as
Rachmaninoff's "Ostrovok" or "The Isle." Moreover, the
reader would occasionally be unable to tell what was
the language of a musical setting published on the
continent of Europe, unless a foreign tongue was listed
under the "g" field. The lack of any other language
there would automatically signify that the English
words were used even by a Dutch or German composer.
     A word is owed also on the subject of the symbols
used in the "g" field. It would have been easy to give
the explanatory parameters to the computer for a full
printout of "lc" (Library of Congress) or "bm" (British
Museum) or "bn" (Bibliotheque Nationale) and avoid the
need for a legend. However, how repetitious and tedious
it would be to list the British Museum in over half the
entries, or to insert the words "xerox copy in the
collection" instead of the simple "x"! Since the items
under the legend are strictly alphabetical, it seems
possible to justify the slight hardship of having to
refer to the key if one is interested in the source of
information or the place where a rare nonxeroxed item

can be seen. I have not felt obligated to list every
source of information, especially for items that occur
in many collections seen or in several bibliographic
works, but only for those that are excessively rare or
where there may be contradictory information about the
dating of the first edition. Pazdirek does not always
agree with Grove or with the British Museum listing,
for example, and in such cases, I try to list all
sources of information. I have listed Anderson as a
source of information for about fifty or half the
total entries that he gives, excluding those found
separately in other collections, often without any
reference to Anderson's listing. In a few instances
Anderson is incorrect, but I have not wished to point
attention to each one. Several of the indications of
source are really a form of tribute to the graciousness
of particular institutions in helping me to search out
and copy pieces unobtainable in more likely places. As
an example, R. Guerini's setting of "A Widow Bird" came
to my attention via the catalogue of the National
Library in Edinburgh. I waited two years to see a copy
of the song in the British Museum, only to find it
missing, but my xeroxed copy represents the example
that I finally saw in the East Berlin music library.
Many of the eighty or ninety items seen in Berlin first
came to my attention in London, and for these there is
likely to be no reference to Berlin under "g". All of
this demonstrates that a reader who wishes to see a
copy of the music can usually rely upon my listing for
its location in a mentioned collection, but he should
check any large unmentioned local collection that may
very well have a Shelley piece listed, especially if
modern. It is my hope that the New York Public Library
Music Division will be able to furnish to anyone who
wishes it a xeroxed copy of either the original
publication or of the xerox copy in my collection after
it has all been transferred to its holdings. For the
most part the xerox copies are clear and capable of
being reproduced for study purposes. Those from the
Bibliotheque Nationale could be had only as microfilms
and are less distinct in their printed-out form than
the straight xeroxes of the British Museum.

V. ACKNOWLEDGMENTS

     I wish to express my gratitude for indispensable
aid in collecting and producing THE MUSICAL SETTINGS OF
SHELLEY'S POEMS to the following individuals and

organizations:

For generous financial aid--The New York State
University Research Foundation, which provided summer
leisure time for traveling to collections in Europe and
which enabled me to have the entire text keypunched
through paid aides who worked in the computer
laboratory of the Bronx Community College; and The Carl
and Lily H. Pforzheimer Foundation, which furnished a
substantial sum for xeroxing and microfilming over 500
pieces of music, chiefly in Europe, not found in the
New York Public Library music collection and eventually
to be deposited therein.

For the assistance specified--Martin Bailey of the
Senate House Library of London University, who helped
me to check on items in the British Museum music
collection which occasionally needed urgent
verification; Mr. George Kazasoglou of Greece, who
kindly responded to my inquiries about his composition;
Mr. Philip Miller, "emeritus" head of the NYPL music
division, who helpfully discussed my project; Dr. F. R.
Noske of the University of Amsterdam, who helped me to
examine the music library there; Mr. Norman Mangouni,
of the New York State University Press, who encouraged
me with the prospect of a publisher; Dr. Donald Reiman,
of The Carl H. Pforzheimer Library, who helped me with
rare Shelley materials; and, above all, my wife Dr.
Alice M. Pollin, who contributed more than I can
describe through her knowledge of music, languages,
computerization processes, and, especially, her
unfailing good judgment and patience.

For the kind permission to xerox original copies,
for the use of catalogues, for donated copies of music,
and for other assistance--Edwin Ashdown Ltd., Boosey
and Hawkes, Breitkopf and Hartel, Curwen Music Co.,
Galliard, Ltd., Paterson's of London, Schirmer's music
store in New York, B. Schott in Mainz, Donemus of
Amsterdam (Andre Surres), and other music publishers.

For the use of catalogues, collections, and other
facilities, usually in person but occasionally through
helpful correspondence--American Composer's Alliance of
New York; American Society of Composers, Artists, and
Performers (ASCAP); the Amsterdam Music Library (Dr. P.
W. van Reijen); the Bibliotheque Nationale of Paris
(especially V. Fedorov); Bibliotheque Royale of
Brussels; the Biblioteca Nacional of Madrid, Music
Section; Baylor University Armstrong Browning Library,
Waco, Texas (Mrs. Sally East); Boston Public Library,
Music Division (Ruth Bleecher); Bodleian Library of

Oxford University (and Prof. F. W. Sternfeld); British
Broadcasting Company library (especially its head, John
H. Davies); Bronx Community College, especially Dr.
James A. Colston, President, and Dean Bernard P.
Corbman, both of whom constantly lent their
encouragement and interest, the BCC Computer
Laboratory, directed by the cooperative Meyer Shopkow
and including in its personnel Kenneth Weisman, whose
aid in programming the text made the final production
possible, Cedric White, machine operator, and Richard
Stein, zealous keypunch aide, and the BCC library, in
which Oksana Klymowycz helped greatly with translations
of Russian entries and Juliana Skurdenis and Jean
Kolliner provided the aid of specially ordered Shelley
materials, under the general direction of Dr. Edward
Terry; Broadcast Music Incorporated library (BMI); The
British Museum, especially A. H. King, head of the
music room, and Mr. Bancroft, superintendent of the
reading room; the Central Music Library, Boro of
Westminster, London; the Composer's Guild, publisher of
COMPOSER, which circularized my questionnaire; the
Copenhagen University Music Library (Gerda Schiotz);
the Copyright Office, division of the Library of
Congress (especially Mrs. Layton); the Deutsche
Staatsbibliothek, in East Berlin (Evelyn Bartlitz); the
Hamburg Music Library (Dr. K. Richter); the Harvard
University Libraries, including the Houghton Library
(especially Mrs. Jakeman); the Library of Congress,
music division, especially the director, William
Lichtenwanger, the head of the reference section, James
B. Boxley, the assistant librarians Carroll D. Wade and
Wayne D. Shirley; the Moscow Institute of Theatre,
Music, and Cinema (Larissa Mikhailovna Kutateladze);
the Moscow Tanayev Musical Library (V. D. Magnitskaia);
the Munich Bavarian State Library (Dr. Dorfmuller),
music section; the Newberry Library of Chicago; the
New York Historical Society Library; the New York
Public Library, Music Division at Lincoln Center; the
Royal College of Music in London (Jane Harington and
William Stock); the Royal College of Music in London
(Barbara Banner); the Swedish Music Information Center
of Stockholm; the Princeton University Music Library
(Paula Morgan); the Vienna National Library (Dr.
Leopold Nowak); and the West Berlin Music Library at
Dahlem.

PROGRAMMING THE BOOK
by Kenneth S. Weisman

The purpose of this introduction is to clarify for
the reader some of the more technical aspects involved
in the production of a computerized book. Normally, the
publication of a scholarly work requires that a type-
written manuscript be submitted to the publisher, who
then uses this information in order to set up "proofs"
of what the final pages of the book will look like in
print. But the use of a computer makes all this
unnecessary. If, instead of just relying on a
typewriter, the author turns out a text in a form
suitable for computer printout, then the "proofs" can
be made under his close supervision "at home," leaving
only the finalized copy to be sent to the publisher or
printer. Thus, there are two obvious advantages to the
above mentioned computerized procedure, namely, (1) the
overall reduction in the total cost of the book and (2)
the relative ease with which the author can make last-
minute additions, deletions, and/or minor adjustments
to the finalized manuscript.

Computers and books are not a new phenomenon--there
are more computerized texts being produced today than
ever before. I feel that I have been most fortunate to
have worked with Dr. Burton Pollin on this particular
book, as he has the rare quality of being able to
communicate, both clearly and correctly, the exact
specifications required. This is especially important
when you consider that the computer performs only those
functions for which it is programmed, and the computer
programmer/analyst can provide instructions regarding
only that of which he has complete knowledge and/or
comprehension. Thus, the computer will not be aware of
any non-verbalized assumptions.

In the basic preparation of the text, itself, as
well as the introductory material and the "legend," all
input data were fed to the computer in the form of keypunched cards. However, the indexes, at the end of
this book, were extracted by the computer from the text
itself, and then compiled into their finalized form.
This latter procedure will be explained more fully
below.

The first efforts involved formatting the text or
body of the book, where each entry was composed of a
variable amount of the input data cards, and where the
different fields of information that made up an entry,
were preceded by a rubric to show what each field

contained. Thus, /C stood for "composer"; /T, for
"title"; /D, for "descriptive matter"; /P, for
"publisher information"; and /G, for "general
miscellany". Moreover, because the input was hand-
punched, there was no need to worry about the right-
hand margin occurring in the middle of a word. That is
to say, one just punched until he reached the end of
the 80-column card, and then continued, at the
beginning of the next card, punching that word, even if
it were broken up illogically, as in "th" on one card
and "e" on the next. The only exception to this was the
/C field, which always began on a new card.
     During the construction of this book, there has
been a slight variation in the width of a page.
Initially, we envisioned the use of a 45-character
line. In view of this, the input cards were transferred
onto magnetic tape, then sorted according to the
contents of the /C field, and formatted in such a way
that there would be a maximum of 45 characters per
line, including spaces between words, with only whole
words on a line, as many as possible to fill up the 45
characters. There was only one exception to this rule,
i.e. every /C field (and its preceding item number)
must be started on a new line. For final output, the
length of the line was expanded to 56 characters.
     The machine we used was an IBM 029 keypunch which
had only one set of keys, for upper-case letters; (in
order to produce lower-case letters, two keys are
required). Thus, we assumed all letters to be lower-
case unless preceded by an added asterisk (*).
However, quoted titles and alpha-numeric book catalog
numbers were also to be capitalized. And since one
asterisk per letter was both tiresome and monotonous,
it was decided to capitalize all letters between one
asterisk and the next, unless a space intervened. Thus
when it encountered an asterisk, the computer was
required to scan ahead until the next asterisk or
blank, whichever came first, and to act accordingly.
Moreover, when two asterisks were found, the word was
expanded via a special algorithm such that all letters
between those delimiters were preceded by their own
asterisks.
     Now that we had the tape, and not the unwieldy tab
cards, we could, at will, produce lists for editing and
checking purposes. For example, we printed out the /P
and /T fields to check for consistency and correctness
of both spelling and punctuation. A composer listing
was used to point up all descrepancies in the form of

various repeated authors' names. We also produced a
listing of those records which did not contain /G
fields. In addition, the number of entries in the text
itself was increased by a special-purpose program
designed in such a way that new material could be
inserted into proper alphabetic sequence. For the final
print-out of the text, the internally stored format had
to undergo some slight modifications. Thus, the /C
rubric was eliminated entirely, and in the interest of
reading ease, the slash designating each of the other
separate fields became hairpin brackets (<>). Thus, for
example, the early title listing program had to be
modified from searching for /T to searching for <T>.

      We produced the title and language indexes using a
program that stored the required parameters and then
searched the text for these key words. The index of
first lines was derived from the listing of titles.
There was one exception, however--the index of dates,
which was merely a collection of all the dates found in
the <P> field.

      For the introduction, we used a technique similar
to that of the text--it also came on cards. In general,
paragraph and section headings started on new cards.
The major difference, therefore, was in capitalization.
Because book titles were to appear in upper-case, the
"asterisk to asterisk" method was not viable, since
there were whole phrases with many embedded blanks, a
fact which meant that the computer would have to scan
many records ahead to see if the next asterisk was a
delimiter (one record here is equal to one input card).
Thus, a new symbol had to be invented, called an
"escape character". This was designated by the 0-2-8
multiple punch key, which prints out as a space; the
asterisk is then used as the termination character.

      The storage of the introduction differed from that
of the text since it contained both upper and lower-
case letters and no asterisks. In the final stages of
the programming for the introduction, the only tasks
that remained were the paging (in Roman numerals, not
the normal computer numbers) and length of line. The
"legend program" was in the form of card to printer,
using a maximum line length and asterisks for upper-
case letters.

      Insofar as computer methodology is concerned, the
major programming technique used in this book involved
the use of the "flap-back", a procedure whereby the
output consists of only whole words on a line, within a
maximum line length. This technique is also applicable

to things like library catalog cards, or, in general,
any text processing where the input consists of a
string of characters. The general procedure requires a
"scratch-pad" that contains the discrete segment on
which you are working. Upon completion of the
formatting of this segment, you then check to see if it
fits on the current line. If so, you insert it and
decrease the amount of space (a counter) in that line.
If not, you print out the current line, and make your
"scratch-pad" word the first item of the next line.

In fine, this book has proved to be an interesting
application of computer text processing and string
manipulation to a humanities project. Good
specifications have greatly aided the programming
effort. Aside from the more technical aspects of such
an endeavor, I have been able to develop a greater
familiarity with the works of Percy Bysshe Shelley. In
addition, I have been able to work with new programming
techniques especially formulated for this particular
type of computer program and have derived a great deal
of personal satisfaction in seeing this project come to
fruition.

August 1973

GUIDE TO ALL ABBREVIATICNS USED IN THE TEXT AND
IN THE <G> FIELD, REFERRING CHIEFLY TO SOURCES
IN TEXTS AND LIBRARY COLLECTICNS
(FOR DETAILS SEE THE INTRODUCTION)

amc = American Music Center, a music library in
    NYC, maintained largely by contributing composers
and = Anderson, author of the supplementary appendix
    to William Sharpe's 1886 biography of Shelley
bbc = British Broadcasting Company Catalogue to
    songs
bcm = British Catalogue of Music Copyrights (issued
    annually)
bl = Blume, editor of MUSIK IN GESCHICETE UND
    GEGENWART
bm = British Museum music collection and catalogues
bmi = Broadcast Music Incorporated, its catalogues
    and collections
bn = Bibliotheque Nationale music library, Paris
bodleian = Bodleian Library of Cxford University,
    especially its Shelley music collection
bpl = Boston Public Library catalogue or its collection
    of music
cc = Catalogue of USA music copyrights
copy in collection = indication that a printed
    cr published copy of the composition is in
    the collection that has been donated to the
    NYPL at Lincoln Center, where it may be seen
<d> = description of the musical composition
don or Donemus = Donemus (Dutch Music Publishers
    Association) which publishes the quarterly
    SPECULUM SONORIS, occasionally mentioned
ed = Edinburgh National Library catalogue and
    collection
eu and ep = the letters prefixed by LC, copyright
    division, to unpublished and published music,
    respectively
<g> = general information, such as the language
    of a song, the source of information, the
    place or places where it may be found, and
    the inclusion of a xeroxed cr printed copy
    in this collection, now donated to NYPL
gr or grove or Grove = GROVE'S DICTIONARY OF
    MUSIC (revised by Eric Blom)
grove, su = Supplement to GROVE'S DICTIONARY
lc = Library of Congress catalogues of music and
    also of copyrights; also its collections
mn = MUSICAL NEWS article of 16 December 1922,
    p. 564
nuc = NEW UNION CATALOGUE OF MUSIC AND PHCNORECORDS

GUIDE TO ALL ABBREVIATIONS USED IN THE TEXT AND IN THE <G> FIELD, REFERRING CHIEFLY TO SOURCES IN TEXTS AND LIBRARY COLLECTIONS
(FOR DETAILS SEE THE INTRODUCTION)

(U. S. government)

nn = New York Public Library, usually the collection
of music at Lincoln Center

nypl or NYPL = New York Public Library, usually
the collection of music at Lincoln Center

<p> = publication data, including the place, publisher,
and date of the composition

paz = F. Pazdirek, UNIVERSAL HANDBUCH DER MUSIK
LITERATUR, Vienna, 1904

q = information derived from a questionnaire,
circulated among composers in the USA and,
via the magazine COMPOSER, in England

Royal Academy = Royal Academy library, London

Sears = SEARS'S CATALOGUE OF SONGS, also the supplement
when specified

<t> = title of the musical composition, with the
title of Shelley's poem included if different

usi = UNITED STATES INFORMATION SERVICES CATALOGUE
OF PUBLISHED MUSIC BY AMERICAN COMPOSERS (1964)

x = A xeroxed copy of the original musical composition
has been included in the whole collection,
donated to the NYPL, Lincoln Center, where
it may be seen.

Yale = Yale Music Library

PART I
The Bibliography

1 Adomowski, Timothee <t> I arise from dreams of thee <p> ms. <d> song, in Harvard Library

2 Agnew, Roy E. <t> Dirge: Rough wind <p> Curwen, London, 1924 <d> solo vcice. Curwen 2340. 2p. <g> bm, x

3 Ahnell, Emil G. <t> Love's philcsophy <p> ms. <d> unperformed. Kentucky Wesleyan College <g> q

4 Ahnell, Emil G. <t> Music, when soft voices die <p> ms. <d> unperformed. Kentucky Wesleyan College <g> q

5 Ahnell, Emil G. <t> Remembrance: Swifter far <p> ms. <d> unperformed. Kentucky Wesleyan College <g> q

6 Aide, Hamilton <t> A lament: Swifter far <p> C. Lonsdale, London, 1877 <d> 4p. <g> bm, and, ed, paz

7 Aitken, George <t> Music, when soft voices die <p> B. Schott, London and Mainz, 1904 <d> 2p. <g> bm, x, mn

8 Albert, Boubee <t> Thou art fair (To Sophia) <p> E. Ascherberg, London, 1893 <d> song with violoncello obbligato <g> mn, bm

9 Alcock, Gilbert A. <t> Music, when soft voices die <p> Joseph Williams, London, 1928 <d> St. Cecilia Collection of Two-Part Songs, Series 18, no. 22. First issued in 1910 as St. Cecilia Series of two-part songs, Series 12, no. 5. 3p. <g> bm, x

10 Allen, Creighton <t> The dawn: The pale stars are gone <p> Merl A. Reid, New York, 1954 <d> in Shelley Songs, Cycle of Ten Songs, pp. 1-2 <g> nn

11 Allen, Creighton <t> Winter song: A widow bird <p> Merl A. Reid, New York, 1954 <d> Shelley Songs. pp. 3-4 <g> nn

12 Allen, Creighton <t> To a maiden: I fear thy kisses <p> Merl A. Reid, New Ycrk, 1954 <d> in Shelley Songs, pp. 5-7 <g> nn

13 Allen, Creighton <t> Autumn: If I walk in autumn's even <p> Merl A. Reid, New York, 1954 <d> in Shelley Songs, pp. 8-9 <g> nn

14 Allen, Creighton <t> The world's wanderers: Tell me, thou star <p> Merl A. Reid, New York, 1954 <d> in Shelley Songs, pp. 10-11 <g> nn

15 Allen, Creighton <t> Mutability: The flower that smiles <p> Merl A. Reid, New York, 1954 <d> in Shelley Songs, pp. 12-16 <g> nn

16 Allen, Creighton <t> A dirge: Rough wind, that moanest loud <p> Merl A. Reid, New York, 1936; 1954 <d> in Shelley Songs, pp. 17-18 <g> nn

17 Allen, Creighton <t> Remembrance: Swifter far <p> Merl A. Reid, New York, 1954 <d> in Shelley Songs, pp. 19-21 <g> nn

18 Allen, Creighton <t> Evening: When soft winds <p> Merl A. Reid, New York, 1954 <d> in Shelley Songs, pp. 22-23 <g> nn

19 Allen, Creighton <t> To the moon: Art thou pale <p> Merl A. Reid, New York, 1954 <d> in Shelley Songs, pp. 24-26 <g> nn

20 Allen, Creighton <t> The poet's world: On a poet's lips I slept <p> Schirmer, New York, 1928 <d> Song for medium or high voice with piano accompaniment. Pub. no. 34004. 3p. <g> lc

21 Allen, Edward <t> Music, when soft voices die <p> Frank Harding, New York, 1913 <d> no. 1 of Four Songs, pp. 2-3 <g> x, lc

22 Allman, George Joseph Oliver <t> Good night? ah no <p> T. Prowse, London, 1845 <d> for middle voice. 4p <g> bm, x, nn

23 Alvstad, Vivian Loretta <t> Love's philosophy (by Shelly--sic) <p> EU239227, 21 May 1951

24 Ambrose, Paul <t> Serenade, op. 12, no. 1 (presumably Indian serenade) <p> C. Litson, Boston, 1898 <g> lc, not seen

25 Anderson, William H. (published under pseudonym of
     Hugh Garland) <t> Music, when soft voices die <p>
     Western Music Co., Vancouver, 1947 <d> SSA. No.
     3025, Western Choral Series. practice piano only.
     2p <g> lc

26 Anderton, Thomas <t> The skylark (for To a skylark)
     <p> Seeley, Jackson, and Halliday, London, 1871
     <d> Songs and Etchings, pp. 18-23 <g> bm, x

27 Andrews, Richard H. <t> Mary dear <p> Duncan Davison,
     London, 1870 <d> no words. 3p. for the pianoforte.
     based on H. Glover's piece, q.v. <g> bm, x

28 Andriessen, Jurriaan <t> Ariette: As the moon's soft
     splendour <p> Donemus, Amsterdam, 1960 <d> in Four
     English Songs, for tenor and piano, pp. 4-5 <g>
     copy in collection

29 Anonymous <t> Men of England: Men of England,
     wherefore plow <p> Swan Sonnenschein, London,
     1888, 1892, 1897 <d> no. 29 in Chants of Labour: A
     Song Book of the People with Music, pp. 46-47, ed.
     by Edward Carpenter. SATB, a capella, to the air:
     Now the rosy morn appearing (the music printed)
     <g> bm, x

30 Anonymous <t> One word is too often profaned <p> ms.
     <d> 2p. <g> Harvard Library

31 Anonymous <t> To liberty: God prosper, speed, and
     save <p> Swan Sonnenschein, London, 1888, 1892,
     1897 <d> no. 34 in Chants of Labour: A Song Book
     of the People with Music, p. 66, ed. by Edward
     Carpenter. SATB, a capella, to the "National
     Anthem." The music is not given, only Shelley's
     six stanzas. <g> bm, x

32 Antheil, George <t> When soft winds <p> Weintraub
     Music Co., New York, 1951 <d> SATB and keyboard.
     no. 1 in Eight Fragments from Shelley <g> usi, lc

33 Antheil, George <t> To the moon: Bright wanderer <p>
     Weintraub Music Co., New York, 1951 <d> SATB and
     keyboard. no. 2 in Eight Fragments from Shelley
     <g> usi, lc

34 Antheil, George <t> When the lamp is shattered <p> Weintraub Music Co., New York, 1951 <d> no. 3 in Eight Fragments from Shelley. SATB and keyboard instrument <g> usi, lc

35 Antheil, George <t> Dirge: Rough wind that moanest <p> Weintraub Music Co., New York 1951 <d> no. 4, in Eight Fragments from Shelley <g> bmi, lc

36 Antheil, George <t> To-morrow (Where art thou) <p> Weintraub Music Co., New York, 1951 <d> SATB and keyboard. no. 5 in Eight Fragments from Shelley <g> usi, lc

37 Antheil, George <t> Sonnet to Byron <p> Weintraub Music Co., New York, 1951 <d> SATB and keyboard. no. 6 in Eight Fragments from Shelley <g> usi, lc

38 Antheil, George <t> I faint, I perish <p> Weintraub Music Co., New York, 1951 <d> SATB and keyboard. no. 7 in Eight Fragments from Shelley <g> usi, lc

39 Antheil, George <t> I stood upon a heaven-cleaving tower <p> Weintraub Music Co., New York, 1951 <d> SATB and keyboard. no. 8 in Eight Fragments from Shelley <g> usi, lc

40 Arensky, Anton <t> Out of olden days <p> P. Jurgenson, Moscow and Leipzig, 1905 <d> op. 71, no. 1. 3p. <g> East Berlin, x

41 Arensky, Anton <t> Over the sea slept a pine forest (for To Jane. The recollection?) <p> P. Jurgenson, Moscow and Leipzig, 1905 <d> op. 71, no. 2. 6p. <g> East Berlin, x

42 Arensky, Anton <t> The pine trees embrace each other <p> P. Jurgenson, Moscow and Leipzig, 1905 <d> op. 71, no. 3. 5p. <g> East Berlin, x

43 Arensky, Anton <t> How quiet everything is <p> P. Jurgenson, Moscow and Leipzig, 1905 <d> op. 71, no. 4. 4p. <g> East Berlin, x

44 Arensky, Anton <t> Your long-enduring down-cast look <p> P. Jurgenson, Moscow and Leipzig, 1905 <d> op.

71, no. 5. 6p. <g> East Berlin, x

45 Argento, Dominick <t> Ode to the west wind <p> Boosey
   and Hawkes, New York, 1956 <d> Concerto for
   soprano and orchestra <g> lc, q

46 Arkwright, Mrs. Robert (Frances Crauford) <t> I arise
   from dreams <p> C. Lonsdale, London, 1866 <d> no.
   3 in a Sixth Set of Six Songs. no. 7 in Sixteen
   Vocal Compositions, in C. Lonsdale's Musical
   Circulating Library (1872?), nos. 5-10 forming the
   sixth volume of Mrs. Arkwright's Songs <g> ed,
   and, bm, x

47 Arnatt, Ronald Kent <t> Five songs to poems by
   Shelley <p> EU244938, 23 July 1951 <g> lc, but
   unseen

48 Arnell, Richard Anthony Eryer <t> Ode to the west
   wind <p> ms., 1954 <d> for soprano and orchestra
   <g> gr, su

49 Arnold, George B. <t> The colour from the flow'r is
   gone <p> Addison, Hollier, Lucas, London, 1859 <d>
   4p. <g> and, bm, x

50 Arnold, George B. <t> The flower that smiles <p>
   Novello, London, 1878 <d> 4p. <g> bm, x, and

51 Arnold, George B. <t> Music, when soft voices die <p>
   Novello, London, n.d. <d> four-part song, ATBB and
   piano ad lib. 3p. no. 1 <g> Bodleian, x

52 Arnold, George B. <t> Orphan hours, the year is dead
   <p> Addison, Hollier, Lucas, London, 1859 <d> 4p.
   <g> bm, x

53 Arnold, George B. <t> A widow bird <p> Novello,
   London, n.d. <d> duet for two sopranos. 5p <g>
   Bodleian, x

54 Aschaffenburg, Walter <t> Ozymandias <p> ms. <d> for
   orchestra <g> q

55 Ashe, John Harold <t> Love's philosophy <p> John
   Harold Ashe, publisher (facsimile publication),
   Townesville, Queensland, Australia, 1947 <d> 2p.
   <g> lc

56 Ashe, John Harold <t> O world! O life! <p> John
     Harold Ashe, publisher (facsimile publication),
     Townesville, Queensland, Australia, 1947 <d> 3p.
     <g> lc

57 Ashe, John Harold <t> A widow bird <p> John Harold
     Ashe, publisher (facsimile publication)
     Townesville, Queensland, Australia, 1947 <d> 2p.
     <g> lc

58 Ashton, Archie Thomas Lee <t> The heart's devotion: I
     fear thy kisses <p> Paterson, Edinburgh, 1908 <d>
     no. 3 in Four Old English Love Lyrics. 12p. no. 3,
     pp. 8-9 <g> lc, bm, x

59 Atkinson, Frederick Cook <t> A widow bird <p> Weekes,
     London, 1876 <d> no. 3 in Six Songs <g> and, ed,
     bm, x

60 Austin, Ernest <t> Hymn of Apollo: The sleepless
     hours who watch me. op. 39 <p> J. H. Larway,
     London, 1917 <d> orchestra and chorus, SATB,
     doubled. piano transcription. 60p. <g> bpl, x

61 Austin, Frank <t> Fragments of an unfinished drama:
     He came like a dream <p> Ashdown, London, 1883 <d>
     4p. <g> ed, bm, x

62 Backer-Grondahl, Agathe <t> Love's philosophy <p> ms.
     <d> in the BBC library.

63 Backer-Grondahl, Agathe <t> To the queen of my heart,
     op. 1 (Til Mit Hjertes Dronning), falsely
     attributed to Shelley <p> Wilhelm Hansen,
     Copenhagen, 1867 (in British Museum) <d> in Three
     Songs (Tre Sange), dated 1847 in Grove. also in
     song-album of Nordiske Kinder, Wilhelm Hansen,
     Copenhagen, 1895, pp. 16-20 and in Tre Sange, op.
     1, no. 3, F. Harris, London, 1907. also advertised
     by Stanley Lucas, Weber et al. in 1897. in E, F
     sharp and G <g> bm, bl, Grove, x, Danish

64 Baddeley, St. Clair <t> Music, when soft voices die
     <p> Stanley Lucas, Weber and Co., London, 1883 <d>
     no. 2 of Sechs Lieder. words in English, pp. 4-5.
     <g> bm, x

65 Bailey, Judith Margaret <t> Music <p> ms., 1969 <d>

baritone and piano. in Three Settings of Poems by Shelley <g> q

66 Bailey, Judith Margaret <t> To the moon: Art thou pale <p> ms., 1969 <d> baritone and piano. in Three Settings of Poems by Shelley <g> q

67 Bailey, Judith Margaret <t> A widow bird <p> ms., 1969 <d> baritone and piano. in Three Settings of Poems by Shelley <g> q

68 Bainton, Edgar Leslie <t> The cloud <p> Curwen, London, 1912 <d> Unison song, no. 71362. 4p. <g> bm, x

69 Bainton, Edgar Leslie <t> Summer (for Summer and winter?) <p> J. Williams, London, 1924 <d> trio for female voices. St. Cecilia Part-Songs. Series 14, no. 20 <g> bm

70 Baird, Margery Anthea <t> To a skylark <p> ms., 1953-54 <d> baritone solo, four-part chorus and small orchestra <g> q

71 Bairstow, Edward Cuthbert <t> I arise from dreams <p> Williams, London, 1903; republished 1943 <d> no. 4 of Six Songs. 4p. <g> bm, x, bbc

72 Bairstow, Edward Cuthbert <t> Music, when soft voices die <p> Winthrop Rogers and Son, London, 1929 <d> Winthrop Rogers Edition of Choral Music for Festivals, Series 3. TTBB <g> bm, x

73 Bairstow, Edward Cuthbert <t> On a poet's lips I slept <p> Winthrop Rogers, London, 1929 or Hawkes and Son <d> Winthrop Rogers Edition of Choral Music for Festivals, Series 1. for SSA .5p. <g> bm, x, bbc

74 Bales, Richard <t> Ozymandias <p> Peer International Corp. New York, 1953 (and 1958) <d> 3p. also for medium voice and small orchestra. New York, Southern Music Publishing Company, 1958. 6p. <g> lc, x

75 Ball, William Ernest <t> Love's entreaty: The fountains mingle <p> Boosey, London, 1919 <d> 6p. <g> lc, x, bm

76 Banister, Henry Charles <t> A widow bird, op. 20, no.
   2 <p> Duncan Davison, London, 1870 <d> no. 2 of
   Two Winter Songs. 4p. <g> and, bm, x

77 Bantock, Granville <t> Arethusa <p> Boosey, London,
   1927 <d> for six-part women's chorus, a capella.
   no. h.12276. 32p. <g> bm, x

78 Bantock, Granville <t> Dreams: The flower that smiles
   <p> W. Paxton, London, 1938 <d> a capella chorus.
   7p. <g> bm, x

79 Bantock, Granville <t> Hymn of Pan <p> Swan, London,
   1922 <d> song, 10p. <g> bm, x

80 Bantock, Granville <t> Music, when soft voices die
   <p> J. Curwen, London, 1912 <d> a capella chorus.
   Choral handbook, no. 991 SATBB, unaccompanied <g>
   bm, x

81 Bantock, Granville <t> On Himalay: Far away on
   Himalay <p> Novello, London and Gray, New York,
   1932; Novello, London, 1908 <d> female chorus a
   capella. no. 1062 of Novello's part-song book,
   second series. 6p. <g> bm, x

82 Bantock, Granville <t> One with eyes the fairest,
   from Cyclops of Euripides <p> Musical Times,
   London, August, 1909 <d> Musical Times no. 798.
   Novello's tonic sol-fa series, no. 1785 <g> bm, x

83 Bantock, Granville <t> Ozymandias <p> Swan, London,
   1924 <d> no. 44 of Swan edition. 5p. <g> bm, x

84 Bantock, Granville <t> Prometheus Unbound: Life of
   life (Spirit song), Act II, v <p> Novello, London,
   ca. 1909; Goodwin and Tabb, London, 1947 <d>
   Novello's Part-Song Book, series 2, no. 1128 (8
   parts) and Tonic-Sol-Fa series, no. 2038; in 1947
   edition (copy in the collection) a song for one
   middle voice of 7p. <g> bm, x

85 Bantock, Granville <t> Wake the serpent not
   (Fragment) <p> Novello, London, 1908 and 1909 <d>
   Musical Times, vol. 49, pp. 653-56. also no. 4 of
   (4) Hebridean Songs. also no. 1128 of Novello's
   Part-Song Book (1909) for SATB chorus with

rehearsal piano and in Novello's tonic sol-fa
series, no. 2038 <g> nn, x

86 Bantock, Granville <t> A widow bird <p> Swan, London,
   1932 <d> no.3 in Five Songs of Shelley <g> bm, x,
   bbc, ed, lc

87 Bantock, Granville <t> Wine of Eglantine
   (Elfenmusik): Trunken bin ich von Honigwein
   (German translation by K. Hill) <p> Breitkopf and
   Hartel, Leipzig, 1909 <d> for S, MS, and A, with
   piano. 6p. <g> nn, German

88 Bantock, Granville <t> Witch of Atlas <p> Novello,
   London, 1903 <d> Symphonic tone poem, no. 5,
   arranged for piano by Josef Holbrooke. Orchestra
   score, 58p. <g> bm, x

89 Bantock, Granville <t> The world's wanderers <p>
   Joseph Williams, London, 1937 <d> a capella chorus
   or quartet of mixed voices, SCTB. no. 19 of vol.
   21 of St. Cecilia Choral Series <g> bm, x

90 Barber, Edwin Masterman <t> Love's philosophy <p>
   Farmer and Co., Nottingham, 1893 <g> ed, bm, x

91 Barber, Samuel <t> Prometheus Unbound, music for a
   scene, II, v. op. 8 <p> Schirmer, New York, 1936
   <d> for orchestra. Schirmer's study score, no. 11.
   18p. preface of 2p. by L. Gilman on Barber's aim.
   No words in score, but Barber cites several lines
   as epigraph. <g> nn, lc

92 Barbour, Florence Newell <t> O wild west wind <p> A.
   P. Schmidt, Boston and New York, 1921-23 <d> no. 4
   of Six Song Pictures. 6p. <g> bm, x

93 Barbour, Florence Newell <t> Tell me, thou wanderers
   <p> A. P. Schmidt, Boston and New York, 1921-23
   <d> no. 3 of Six Song Pictures, pp. 3-7 <g> m, x

94 Barker, Laura Wilson (afterwards Taylor) <t> Spirit
   of delight <p> Cramer, Beale and Co., London, 1847
   <d> no. 5 of Six Songs. 13 p. <g> bm, x

95 Barker, Laura Wilson (afterwards Taylor) <t>
   To-morrow, Canzonet: Where art thou <p> Cramer,
   Beale and Co., London, 1847 <d> no. 4 of Six

Songs. 4p. <g> bm, x

96 Barnett, Alice <t> I arise from dreams <p> C. F.
   Scmary, Chicago, 1908 <g> nn (missing), lc

97 Barnett, Alice <t> Music, when soft voices die <p>
   Schirmer, New York, 1926 <d> 3p. <g> bm, x

98 Barnett, David <t> To night: Swiftly walk. op. 11 <p>
   Evans Music Co., Boston, 1941 <d> pp. 2-11 <g> lc,
   x

99 Barnett, James G. <t> I arise from dreams <p> Firth
   and Hall, New York, 1845 <d> 4p. <g> nn

100 Barnett, John G. <t> Lyric Illustrations of the
    Modern Poets: A collection of twelve vocal
    compositions, the poetry selected from the works
    of Lord Byron, Shelley, etc. <p> D'Almaine and
    Co., London, 1834 in the Athenaeum magazine of
    October 11, 1834, p. 753; London, 1837 for
    individual songs, in Anderson; Hutchings, and
    Romer, London, 1877 for the volume in the Boston
    Public Library with a changed title and three more
    non-Shelley songs added: Lyrical Illustrations of
    Modern English Poets. A Collection of Songs for
    Soprano, Contralto, Tenor and Bass Voices <g> and,
    bpl, ed, x

101 Barnett, John G. <t> Queen Mab selection: Hark,
    whence that rushing sound <p> London, 1834 and
    1877 <d> Lyrical Illustrations, pp. 1-15, for
    tenor voice. <g> x, bpl, and

102 Barnett, John G. <t> Prometheus Unbound selection: No
    change, no pause <p> London, 1834 and 1877 <d> pp.
    16-30 in Lyrical Illustrations, called cantata for
    a bass <g> and, bpl, x

103 Barnett, John G. <t> I arise from dreams <p> London,
    1834 and 1877 <d> in Lyrical Illustrations, pp.
    31-35. called canzonet for tenor or soprano <g>
    and, x

104 Barnett, John G. <t> Rarely, rarely, comest thou <p>
    London, 1834 and 1877 <d> Lyrical Illustrations,
    pp. 36-41, called song for soprano <g> x, and, bpl

105 Barnett, John G. <t> One word is too often profaned
     <p> London, 1834 and 1877 <d> Lyrical
     Illustrations, pp. 42-45, called canzonet for a
     tenor <g> x, bpl (see J. Bennett below)

106 Barnett, John G. <t> My faint spirit <p> London, 1834
     and 1877 <d> in Lyrical Illustrations, pp. 46-50,
     called song for soprano <g> bpl, x

107 Barnett, John G. <t> When passion's trance is
     overpast <p> London, 1834, 1877, and 1914 <d>
     Lyrical Illustrations, pp. 90-92. called
     canzonetta. also on p. 303 of R. Dunstan's 600
     English and Dutch Songs, published by Schofield
     and Sims, Huddersfield, 1914, song no. 522, titled
     I should not weep: When passion's trance. See R.
     Dunstan. <g> bm, bpl, x

108 Barnett, John G. <t> The cloud <p> London, 1877 <d>
     Lyrical Illustrations, pp. 93-105, called a scena
     for mezzo soprano <g> bpl, x

109 Barnett, John G. <t> When the lamp is shattered <p>
     Cramer, Beale and Chappell, London, 1860 <d> 5p.
     no. 2 of "A Series of Contralto Songs" <g> and,
     bm, x

110 Barricelli, Jean-Pierre <t> Indian serenade, op. 12,
     no. 3 <p> EU147105, 20 September 1948

111 Barrington-Baker, G. <t> Time long past: Like the
     ghost of a dear friend dead <p> Novello, London,
     1924 <d> SATB, no. 15125. 4p. <g> bm, x

112 Barry, Katherine <t> Music, when soft voices die <p>
     Reeder and Walsh, London, 1922 <d> Four Song
     Cameos. 3p. <g> lc, x

113 Barton, Claude <t> Good night? ah no, the hour is ill
     <p> Novello, London, 1893 <d> Orpheus 221 <g> bm,
     x

114 Bauer, Harold <t> The fountains mingle <p> Oliver
     Ditson, Boston, 1902 <d> 6p. <g> Harvard Library,
     lc, x

115 Bax, Arnold <t> Enchanted summer from Prometheus
     Unbound: The path through which those lovely twain

<p> Sidney Riorden, London, 1911 <d> SATB plus
soprano solo. 43p. piano accompaniment <g> bm, x

116 Bayley, T. Harold R. <t> Music, when soft voices die
<p> Joseph Williams, London, 1902 <d> two-part
songs for treble voices. no. 19 of series 2. 4p.
J. W. 13588. two-part songs, series 2, no. 29. <g>
bm, x

117 Bayliff, Mary Lane <t> Threnos: O world <p> Weekes,
London, 1904 <d> no. 1 of Two Songs. 1p. <g> bm, x

118 Bayliff, Mary Lane <t> Music: Music, when soft voices
die <p> Weekes, London, 1904 <d> no. 2 of Two
Songs. 1p. <g> bm, x

119 Beach, Mrs. H. H. A. <t> As the moon's soft splendour
(Ariette) <p> Arthur P. Schmidt and Co., Boston,
1886 and 1893 <d> Lyric Fancies, album of songs,
vol. 2 (in NYPL) as separately published by
Schmidt, four pages, entitled Ariette by Shelley.
An Ariette for Music. To a lady singing to her
accompaniment on the guitar <g>   nn

120 Beaumont, Ida <t> Indian serenade <p> St. Clements,
London, 1895 <d> 4p. <g> bm, x

121 Becker, John Joseph <t> I fear thy kisses <p> ms.,
193- <d> no. 3 of Three Songs for Soprano, Piano
and String Quartet. two forms: one for voice and
string quartet and one for voice and piano, the
first on 5 leaves, the second on 2 <g> nn

122 Bedford, Herbert <t> Serenade (Serenade for Baritone)
<p> not found <d> for voice and orchestra. given
by Grove <g> paz, grove

123 Beeson, Jack <t> The moon (The waning moon): And like
a dying lady <p> ms., 1952 <d> widely performed
<g> q

124 Behrend, A. H. <t> A widow bird <p> Novello, London,
1908 <d> no. 8 in Through the Year. A Cantata for
Ladies' Voices. unison song with piano
accompaniment. pp. 54-56. Also published in tonic
sol-fa notation <g> bm, x

125 Bell, H. Poynter <t> Love's philosophy (by Percy B.
    Shelly, sic) <p> Berandol Music, Toronto, July,
    1948 (listed by BMI) <d> 3p. <g> lc

126 Bell, William Henry <t> Men of England: Heirs of
    glory <p> Lansbury's Labour Weekly, 28 November
    1925 <d> p. 16 in I, no. 40 <g> x, nn (42nd Street
    collection)

127 Bement, Edward <t> Music, when soft voices die <p>
    EU13960, 3 December 1919 <g> lc

128 Bendelari, Augosto <t> I arise from dreams of thee
    <p> Oliver Ditson, Boston, 1863 <d> 4p. <g> nn

129 Bendixen, Louise <t> Darkness has dawned in the East
    (Hellas) <p> Wessel and Stapleton, London, 1846
    <d> 5p. <g> bm, x

130 Bendixen, Louise <t> As the moon's soft splendour <p>
    Wessel and Stapleton, London, 1846 <d> title on
    the cover of Darkness has dawned. Song is
    unobtainable.

131 Bendixen, Louise <t> My faint spirit <p> Wessel and
    Stapleton, London, 1846 <d> title on the cover of
    Darkness has dawned. Song is unobtainable.

132 Benkman, Siegfried <t> To a skylark <p> 13 September
    1937, EU152186

133 Bennett, Alfred William <t> I arise from dreams <p>
    1854 <g> in Anderson only

134 Bennett, George John <t> Twelve Songs Set to Poems of
    Shelley and Rossetti <p> Novello, London and New
    York, 1886 <d> for the Shelley songs see the
    entries below <g> bm, mr, paz

135 Bennett, George John <t> I fear thy kisses <p>
    Novello, London, 1886 <d> no. 1 in Twelve Songs,
    2p. <g> bm, x

136 Bennett, George John <t> To Jane: The keen stars <p>
    Novello, London, 1886 <d> no. 2 in Twelve Songs,
    pp.3-5 <g> bm, x

137 Bennett, George John <t> Love's philosophy <p>

Novello, London, 1886 <d> no. 3 of Twelve Songs,
pp. 6-9 <g> bm, x

138 Bennett, George John <t> Music, when soft voices die
<p> Novello, London, 1886 <d> no. 4 in Twelve
Songs, pp. 10-13 <g> bm, x

139 Bennett, George John <t> Mutability: The flower that
smiles today <p> Novello, London, 1886 <d> no. 5
in Twelve Songs, pp. 14-16 <g> bm, x

140 Bennett, George John <t> On a dead violet (On a faded
violet) <p> Novello, London, 1886 <d> no. 6 in
Twelve Songs, pp. 17-19 <g> bm, x

141 Bennett, George John <t> When passion's trance <p>
Novello, London, 1886 <d> no. 7 in Twelve Songs,
pp. 20-22 <g> bm, x

142 Bennett, George John <t> Rarely, rarely, comest thou
<p> Novello, London, 1886 <d> no. 8 in Twelve
Songs, pp. 23-26 <g> bm, x

143 Bennett, J. (James?) <t> One word is too often
profaned <p> 1837 <d> given only in Anderson,
probably a misprint for John G. Barnett, q.v.

144 Bennett, Richard Rodney <t> A widow bird <p>
Universal ed., London, 1966 <d> no. 2 in a suite
of five pieces for small orchestra and voice,
adapted from two books of songs (The Aviary and
The Insect World). pp. 12-14 in the score <g> nn,
ed

145 Bennett, Wentworth <t> Good night? ah no <p> Enoch
and Sons, London,1886 <d> 7p. <g> ed, bm, x

146 Bennett, William Sterndale <t> The past: Wilt thou
forget the happy hours (Entflohenes Gluck: Ob wohl
dein Herz), op. 23, no. 5 <p> Coventry and
Hollier, London, n.d.; Augener, London, 1886, no.
8810; Lamborn Cock, London, 1860 <d> also no. 5 in
collection of Six Songs with English and German
words, German words by W. Gerhard. 5p. Published
also in Leipzig by F. Kistner. Also reprinted in
Cavendish Music Book, of Boosey, as no. 85, pp.
14-17 <g> bm, x, ed, paz, Yale, German

147 Benson, Lionel Solomon <t> I fear thy kisses <p>
    Metzler, London, 1879 <d> 4p. <g> bm, x, and, ed

148 Berdahl, Arthur C. <t> dirge: Rough wind that moanest
    <p> ms., ca. 1936 <d> SSA and kettledrum or string
    bass. performed 1936 <g> q

149 Berdahl, Arthur C. <t> Mutability: The flower that
    smiles <p> ms. <g> q

150 Berdahl, Arthur C. <t> Threnos: O world <p> ms. <d>
    SSATB <g> q

151 Bergh, Arthur <t> Music, when soft voices die. op.
    37, no. 1 <p> Wesley Webster, San Francisco, 1947
    <d> for medium voice. 2p. <g> lc

152 Berwald, William <t> Indian serenade <p> G. Schirmer,
    New York, 1931 <d> four-part chorus. 8p. <g> lc, x

153 Besly, Edward Maurice <t> Music, when soft voices
    die. op. 11, no. 1 <p> Boosey, London, 1922 <d> 3
    forms; in D flat, E flat, and F. 3p. <g> bm, bbc,
    x

154 Besly, Edward Maurice <t> Song of Proserpine: Sacred
    goddess, Mother Earth <p> Boosey, London, 1922 <d>
    5p. <g> bm, x

155 Betjemann, Gilbert R. <t> As the moon's soft
    splendour (To a lady singing) <p> Novello, London,
    1891 <d> medium voice. 4p. Listed as in ms. in
    concert of the Shelley Society, 11 May 1887 <g> nn

156 Beuthin, J. S. <t> I arise from dreams <p> John
    Shepherd, London, 1855 (BM, 1857) <d> four-part
    song, SSTB. four parts in single sheets. 5p. <g>
    bm, and, x

157 Bexfield, W. R. <t> A serene winter's night <p>
    Novello, London, 1847 <d> Reviewed in Dramatic and
    Musical Review, no. 174, 26 June 1847, pp. 312-13.
    Copy not available.

158 Bimboni, Alberto <t> Clouds: I bring fresh showers
    <p> G. Ricordi, New York, 1925 <d> SATB chorus and

piano, plus contralto solo. 23p. <g> bm, x

159 Birch, Robert Fairfax <t> I fear thy kisses. op. 34,
    no. 2 <p> J. Patelson, New York, 1955 <d> baritone
    or bass. 2p. <g> lc

160 Birch, Robert Fairfax <t> To the moon <p> J.
    Patelson, New York, 1954 <d> 1p. <g> copy in
    collection

161 Bischoff, J. W. <t> I arise from dreams <p> Arthur P.
    Schmidt, Boston, 1910 <d> S or T. 3p. <g> bm, x

162 Blake, Ernest <t> A dirge <p> Breitkopf and Hartel,
    London, 1908 <d> in Ten Poems by Percy Bysshe
    Shelley for voice and piano, pp. 2-3 <g> lc

163 Blake, Ernest <t> I fear thy kisses <p> Breitkopf and
    Hartel, London, 1908 <d> in Ten Poems by Percy
    Bysshe Shelley for voice and piano, pp. 4-7 <g> lc

164 Blake, Ernest <t> Love's philosophy <p> Breitkopf and
    Hartel, London, 1908 <d> no. 3 in Ten Poems by
    Percy Bysshe Shelley for voice and piano, pp.
    8-15. end of volume. apparently no more published
    <g> lc

165 Bliss, Arthur <t> Three Songs for Girls' or Boys'
    Voices; nursery rhyme by Percy Bysshe Shelley and
    anonymous (A widow bird) <p> Novello, London, 1968
    <d> A widow bird, no. 2 of Three Songs, of 17 p.
    <g> bm, lc

166 Blower, Maurice <t> Tell me, thou star <p> J. Curwen,
    London, 1955; Schirmer, New York, 1955 <d> SA with
    piano, staff and tonic sol-fa notation. choruses
    for equal voices, no 2339. 4p. <g> copy in
    collection, lc, bm

167 Blume, Alfred <t> Music, when soft voices die <p>
    Novello, Ewer, London, 1891 <d> 2p. <g> x, bm

168 Blumenfeld, Sigismund <t> Death: they will die and
    there is no return. op. 22 in Trois Melodies <p>
    M. P. Belaieff, Leipzig, 1910 <d> Song 1, pp. 3-4
    in memory of Rimsky Korsakoff <g> x, Berlin,
    Russian

169 Blumenfeld, Sigismund <t> To the moon: Wanderer of
    the skies, o sad moon. op. 22 in Trois Melodies
    <p> M. P. Belaieff, Leipzig, 1910 <d> no. 2, pp.
    5-7 For Andrei Dm. Stascv <g> x, Berlin, Russian

170 Blumenfeld, Sigismund <t> C Mary: O Mary, my far-away
    friend (To Mary. op. 22, in Trois Melodies <p> M.
    P. Belaieff, Leipzig, 1910 <d> no. 3, pp. 8-11 for
    Grigorii Nik. Timofeev <g> x, Berlin, Russian

171 Blyton, Carey <t> To the moon <p> ms., 1956-60 <d>
    no. 2 of Lachrymae. In memoriam John Dowland. Five
    Songs for High Voice and String Quartet or
    Orchestra. Available for hire from Stainer and
    Bell. 4p. in 45p. <g> q

172 Bcase, Kate <t> Serenade: Good night? Ah no <p>
    Novello, London, 1900 <d> 3p. <g> bm, x

173 Bcase, Kate <t> Spirit of delight: Rarely, rarely,
    comest thou <p> Novello, London, 1900 <d> 4p. <g>
    x, bm

174 Bonavia, Ferrucio <t> Autumn--a dirge: The warm sun
    is failing <p> Augener, London, 1935 <d> a
    capella, for male quartet or chorus. no. 17482.
    3p. <g> bm, lc

175 Bcoth, Daisy <t> Love's philosophy <p> 12 June 1928,
    EU693358

176 Bcoth, Thomas Lykes <t> Czymandias <p> 1953 <d> 6p.
    in Library of Congress under EU32723, of 26
    January 1960, but application states "previously
    published 6 August 1953, A107765" <g> lc, not seen

177 Bcrnschein, Franz Carl <t> Arethusa <p> Fischer, New
    York, 1926 <d> soprano solo, SSA, and piano. 24p.
    no. 5658 <g> nn

178 Bcrnschein, Franz Carl <t> Indian serenade <p>
    Clayton F. Summy, Chicago, 1907 <g> listed in lc

179 Bcrton, Alice <t> Love's philosophy <p> possibly in
    ms., 1887 <d> sung at the Shelley Society Song
    Evening, 11 May 1887, item 18 cn the program. Not
    listed as in ms., like Betjemann's <g> not found

180 Borton, Alice <t> Rarely, rarely, comest thou <p>
    Stanley Lucas, Weber, London, 1881 <d> 5p. <g> ed,
    bm, mn, x

181 Borton, Alice <t> Remembrance: Swifter far than
    summer's flight <p> Stanley Lucas, Weber, London,
    1881 <d> 5p. <g> bm, ed, x

182 Boughton, Rutland <t> The cloud: I bring fresh
    showers <p> Stainer and Bell, London, 1925 <d> for
    women's chorus, SSA. S and B 3175. 25p. <g> bm, x

183 Bracken, Edith <t> The faded violet <p> 19th century
    <d> Listed on the back of a piece of 19th century
    music in the British Museum. Not found anywhere

184 Bracken, Edith <t> One word is too often profaned <p>
    19th century <d> the same as above item.

185 Brackett, Frank H. <t> From dreams of thee (Indian
    serenade) <p> Theodore Presser, Philadelphia, 1905
    <d> no. 4744. 5p. <g> bm, x

186 Bradshaw, N. <t> Music, when soft voices die <p>
    Lamborn Cock, and Addison, London, 1869 <d> 4p.
    <g> x, bm

187 Brainard, H. L. <t> Music, when soft voices die <p>
    John Church, Cincinnati, 1902 <d> 2p. <g> lc, x

188 Brainard, H. L. <t> A widow bird <p> Boston Music Co.
    (G. Schirmer, Jr.), Boston, 1906 <d> 3p. <g> x, bm

189 Bram, Marjorie Aimee <t> Lament <p> EU226763, 13 July
    1940

190 Braun, Charles <t> I fear thy kisses <p> Pitt and
    Hatzfeld, London, 1900 <d> no. 2 of Six Songs, <d>
    pp. 6-7 <g> nn

191 Braun, Charles <t> Love's philosophy <p> Pitt and
    Hatzfeld, London, 1900 <d> no. 1 of Six Songs, pp.
    1-5 <g> nn

192 Brearley, Herman <t> As the moon's soft splendour <p>
    Landry and Co., London, 1922 <d> Part-songs no.

108, SATB. Rehearsal piano only. J.228.L 7p. <g>
bm, x

193 Brewer, Alfred Herbert <t> I fear thy kisses <p>
Novello, London, 1912 <d> The Orpheus, New Series,
no. 538. 3p. <g> bm, x

194 Brewer, Alfred Herbert <t> Love's philosophy <p>
Novello, London, 19-- <d> ATTB. Orpheus Part-Songs
no. 340 listed in Novello catalogue 5C of 1915 <g>
not seen

195 Brewer, Alfred Herbert <t> Queen of my heart (false
attribution to Shelley) <p> Novello, London, 1912
<d> The Orpheus, New Series, no. 539. 8p. <g> bm,
x

196 Brewer, Alfred Herbert <t> A widow bird sat <p>
Joseph Williams, London, 1924 <d> A miniature
suite for voice and piano, no. 2, pp. 4-5, in
Miller's Green <g> bbc, bm

197 Brian, Havergal <t> Music, when soft voices die <p>
not published <d> composed in 1919 and sold to
Enoch and Sons, whose business was acquired by
Ashdown, and still unpublished. (Information from
the composer)

198 Brian, Havergal <t> On a poet's lips I slept <p>
unpublished, 1919. Same situation as in above
entry.

199 Brian, Havergal <t> Prometheus Unbound <p>
unpublished cantata. 1937-44 <d> Cantata for solo,
chorus, orchestra. First two acts complete.
Autographed vocal score only in BBC library. PL
3608. Performed by BBC.

200 Brian, Havergal <t> The Cenci <p> Unpublished opera
in 8 scenes, 195- <d> Autograph in BBC library.
vocal score and orchestra, Miscellaneous Score
6908.

201 Bright, Houston <t> Clouds that veil the midnight
moon (Mutability) <p> Shawnee Press, Delaware
Water Gap, 1971 <d> for SSA chorus with piano.
stanza one of Mutability plus a stanza by Houston
Bright. 7p. <g> q, copy in collection

202 Bright, Houston <t> Lament of the enchantress: He
    came like a dream (Fragments of an Unfinished
    Drama) <p> Associated Music Publishers, New York,
    1963 <d> SATB with rehearsal piano. 6p. <g> usi,
    copy in collection

203 Bright, Houston <t> Star, moon, and wind (for Tell
    me, thou star) <p> Shawnee Press, Delaware Water
    Gap, Pennsylvania, 1967 <d> Waring Workshop
    Series, A 896. SATB. rehearsal piano part. 7p. <g>
    copy in collection

204 Bright, Houston <t> The tale untold (Fragment: A tale
    untold) <p> Shawnee press, Delaware Water Gap,
    1970 <d> for SSA chorus with piano. Shelley's
    stanza with two words changed (sang and daedal).
    7p. <g> q, copy in collection

205 Bright, Houston <t> Trilogy for Women's Voices.
    Dirge: Rough wind that moanest <p> Shawnee Press,
    Delaware Water Gap, Pennsylvania, 1967 <d> Words
    by Shelley, Emily Bronte, and anonymous. SSAA, a
    capella. no. 2 of Trilogy, pp. 8-10 <g> lc, copy
    in collection

206 Bright, Houston <t> When the lamp is shattered <p>
    Shawnee Press, Delaware Water Gap, 1970 <d> for
    SATB chorus with rehearsal piano. 7p. <g> q, copy
    in collection

207 Bright, Houston <t> Winter night on the mountain: The
    cold earth slept below <p> Shawnee Press, Delaware
    Water Gap, Pennsylvania, 1964 <d> SATB, a capella.
    Contemporary Series A 763. 8p. <g> lc, copy in
    collection

208 Britten, Benjamin <t> Nocturne for Tenor Solo, Seven
    Obligato Instruments and String Orchestra. op. 6,
    no. 1. Shelley section taken from Prometheus
    Unbound: On a poet's lips I slept <p> Boosey and
    Hawkes, London, 1963 <d> 69p. for the whole.
    Shelley section pp. 1-7 for voice and strings.
    text in English and German, translated by Ludvig
    Landgraf <g> nn, German

209 Bruguiere, Emile Antoine <t> I arise from dreams <p>
    Breitkopf and Hartel, New York, 1901 <d> 7p. Mich
    erweckt ein susser Traum. Deutsch von F. H.

Schneider <g> not found, but listed in lc, German

210 Buck, Dudley <t> Prometheus Unbound, Chorus of
    spirits and hours: From unremembered ages. op. 90
    <p> Schirmer, New York, 1905; Curwen, London, 1905
    <d> male chorus and tenor solo, with piano, flute,
    string quintet. 39 p. Called new and revised
    edition. 27 p. in Curwen piano and chorus and solo
    edition <g> x, bpl, bm

211 Buck, Percy C. <t> Music, when soft voices die <p>
    Sydney Acott, Oxford, n.d. <d> no. 3 of Three
    Songs for Bass Voice, pp. 8-9 <g> nn

212 Budd, Alfred (Lee), Jr. <t> When the lamp is
    shattered <p> EU317405, 7 December 1942

213 Bugge, Magda <t> Vandrerne (World's wanderers): Klare
    Stjerne Du som foer <p> Wilhelm Hansen,
    Copenhagen, 1895 <d> p. 21 in Sang-Album af
    Nordiske Kunder <g> East Berlin, x, Danish

214 Bullard, Frederick Field <t> De profundis: Rarely,
    rarely, comest thou <p> Miles and Thompson,
    Boston, 1894 <d> no. 2 in Four Poems by Shelley
    Set to Lyric Music, op. 17 <g> Harvard Library
    (Houghton), x

215 Bullard, Frederick <t> From dreams of thee (Indian
    serenade) <p> 1894. See above. <d> no. 3 in Four
    Poems, 5p. in G and E <g> Harvard, x

216 Bullard, Frederick <t> Hymn of Pan: From the forests
    <p> 1894. See above. <d> no. 4 in Four Poems. 7p.
    in G and E flat <g> Harvard, x

217 Bullard, Frederick <t> To a skylark <p> 1894. See
    above. <d> no. 1 in Four Poems. 6p. in E flat and
    C <g> Harvard, x

218 Bulow, Hans von <t> The mask of anarchy <p> ca. 1863
    <d> Shelley's Song to the men of England and The
    mask of anarchy are variously maintained to be the
    inspiration of Georg Herwegh's Bundeslied which
    Ferdinand Lassalle requested von Bulow to set to
    music as a worker's song. The latter did so under
    the name of W. Solinger, concerning which see

Bulow's Briefe (Leipzig, 1898), IV, 346-348, wherein the song is printed, IV, 629-634, for TTBB. Concerning this much mooted question of Herwegh's use of Shelley's ideas, words, and meter see Solomon Liptzin, Shelley in Germany (New York, 1924), pp. 71-74. <g> Columbia University, x

219 Burnham, R. <t> Music, when soft voices die <p> Novello, London, 1920 <d> 2p. French translation by Maurice Boucher also given (Quand tu ne seras plus la) <g> bm, x, French

220 Burrows, Benjamin <t> O gentle moon <p> Augener, London, 1917 <d> no. 1 in Three Songs <g> lc

221 Burt, Joe Evan <t> Ozymandias <p> ms., 1969 <d> voice and orchestra <g> q

222 Bush, Alan D. <t> To the men of England <p> J. Curwen, London, 1928 <d> chorus, a capella, with rehearsal piano. 9p. SATB for the London Labour Choral Union. Curwen Choral Handbook no. 1243. 9p. <g> ed, bm, x

223 Bush, Geoffrey <t> Music, when soft voices die <p> Elkin, London, 1956 <d> SATB. Elkin choral series no. 2428, with tonic sol-fa notation. 4p. <g> bm, bbc

224 Bush, Geoffrey <t> A Summer Serenade (Music, when soft voices die) <p> Elkin, London, 1951 <d> item is probably the same as above entry (not seen). Part 6, pp. 53-58, is for tenor and SATB, with rehearsal piano <g> bm, x

225 Bush, Geoffrey <t> Ozymandias <p> Novello, London, 1967 <d> no. 2 of Two Shelley Songs for SATB, a capella. 8p. Musical Times, 1498 <g> lc

226 Bushell, Donald <t> The Cenci ("special music") <p> unpublished, 1940 <d> according to the program in NYPL, Donald Bushell wrote the music for a production of the play, produced at the Civic Playhouse of Bellingham, Washington, March 6-9, 1940, under the auspices of the Bellingham Theatre Guild, with Jeanne Mousc as Music Director. Beatrice's "Song: False friend, wilt thou smile" was based on an adapted version of Schumann's

Romance, op. 28, no. 2. <g> music not seen or available

227 Butcher, Frank C. <t> Love's philosophy. op. 3, no. 1 <p> Luckhardt and Belder, New York, 1908 <d> chorus for male voices. no. 50 of collection of quartettes and choruses for mixed voices. pp. 2-7 <g> lc, x

228 Butler, Eugene <t> Music, when soft voices die <p> Art Masters Studios, Minneapolis, 1966 <d> Art Masters choral music, no. 10 17. 3p. EP220860. <g> lc

229 Butterworth, Arthur <t> Le vent vert (for Summer and winter): It was a bright and cheerful afternoon <p> ms., London, 1960 <d> orchestral scherzo. available from Hinrichsen, London. Scored for flutes, oboes, clarinets, bassoons, horns, timpani, percussion, harp, strings. no voice. 34p. performed by BPC et al. <g> g

230 Butterworth, George S. K. <t> I fear thy kisses <p> Augener, London, 1919 <d> 3p. <g> bbc, ed, bm, x

231 Button, H. Elliot <t> The flower that smiles today <p> Novello and Co., London, 1898 <d> Novello's Part-Song Book, Series 2, no. 810 <g> lc

232 Button, H. Elliot <t> A lament: Swifter far <p> Novello, London, 1910 <d> A German folk song, arranged for SATB by H. E. Button, with words by Shelley, rehearsal piano. no. 1209 of Novello's, Part-Song Book, 2nd series. 4p. <g> bm, x

233 Button, H. Elliot <t> O Mary dear (To Mary) <p> Novello, London, ca. 1910 <d> included on program of Keats-Shelley Memorial Concert of 20 March 1907. no indication of nature of score, whether printed or ms. listed in Novello's catalogue 5A of 1912 as Part-Song no. 871 <g> not seen

234 Buzzi-Peccia, Arturo <t> Nothing in the world is single (Love's philosophy) <p> Presser, Philadelphia, 1924 <d> 5p. "Words after Shelley" <g> lc

235 Cain, Noble <t> The Indian serenade (Indian serenade)

<p> Raymond A. Hoffman Co., Chicago, 1932 <d>
TTBB. rehearsal piano. 7p <g> bpl, x

236 Cain, Noble <t> Music, when soft voices die <p>
Harold Flammer, Inc., New York, 1939 <d> four-part
chorus of women's voices <g> lc

237 Cain, Noble <t> Queen Mab: How beautiful this night
(IV, i) <p> Schirmer, New York, 1961; Chappell,
London, 1961 <d> eight-part mixed chorus. 7p. <g>
lc, bcm

238 Cain, Noble <t> Rarely, comest thou (A lament) <p>
Raymond A. Hoffman Co., Chicago, 1930 <d> no. 20
of A Series of A Cappella Choruses. 12 voices,
SATB. rehearsal piano. Dedicated to the St. Olaf
Choir, F. Melius Christiansen, Conductor. 16p. <g>
bpl, x

239 Callcott, William Hutchins <t> Music, when soft
voices die <p> Lamborn Cock, London, 1847 <d> no.
6 of Lays of Germany for Two Voices by the Most
Celebrated German Composers (11 in all) with the
Original Words and an English Translation edited
and arranged with an accompaniment for the
Pianoforte by William Hutchins Calcott. This song
is Leise, Leise, by C. M. von Weber. 3p. <g> and,
Bodleian, x

240 Camp, John Spencer <t> Indian song (Indian serenade)
<p> Oliver Ditson, Boston, 1903 <d> 6p. <g> bm, x

241 Campbell, Colin Macleod <t> Love's philosophy <p>
Augener, London, 1934; also 1955 (see below) <d>
low and high forms, 4p. Also published as Three
Shelley Songs, op. 173, for women's voices, SSA.
9p. with piano. Augener ed. has 4p. the rest of
the set probably not published. in LC, G. Ricordi,
New York, 1955. Listed as EP94738. <g> bm, x (seen
for solo voice only)

242 Canale, Orlando <t> The Indian serenade <p> EU35010,
23 August 1946

243 Candlyn, T. Fredrick H. <t> Music, when soft voices
die <p> Arthur P. Schmidt, Boston, 1920 (also 1926
and 1947) <d> SSA and piano. octavo ed, no. 910.

3p. pub. by Schmidt 1926 and 1947 in Cctavo Series
for Men's voices no. 553, TTEB, with rehearsal
piano part. 3p. <g> lc, bm

244 Carmichael, Mary G. <t> My faint spirit. op. 12 <p>
Czerny, London, 187- <d> no. 7 in Poems set to
Music. Song from the Arabic (an imitation). 4p.
<g> bpl, x

245 Carter, O. L. <t> Indian serenade <p> Oliver Ditson,
Boston, 1893 <d> 5p. <g> lc, x

246 Carter, T. P. <t> The world's wanderers <p> EU440171,
17 December 1918

247 Caseley, J. H. <t> Music, when soft voices die <p>
Weekes, London, 1903 <d> 4p. <g> bm, x

248 Casey, Samuel Ward <t> Music, when soft voices die
<p> Banks and Son, York, 1919 <d> no. 957 of York
Series of Glees, Part-Scngs, etc. for Male Voices
<g> bm

249 Castelnuovo-Tedesco, Mario <t> The fountains mingle.
op. 173 <p> G. Ricordi, New York, 1955 <d> SSA and
piano. 7p. <g> bm, x

250 Castelnuovo-Tedesco, Mario <t> Indian serenade <p> A.
Forlevesi, Florence, 1925 <d> high voice, 6p. no.
11259. With Italian translation. <g> lc, Italian

251 Castelnuovo-Tedesco, Mario <t> Lament. op. 153, no. 3
<p> Leeds Music, New York, 1954 <d> SSA. 7p. <g>
bm

252 Castelnuovo-Tedesco, Mario <t> The moon: And, as a
dying lady (sic). op. 154, no. 7 <p> Leeds Music,
New York, 1954 <d> SSA. 6p. <g> bm, x

253 Castelnuovo-Tedesco, Mario <t> Music, when soft
voices die <p> Leeds Music, New York, 1951 <d> SSA
plus piano. 4p. <g> x, bm

254 Castelnuovo-Tedesco, Mario <t> Cne word is too often
profaned <p> G. Ricordi, New York, 1955 <d> op.
173. SSA and pianc. 8p. <g> x

255 Castelnuovo-Tedesco, Mario <t> When the lamp is

shattered. op. 173 <p> G. Ricordi, New York, 1955
<d> SSA and piano. 12p. chorus of women's voices
<g> x, bm

256 Centanini, G. P. <t> The world's wanderers <p> John
    Church Co., Cincinnati, 1914 <d> no. 1 of Three
    Shelley Lyrics, pp. 5-9. <g> lc, x

257 Centanini, G. P. <t> The past <p> John Church Co.,
    Cincinnati, 1914 <d> no. 2 of Three Shelley
    Lyrics, pp. 13-17 <g> lc, x

258 Centanini, G. P. <t> The cloud <p> John Church Co.,
    Cincinnati, 1914 <d> no. 3 of Three Shelley
    Lyrics, pp. 21-31 <g> lc, x

259 Chadwick, Cecil <t> To Jane: The keen stars <p>
    Boosey and Hawkes, London, 1947 <d> 4p. <g> bbc, x

260 Chadwick, George Whitefield <t> Adonais, overture for
    orchestra <p> 1898. holograph in ink in LC <d>
    62p. gift to LC in 1956 <g> lc

261 Challinor, Frederick Arthur <t> Music, when soft
    voices die <p> Bayley and Ferguson, London;
    Schirmer, New York, 1907 <d> TTBB and rehearsal
    piano. Choral album no. 761. 5p. also in tonic
    sol-fa series <g> bm, x

262 Chapman, Thomas <t> World's wanderers <p> Monthly
    Musical Record, Vol. 22, pp. 179-81, August 11,
    1892 <g> bm, x

263 Chavez, Carlos <t> Three Nocturnes. To the Moon: Art
    thou pale for weariness <p> G. Schirmer, New York,
    1946 <d> no. 2 of the set. 2p. <g> bm, x

264 Cherry, Alexander <t> Mutability: The flower that
    smiles <p> Wood, London, 1889 <d> 4p. <g> ed, bm,
    x

265 Christopher, Cyril S. <t> Love's philosophy <p>
    Paterson, Edinburgh, 1937 <d> pp. 8-11 in Five
    Songs <g> bbc, lc, x

266 Christopher, Cyril S. <t> Music, when soft voices die
    <p> Paterson, Edinburgh, 1937 <d> pp. 6-7 in Five

Songs <g> bbc, bm, x

267 Clark, Horace <t> I arise from dreams <p> C. W.
    Thompson, Boston, 1908 <d> women's voices <g> lc

268 Clarke, Henry Leland <t> O wild west wind <p>
    American Composers Alliance facsimile ed., New
    York, 1962 <d> for men's chorus and piano, TTBB.
    24p. <g> x

269 Clarke, Henry Leland <t> Spirit of delight: Rarely,
    rarely, comest thou <p> American Composers
    Alliance facsimile ed., New York, 1954 <d> voice
    and piano. 8p. <g> x

270 Clarke, Henry Leland <t> To suffer woes (from
    Prometheus Unbound) in Songs of Faith in Man for
    Religious Liberals <p> Hodgin Press, Los Angeles,
    1960 <d> hymn, four parts, on p. 22. See also
    Michael Wise. <g> x

271 Clarke, Reginald <t> Music, when soft voices die. op.
    19, no. 1 <p> Weekes, London, 1900 <d> no. 1 of
    two two-part songs. 3p. <g> bm, x

272 Clarke, Reginald <t> A summer day: The whispering
    waves were half asleep. op. 19, no. 2. <p> Weekes,
    London, 1900 <d> no. 2, of two two-part songs. 3p.
    <g> x

273 Clarke, Robert Conigsby <t> Love's philosophy <p> C.
    Woolhouse, London, 1902 <d> 4p. <g> bm, x

274 Clements, John <t> Music, when soft voices die <p>
    Banks and Son, York, 1936 <d> SATB. York series of
    anthems and glees, no. 126 3p. <g> bm

275 Clokey, Joseph Waddell <t> Music, when soft voices
    die <p> C. C. Birchard, Boston, 1940 <d> SSA. no.
    1333 Laurel Octavo. 3p. <g> bm, x

276 Cobham, Maurice <t> La Chanteuse; a series of vocal
    music. Poetry by Coleridge and Shelley. (The
    spirit song: Weave, weave the dance.) <p> C.
    Jefferys, London, 1849 <d> SA duet and piano. no.
    3 of the five songs in La Chanteuse <g> x, bm

277 Cobham, Maurice <t> Away, unlovely dreams, away, in

La Chanteuse <p> C. Jefferys, London, 1849 <d> no. 4 of La Chanteuse, for solo and final chorus and piano, 7p. <g> bm, x

278 Ccerne, Louis Adolphe <t> I arise from dreams. op. 164, no. 1 <p> Oliver Ditson, Boston, 1921 <d> for high voice in C. 4p. <g> x

279 Coke, Roger Sacheverell <t> The Cenci. Opera. op. 41 <p> ms., 1940-55 <d> Coke's libretto. Performed Nov. 5, 1959 by Eugene Goosens, London Symphony Orchestra and Imperial Opera Co. <g> Grove

280 Ccke, Roger Sacheverell <t> I dreamed that as I wandered. op. 17 <p> Chappell, London, 1936 <d> no. 1 of Six Songs for soprano or tenor voice. 5p. <g> x, bm

281 Ccke, Roger Sacheverell <t> On a poet's lips. op. 19 <p> Chappell, London, 1936 <d> no. 4 in Six Songs for soprano or tenor voice. 10p. <g> lc, x

282 Ccke, Roger Sacheverell <t> When the lamp is shattered. op. 19 <p> Chappell, London, 1936 <d> nc. 6 of Six Songs for soprano or tenor voice. 2p. <g> x, lc

283 Ccleridge-Taylor, Avril <t> Love's philosophy <p> ms. <d> song with accompaniment. 4p. <g> q

284 Coleridge-Taylor, Samuel <t> As the moon's soft splendour. op. 37, no. 5 <p> Novello, London, 1899 <d> 5p. <g> bbc, ed, bm, x

285 Ccleridge-Taylor, Samuel <t> Song of Proserpine: Sacred Goddess, Mother Earth <p> Novello, London, 1912 <d> SATB, a capella. rehearsal piano. no. 2040 of Novello's tonic sol-fa series <g> bm, x

286 Ccnverse, Frederick Shepherd <t> I arise from dreams. op. 14 <p> Boston Music Cc., Boston, 1903 <d> for baritone. Also in library of Congress as a holograph by the composer, arranged for small orchestra. 5p. <g> nn

287 Ccoke, Arnold <t> To the moon: And like a dying lady <p> Oxford University Press, London, 1963 <d> no. 1 in Nocturnes, a Cycle of Five Songs for Soprano,

Horn, and Piano, pp. 1-4 <g> nn

288 Cooke, Waddington <t> Love's philosophy <p> Chappell
     and Co., London, 1892 <d> song. 5p. <g> nn, ed,
     bm

289 Coombs, C. Whitney <t> Indian serenade <p> G.
     Schirmer, New York, 1891 <d> for soprano or tenor,
     5p. <g> lc, x

290 Cory, George <t> Good night? ah no <p> General Music
     Publishing Co., New York, 1970 <d> no. 3 of Four
     Songs of Night. 3p. <g> copy in collection

291 Covell, Elizabeth <t> The cloud <p> ms., 1933 <g> lc

292 Covell, Elizabeth <t> To a skylark <p> ms., 1933 <g>
     lc

293 Cowen, Frederick Hymen <t> The fountains mingle with
     the river <p> Joseph Williams, London, 1892;
     Oliver Ditson, Boston, 1892 <d> no. 4 of Four
     Duets for ST, 7p. <g> bbc, bm, x

294 Craig, Lou Urmston (Aoede, pseud.) <t> Jane (for To
     Jane), a Serenade <p> EU361419, 25 June 1944

295 Crandell, John Stanley <t> Good night, from The
     Debutante (words by Thomas Moore and Shelley) <p>
     J. S. Crandell, New York, 1910 <d> duet for
     soprano and baritone in a two-act "musical play".
     Shelley's poem adapted <g> lc

296 Cripps, A. Redgrave <t> When the lamp is shattered
     <p> Lyon and Hall, Brighton, 1938 <d> no. 3 in Six
     Songs, pp. 3-7 <g> bm

297 Crowder, C. F. <t> Swiftly walk o'er the western wave
     <p> J. Fischer, New York, 1913 <d> SATB with
     rehearsal piano, 8p. <g> lc, nn

298 Crowe, Eyre A. <t> Arethusa. A Song <p> Novello,
     London and New York, 1889 <d> 12p. <g> ed, bm, x

299 Culbertson, Della <t> Good night <p> Indicated only
     under 10 June 1907, E134199 by LC, with no further
     information. Seemingly unavailable.

300 Curry, W. Lawrence <t> Music, when soft voices die
    <p> Plymouth Music Co., New York, 1964 <d> SSA.
    4p. John Raymond Choral Series 200 <g> lc

301 Cushing, Charles <t> Music, when soft voices die <p>
    ms. <d> numerous public performances, according to
    questionnaire response <g> q

302 Cuvelier, Andre-Marie <t> Prometheus Unbound: My soul
    is an enchanted boat <p> Maison
    Deswartes-Courtois, Paris, 1940 <d> no. 4 in
    Chansons pour Helene. Melodies anglaises. pp. 4-5.
    text only in English <g> bn, x

303 Dance, Carolin Adelaide <t> Music, when soft voices
    die <p> Robert W. Ollivier, London, 1861 <d> 5p.
    <g> and, bm, x

304 Daniel, Cyrus <t> Music, when soft voices die <p> B
    and W <g> source: amc

305 Dann, Horace <t> Music, when soft voices die <p>
    Paxton, London, 1938; E. B. Marks, New York <d>
    3p. <g> bbc, lc, bm, x

306 Darke, Harold <t> Widow bird <p> Edward Arnold,
    London, 1950 <d> no. 841, E. Arnold's Singing
    Class Series. Unison song and piano. 4p. <g> bm, x

307 David, Paul <t> To the night: Swiftly walk over the
    western wave <p> Augener, London, 1866 <d> SSTB.
    9p. <g> and, bm, x

308 Davies, H. Walford <t> The cloud <p> Sidney Riorden,
    London, 1914 <d> SSA with piano. 12p. <g> ed, bm,
    x

309 Davis, John David <t> The Cenci <p> unpublished <d>
    symphonic ballad produced at Birmingham,
    Bournemouth and other places, probably in the
    1890's. <g> grove

310 Davis, John David <t> Good night, ah no, the hour is
    ill. op. 41, no. 1 <p> Novello, London, 1909 <d>
    song for voice and piano with violoncello obligato
    ad lib. 7p. <g> bm

311 Davis, William Robert <t> Adonais: The one remains
    (LII, i) <p> Galaxy Music Corp., New York, 1939
    <d> short anthem for chorus. Galaxy Music for the
    Church, no. 972 <g> lc

312 Davison, James William <t> I fear thy kisses <p>
    Wessel and Stapleton, London, 1876; also Duncan
    Davison, London <d> 5p. in British Vocal Album <g>
    and, paz, bm, x

313 Davison, James William <t> Swifter far <p> Duncan
    Davison, London, 1845; also Cramer, Beale and
    Chappell, London (1876?) <d> no. 1 of Vocal
    Illustrations of Shelley, 5p. <g> bm, x

314 Davison, James William <t> False friend, wilt thou
    smile (from The Cenci) <p> Duncan Davison, London,
    1845 <d> no. 3 of Vocal Illustrations of Shelley,
    5p. <g> bm, x, paz

315 Davison, James William <t> Rough wind that moanest
    (Dirge) <p> Duncan Davison, London, 1845; also,
    Cramer, Beale and Chappell, London, 1860 <d> no. 2
    of Vocal Illustrations of Shelley. 7p. <g> bm, x

316 Davison, James William <t> There was a little lawny
    islet <p> Duncan Davison, London, 1845 <d> no. 4
    of Vocal Illustrations of Shelley. 5p. <g> bm, x,
    paz

317 Davison, James William <t> Tell me, thou star <p>
    Duncan Davison, London, 1845 <d> no. 5 of Vocal
    Illustrations of Shelley. no copy found

318 Davison, James William <t> Orphan hours, the year is
    dead <p> Duncan Davison, London, 1845 <d> no. 6 of
    Vocal Illustrations of Shelley. no copy found.

319 Day, Alfred <t> Music, when soft voices die <p> ca.
    1847, 1909, London <d> First published in The
    Harmonist, a collection (q.v. in Henry Davison,
    Music in Victorian England, p. 36). The air is
    copied from Davison's Universal Methodist (1847?),
    Vol. 2, p. 216, which says that Dr. Day, physician
    and musical theorist, was author of the celebrated
    treatise on Harmony of 1845 followed by Macfarren
    and others. Republished in W. E. Duncan, The
    Minstrelsy of England, Augener, 1909, II, 231. <g>

bm

320 Day, Grant <t> I arise from dreams <p> EU 205252, 4 October 1939

321 De Marsan, Henry (ed.) <t> The Kiss (Love's philosophy) <p> New York, n.d. <d> Words of Shelley given in The New Singer's Journal, p. 355. Reference to no. 49, Henry De Marsan's New Comic and Sentimental Singer's Journal Containing all the most popular Songs cf the day. Music not given but implied. <g> nn

322 De Stein, E. S. <t> An enchanted boat (Prometheus Unbound, Asia's song) <p> Enoch and Sons, London, 1911 <d> no. 2 in c in IC <g> lc

323 Deane, Allan <t> By Law divine (Love's philosophy) <p> B. F. Wood, Boston, 1913 <d> 3 forms, in G, A, and C. 5p. <g> bm, x

324 Deffner C. H. <t> To night <p> EU985211, 20 March 1967 <d> words adapted

325 Defontaine, M. <t> La Mort (Death): Death is here <p> Durand, Paris, 1956 <d> SATB, a capella, translated by Defontaine. 7p. <g> bn, x, French

326 Deis, Carl <t> Music, when soft voices die <p> Schirmer, New York, 1914 <d> 4p. one of Eight Songs <g> nn

327 Deis, Carl <t> On a faded violet <p> Schirmer, New York, 1914 <d> no. 5 in Eight Songs. for a low voice. 3p. <g> nn

328 Delius, Frederick (also Fritz) <t> Indian love song (Indian serenade) <p> Augener, London, 1892; Breitkopf and Hartel, New York and Cologne, 1910; Oxford University Press, London, 1969 <d> first of the Three Songs, Augener no. 8824. 6p. in each edition. ed. of 1910 includes German translation by Jelka-Rosen. 1969 edition in two parts, all Shelley songs being in part two, edited by Peter Peers <g> nn, bm, lc,   German

329 Delius, Frederick (also Fritz) <t> Love's philosophy <p> Augener, London, 1892; Breitkopf and Hartel,

New York and Cologne, 1910; Oxford University
Press, London, 1969 <d> second of the Three Songs,
Augener no. 8824. 6p. in each edition. ed. of 1910
includes German translation by Jelka-Rosen. 1969
edition in two parts, all Shelley songs being in
part two, edited by Peter Peers <g> nn, bm, lc,
German

330 Delius, Frederick (also Fritz) <t> To my heart's
queen (for To the queen of my heart, a false
attribution to Shelley) <p> Augener, London, 1892;
Breitkopf and Hartel, New York and Cologne, 1910;
Oxford University Press, London, 1969 <d> third of
the Three Songs, Augener no. 8824. 6p. in each
edition. ed. of 1910 includes German translation
by Jelka-Rosen. 1969 edition in two parts, all
Shelley songs being in part two, edited by Peter
Peers <g> nn, bm, lc,   German

331 Demuth, Norman <t> Pan's Anniversary (from Prometheus
Unbound, IV): The pale stars are gone <p> Joseph
Williams, London, 1954 <d> suite for chorus, SATB,
and orchestra or piano, words from Ben Jonson,
Keats and Shelley. 35p. Part V, Nocturne, pp.
30-35 by Shelley <g> bm, ed, x

332 Demuth, Norman <t> Prometheus Unbound <p> ms., 8
December 1948 <d> BBC mss.R3, full score for
orchestra. Probably the same as above. Grove
speaks of incidental music for Prometheus Unbound
<g> bbc, grove

333 Dennee, Charles Frederick <t> Love's argument. op. 29
(Love's philosophy) <p> Arthur P. Schmidt, Boston,
1900 <d> no. 2 of Five Songs. 4p. A.P.S. no. 5316
<g> lc

334 Densmore, John H. <t> Good night? ah no <p> Schirmer,
New York, 1900 and 1909 <d> for middle voice. 7p.
also in LC as no. 1 of Three Songs (1909). no.
E1995-98, for high voice <g> 1900 copy in nn

335 Desormiere, Roger <t> The Cenci <p> unpublished, 1935
<d> background music for Antonin Artaud's version
of The Cenci, based on Shelley and on Stendhal's
1837 account of the Cenci family, produced in
Paris, on May 6, 1935. For the "musical
inventions" as Artaud called them, see

"Playscript" in Simon Watson-Taylor's English translation (London, 1969), with its indication of four 30-foot high bells, loud speakers, thunder claps and wind, and mechanically produced susurrations and other "sinister music," requiring the Ondes Martinot, according to B. L. Knapp, in Antonin Artaud (New York, 1969), p. 117. See also the article on the music by Paule Thevenin. <g> music not available

336 Dexter, Ada <t> On a faded violet <p> Harrison, Birmingham, 1896 <d> 4p. <g> bm, x

337 Diamond, David <t> Music, when soft voices die <p> American Music Pub., New York, 1944 <d> 2p. <g> bbc, nn, x

338 Diamond, David <t> Sonnet: Lift not the painted veil <p> Associated Music Pub., New York, 1946 <d> 3p. <g> bbc, nn, x

339 Dicker, Maurice <t> Life's reverie: Oh world (for O world) <p> Apollo Music Co., London, 1912 <d> 4p. <g> x, Royal Academy

340 Dickinson, Clarence <t> Music, when soft voices die <p> H. W. Gray, New York, 1911 <d> SSTTBB, with rehearsal piano. 3p. Modern Series of Part-Songs for All Voices, no. 32 <g> bm, lc

341 Dickson, Elizabeth (Dolores) <t> Arethusa arose <p> Augener, London, 1861; Charles Jefferys in BM <g> bm, x, paz

342 Dickson, Elizabeth (Dolores) <t> Cythna's lament: When morning came (for Then morning came) <p> Ashdown, London, 1864; Charles Jefferys, in BM <d> 6p. <g> bm, x, paz

343 Dickson, Elizabeth (Dolores) <t> I pant for the music <p> Charles Jefferys, London, 1861 <d> 5p. <g> x, bm

344 Dickson, Elizabeth (Dolores) <t> My faint spirit was sitting in the light of thy looks (Love song--An imitation from the Arabic) <p> Charles Jefferys, London, 1863 <d> 4p. <g> and, bm, x

345 Dickson, Elizabeth (Dolores) <t> Prometheus Unbound:
Dirge of time (Here, oh here, we bear the bier)
<p> Charles Jefferys, London, 1861 <d> 3p. <g>
and, bm, x

346 Dickson, Elizabeth (Dolores) <t> Prometheus Unbound:
Echoes! we listen (Child of ocean) <p> Charles
Jefferys, London, 1861; also Brainard, Chicago,
1861 <d> 7p. <g> and, bm, x

347 Dickson, Elizabeth (Dolores) <t> Prometheus Unbound:
My soul is an enchanted boat <p> Charles Jefferys,
London, 1859 <d> 6p. <g> bm, x

348 Dickson, Elizabeth (Dolores) <t> One word is too
often profaned <p> Ashdown, London; Charles
Jefferys, 1863, in BM <d> 4p. <g> paz, bm, x

349 Dickson, Elizabeth (Dolores) <t> Spring song (Revolt
of Islam): Behold, spring sweeps over the earth
<p> Charles Jefferys, London, 1862 <d> 6p. <g>
and, bm, x

350 Dickson, Elizabeth (Dolores) <t> The rivulet wanton
and wild (from Alastor) <p> Robert Cocks, London,
1865 <d> 5p. <g> and, bm, x

351 Dickson, Elizabeth (Dolores) <t> Skylark: Hail to
thee, blithe spirit <p> Charles Jefferys, London,
1867 <d> 7p. Also in Bocsey's Musical Cabinet. No.
145. Songs of Dolores: Child of Ocean; Echoes, we
listen; the skylark; The dirge of time: Hear, oh
hear (17 pages); <g> paz, bm, x

352 Dickson, Elizabeth (Dolores) <t> Spirit of delight
(Song: Rarely, rarely, comest thou) <p> Charles
Jefferys, London, 1867 <d> 5p. <g> bm, x

353 Dickson, Elizabeth (Dolores) <t> To morrow: Where art
thou, beloved <p> Charles Jefferys, London, 1863
<d> 5p. <g> and, bm, x

354 Diercks, John <t> The world's wanderers <p> Tritone
Press, Bryn Mawr, 1962 <d> 3p. <g> q

355 Dieren (see Van Dieren)

356 Dolores (see Dickson)

357 Doninger, Paul E. <t> A dirge <p> EU166370, 4 March
    1970 <d> for basscon and soprano

358 Doty, George <t> Love's philosophy <p> 22 July 1969,
    EU125733

359 Douty, Nicholas <t> Music, when soft voices die <p>
    Theodore Presser, Philadelphia, 1936 <d>
    Three-part women's chorus, accompaniment for
    violin, violoncello, and piano or harp. SSA. 7p.
    including 1 for violin and 1 for violoncello. no.
    21247 <g> lc

360 Drakeford, Richard Jeremy <t> Music, when soft voices
    die <p> ms. 1953, rev. 1960 <d> 2p. <g> q

361 Drakeford, Richard Jeremy <t> A widow bird <p> ms.,
    1952, rev. 1960 <d> SATE. 3p. <g> q

362 Drinkwater, George <t> One word is too often profaned
    <p> Chappell, London, 1920 <d> 4p. <g> bm, x

363 Duchemin C. J. <t> To morrow: Where art thou, beloved
    <p> Ashdown and Parry, London, 1874 <d> Trio alla
    canone for S, MS and A. Can also be sung by STB.
    7p. <g> bm, x

364 Duke, John <t> Prometheus Unbound: My soul is an
    enchanted boat <p> The Valley Music Press,
    Northampton, Mass., 1953 <d> low to medium voice.
    2p. <g> nn

365 Dunstan, R. and Arthur Lee <t> Music, when soft
    voices die <p> Huddersfield, Schofield and Sims,
    1914 <d> no. 303 in 600 English and Dutch Songs,
    pp. 137-38. S and S Series. four-part chorus a
    capella <g> bm, x

366 Dunstan, R. and Arthur Lee <t> The widow bird <p>
    Huddersfield, Schofield and Sims, Huddersfield,
    1914 <d> No. 488 in 600 English and Dutch Songs,
    with piano accompaniment. S. and S. Series, p.
    281. 3 staves. a capella chorus <g> bm, x

367 Eden, Robert <t> Dreams of thee. Song (Indian
    serenade) <p> Elkin, London; Galaxy, New York,
    1932 <d> 7p. <g> lc

368 Edwards, Walter Strong <t> Love's philosophy <p> J.
    Church, Cincinnati <d> 5p. <g> mn, bm, x

369 Effinger, Cecil <t> Time, a Chorus: Unfathomable sea
    <p> Fischer, New York, 1947 <d> a capella chorus
    <g> Grove, and

370 Eggar, Katharine Emily <t> My soul is an enchanted
    boat (Prometheus Unbound) <p> London, ms. <d>
    voice, string quartet and piano. Chairman of the
    Council of the Society of Women Musicians. <g> q

371 Eisler, Paul <t> Music, when soft voices die <p> G.
    Schirmer, New York, 1920 <d> 2p. <g> bm, x

372 Elgar, Edward W. <t> In moonlight: As the moon's soft
    splendour <p> Novello, London, 1904 <d> Song, the
    words adapted to the Canto Popolare from the
    concert-overture 'In the South' composed by Elgar.
    voice and piano. 4p. <g> ed, bn, bm, x

373 Elgar, Edward W. <t> O wild west wind. op. 53, no. 3.
    <p> Novello, London; Gray, New York, 1908 <d>
    part-song for SATB, a capella. Novello's part-song
    book, no. 1058, second series. 10p. plus text <g>
    lc, bm, grove

374 Elgar, Edward W. <t> Symphony no. 2, in E flat. op.
    63: Rarely, rarely, comest thou, spirit of delight
    (Motto on the fly-leaf) <p> Novello and Co.,
    London 1911 <d> 184p. <g> nn, lc

375 Elkus, Albert Isaac <t> to the moon: Art thou pale
    <p> ms., 1913, corrected 1923 <g> q

376 Elkus, Albert Isaac <t> To the west: Swiftly over the
    western wave (sic for Swiftly walk o'er the
    western wave) <p> ms., 1920 <g> q

377 Ellerton, John Lodge <t> The flower that smiles today
    <p> C. Lonsdale, London, 1839 <d> 4p. <g> x, and,
    bm

378 Ellerton, John Lodge <t> The world's wanderers.
    Canzonet <p> C. Lonsdale, London, 1844 <d> 5p. <g>
    bm, x, and

379 Ellicott, Rosalind F. <t> Radiant sister of the day

(from The invitation) <p> Novello, London, n.d.
(1887?) <d> no. 542 of Novello's part-song book,
second series. four-part song with piano. Sung at
Shelley Song Evening, 11 May 1887. 13p. <g> East
Berlin, x

380 Elliot, Charles S. <t> A morning in May: The sky
above is bright (possibly Matilda gathering
flowers) <p> Arthur P. Schmidt, Boston, 1910 <d>
trio (SSC) for women's voices and piano. 8p. Music
arranged from a Peruvian dance, words arranged
from Shelley <g> East Berlin, x

381 Ellis, Clifford Cowdell <t> I arise from dreams <p>
EU161778, 15 March 1949 1<d> music arranged by
Winifred Sargent and George Nathaniel Benson

382 Elton (?) <t> Love's philosophy <p> T. W. Strong, New
York, n.d. (ca. 1850) <d> An illustration for the
song (included in Elton's Illustrated Songster),
published by T. W. Strong during the second
quarter of the century, is discussed by Kenneth B.
Murdoch, p. 20 (Introduction) in G. S. Jackson,
Early Songs of Uncle Sam (Boston, 1923), but
Elton's book has proved unavailable. <g> not found

383 Elton, Antony <t> To me this world's a dreary blank
<p> ms. <d> no. 1 of Songs of Despair <g> q

384 Elton, Antony <t> Yet now despair itself seems mild
(Stanzas in dejection) <p> ms. <d> no. 4 of Songs
of Despair <g> q

385 Emmanuel, Maurice <t> Promethee enchaine (for
Prometheus Bound) <p> Paris, 1915 <d> Error in
Grove. Not set to Shelley's text, q.v.,
Bibliotheque nationale

386 Engel, Yuly Dmietrievich <t> Dirge: Rough wind <p> P.
Jurgenson, Moscow and Leipzig, 1907 <d> no. 1 of
Three Poems on Shelley (Balmont translation), op.
4. 4p. <g> Russian, East Berlin, bm, x

387 Engel, Yuly Dmietrievich <t> Mutability: The flower
<p> P. Jurgenson, Moscow and Leipzig, 1907 <d> no.
2 of Three Poems (see above). 6p. <g> East Berlin,
x, Russian

388 Engel, Yuly Dmietrievich <t> Music, when soft voices
      die <p> P. Jurgenson, Moscow and Leipzig, 1907 <d>
      no. 3 of Three Poems (see first entry under
      Engel). 8p. <g> Russian, East Berlin, x

389 Faber, Ella <t> Indian serenade <p> Boosey, London,
      1910 <d> 4p. <g> bm, x

390 Fagge, Arthur <t> The cloud: I bring fresh showers
      <p> Ashdown (also Willcocks), London, 1909 <d> 8p.
      <g> bm, mn

391 Fahlgren, Dorothy Jean <t> Music, when soft voices
      die <p> H. T. Fitzsimons, Chicago, 1946 <d>
      sextet, SSAATB, Aeolian Series of Choral Music,
      no. 1057 <g> lc

392 Fairchild, Blair <t> Music, when soft voices die <p>
      C. W. Thompson, Boston, 1905 <d> no. 1207. at head
      of title: Songs by Blair Fairchild. 5p. <g> nn,
      bpl

393 Farebrother, Bernard <t> The cloud <p> Lamborn Cock,
      London, 1869 <d> 5p. <g> and, bm, x

394 Farley, Roland <t> Indian serenade <p> New Music
      Press, New York, 1933 <d> four-part chorus for
      male voices, TTBB, plus piano. 13p. <g> bbc, lc, x

395 Farwell, Arthur <t> Bridal song: The golden gates of
      sleep unbar <p> Schirmer, New York, 1927 <d> high
      or medium voice. op. 43. in Three Poems by
      Shelley. 4p. <g> lc, bm

396 Farwell, Arthur <t> Daughter of ocean: My coursers
      are fed with the lightning <p> Schirmer, New York,
      1927 <d> for high or medium voice; one of Three
      Poems by Shelley. 5p. <g> lc, bm

397 Farwell, Arthur <t> On a faded violet <p> Schirmer,
      New York, 1927 and 1942 <d> in Three Poems by
      Shelley, op. 43, no. 2, 3p. for medium or high
      voice, and reprinted in A New Anthology, pp. 31-33
      <g> bm, lc

398 Farwell, Arthur <t> Song of Proserpine. op. 72, no. 1
      <p> Schirmer, New York, 1943 <d> 3p. in high and

low forms. <g> bbc, nn

399 Fedeli, Luigi <t> Canto Funebre (Dirge: Rough wind)
    <p> Umberto Pizzi, Bologna, 1929 <d> 2p. <g> Rome,
    Academy of St. Cecilia, x, Italian

400 Fedeli, Luigi <t> Tramonto. Frammento (The sunset):
    There late was one <p> Umberto Pizzi, Bologna,
    1929 <d> 2p. lines 18-23 of the poem used <g>
    Rome, Academy of St. Cecilia, x, Italian

401 Feldon, Fred <t> Rose leaves (for Music, when soft
    voices die?) <p> EU104423, March 1969 <d> 1p.
    words adapted by composer

402 Fenney, William J. <t> Music, when soft voices die,
    op. 9, no. 2 <p> Stainer and Bell, London, 1915
    <d> SMSATB and rehearsal piano. S and B Choral
    Library no. 145, S and E 1448, 4p. <g> bm, x

403 Fernstrom, John <t> The isle. op. 62, no. 3 <p> 1943
    <d> no. 3 of Songs of the Sea. voice and piano <g>
    g information from Swedish Radio Music Library,
    Swedish

404 Ferrers, Herbert <t> Love's philosophy <p> Stainer
    and Bell, London, 1913 <d> no. 1 of Two Songs <g>
    lc, x

405 Finney, Ross Lee <t> The martyr's elegy (from
    Adonais): The slave trampled (IV, 6) <p> C. F.
    Peters, New York, 1967. <d> C. F. Peters ed.
    66094. SATB and piano. 30p. <g> lc

406 Fischer, William R. <t> Music, when soft voices die
    <p> R. D. Row, Boston, 1958 <d> SSA and piano. no.
    622 of Row Octavo Series for Women's Voices. 3p.
    <g> bm

407 Fisher, Truman <t> Ozymandias <p> Schirmer, New York
    and London, 1967 <d> three-part woman's chorus,
    Schirmer's Secular Choral Music no. 11445. 11p.
    <g> lc, bcm

408 Fisher, William Arms <t> Prometheus Unbound: My
    coursers are fed with the lightning. op. 3, no. 3
    <p> Schirmer, New York, 1895 <d> MS or baritone.
    in Three Shelley Songs <g> nn, lc

409 Fisher,William Arms <t> A widow bird. op. 3 no. 1 <p>
    Schirmer, New York, 1895 <d> 2p. in Three Shelley
    Songs <g> lc, x

410 Fisher, William Arms <t> The world's wanderers. op.
    3, no. 2 <p> Schirmer, New York 1895 <d> 4p. in
    Three Shelley Songs <g> lc, x

411 Fiske, Milton <t> The world's wanderers <p> EU461652,
    December, 1956

412 Fitzwilliam, Edward Francis <t> Love's philosophy <p>
    D'Almaine, London, 1855 <d> duet for two sopranos
    in Songs for a Winter Night, 17 songs. no. 17. 7p.
    <g> and, ed, bm, x

413 Fleck, Fritz <t> An den Mond (To the moon): Art thou
    pale <p> C. A. Challier, Berlin, 1927 <d> 2p.
    translated by Dr. Ernst Earthel <g> West Berlin,
    x, German

414 Fleming, Alroy <t> A bridal song: Night, with all
    thine eyes look down! <p> Duff Stewart, London,
    1924 <d> no. 6812. in An Album of Love Lyrics. 7p.
    <g> lc, bm, x

415 Fleming, Alroy <t> To Ianthe: I love thee, baby <p>
    Duff Stewart, London, 1924 <d> pp. 9-12 of An
    Album of Love Lyrics, pub. nc. 6812 <g> lc, bm, x

416 Fleming, Alroy <t> One word is too often profaned <p>
    Duff Stewart, London, 1924 <d> pp. 13-15 of An
    Album of Love Lyrics, pub. nc. 6812 <g> lc, bm, x

417 Fletcher, Percy Eastman <t> The cloud <p> Curwen and
    Sons, London; Schirmer, New York, 1911 <d> SSA
    chorus, 11p. <g> bm, x

418 Fletcher, Percy Eastman <t> How beautiful this night
    (A nocturne) <p> J. Curwen, London, 1912 <d> SATB
    and rehearsal piano. 10p. <g> bm, x

419 Fletcher, Percy Eastman <t> I arise from dreams (arr.
    from C. K. Salaman, q.v.) <p> J. Curwen and Sons,
    London, 1909 <d> The Apollo Club, no. 437. Tenor
    solo and TTBB plus rehearsal piano. 12p. <g> bm, x

420 Fletcher, Percy Eastman <t> The islet: There was a
    little lawny islet <p> Musical Times, London, 1911
    <d> no. 850, Vol. 54, Musical Times, December 1,
    1913, pp. 809-815. SATB, with rehearsal piano
    (copyright of Novello) <g> bm

421 Fletcher, Percy Eastman <t> The witches' carnival:
    To-whoo (Shelley's translation of Faust) <p> J.
    Curwen, London, 1913 <d> SSA and piano, Curwen no.
    71371. 19p. <g> bm, x

422 Flowers, George French <t> Good night? ah no, the
    hour is ill <p> Hitchcock's Music Store, New York,
    1882 <d> Hitchcock's Collection of Old and New
    Songs, I, 72-73. Also in C. H. Purday, Navy Song
    Book, p.142, for men's chorus (given in East
    Berlin Catalogue) <g> nn, East Berlin

423 Flowers, George French <t> Shelley's lament: O world
    <p> Dearle and Co., London, 1867 <d> 4p. for bass
    or contralto <g> and, bm, x

424 Foerster, Adolph M. <t> Love's philosophy. op. 55,
    no. 4 <p> H. Kleber, Pittsburgh; Schirmer, New
    York, 1908 (given by LC as 1901) <d> 4p. <g> nn,
    lc

425 Foerster, Adolph M. <t> Unfathomable sea:
    Unfathomable ocean of time. op. 49, no. 5 <p> H.
    Kleber, Pittsburgh; Schirmer, New York, 1900 <d>
    no. 5 of Six Songs. 5p. <g> nn

426 Fogg, Eric <t> Evening: The sun is set; the swallows
    are asleep <p> J. Curwen and Sons, London, 1924
    <d> Edition Michaud. 6p. <g> lc, bm

427 Fogg, Eric <t> The isle: There was a little lawny
    islet <p> Novello, London, 1922 <d> SATB. Musical
    Times no. 952, with rehearsal piano. 4p. <g> bm, x

428 Fogg, Eric <t> Song of Proserpine <p> Curwen, London,
    1921 <d> solo. Curwen no. 2233. 4p. <g> bm, x

429 Fogg, Eric <t> To morrow: Where art thou <p> J.
    Curwen and Sons, London, 1924 <d> part of Edition

Michaud. 3p. <g> lc

430 Fogg, Eric <t> When passion's trance is overpast <p>
     Elkin, London, 1922 <g> bbc, Yale, lc

431 Fogg, Eric <t> A widow bird <p> J. Curwen and Sons,
     London, 1924 <d> 2p. <g> lc

432 Foote, Arthur <t> Indian serenade: I arise from
     dreams. op. 26, no. 7 <p> Arthur P. Schmidt,
     Boston, 1892 <d> tenor voice. 4p. <g> nn, Yale, bm

433 Foote, Arthur <t> Love's philosophy <p> Arthur P.
     Schmidt, Boston, 1893 <d> p. 26 in Lyric Fancies;
     an Album of Songs, vol. 2, pp. 26-29 <g> nn

434 Ford, Ernest A. <t> Album of Six Songs. Poems by
     Shelley <p> Stanley Lucas, Weber and Co., London,
     1885; reprinted 1893 (26 pages of text) <d> 1p. of
     poetry text and 25 of music. Includes 1. To the
     queen of my heart (falsely attributed to Shelley)
     2. Heart's devotion: I fear thy kisses 3. On a
     faded violet 4. As the moon's soft splendour 5.
     Good night? ah no 6. A bridal song: The golden
     gates unbar. Also issued as Three Songs: Heart's
     devotion; On a faded violet; As the moon's soft
     splendour <g> bm, x, 1893 ed. in lc

435 Ford, Ernest A. <t> As the moon's soft splendour <p>
     Laudy, Paris, 1858; London, 1885 <d> no. 4 of Six
     Songs (see above). no. 3 in Three Songs in F. 3p.
     <g> ed, x, bm

436 Ford, Ernest A. <t> A bridal song: The golden gates
     of sleep unbar <p> London, 1885 <d> no. 6 of Six
     Songs. 6p. <g> bm, x

437 Ford, Ernest A. <t> The fountains mingle with the
     river <p> Boosey, London, 1902 <d> 6p. <g> lc, x

438 Ford, Ernest A. <t> Good night? ah no <p> Laudy,
     Paris, 1858; London, 1881; London, 1885; G. D.
     Russell, Boston, n.d. III, 86-88, Strand Musical
     Magazine of 1896, pp. 92-97 <d> no. 5 1of Six
     Songs, 3p. in A flat and in F (1881 ed.) Boston
     ed. 5p., called Tom Karl's Song Album, no. 16.
     Separately published (1885), in Bodleian copy <g>

bm, ed, Harvard Library (Boston ed.), x

439 Ford, Ernest A. <t> Heart's devotion: I fear thy
kisses <p> Laudy, Paris, 1858; London, 1885 <d>
no. 1 in Three Songs in F. nc. 2 of Six Songs.
Also separately issued in 1885 (Yale copy) <g> bm,
ed, x, Yale

440 Ford, Ernest A. <t> On a faded violet <p> Laudy,
Paris, 1858; London, 1885 <d> no. 3 of Six Songs
(2p.). no. 2 of Three Scngs, in G (3p.) <g> ed,
bm, x

441 Ford, Ernest A. <t> To the queen cf my heart (false
attribution to Shelley) <p> Laudy, Paris, 1858;
London, 1885 <d> no. 1 cf Six Songs (6p). Also
separately issued in 1885 in D flat, C, and B flat
<g> ed, bm, x

442 Ford, Ernest A. <t> Fare-well (poem by Rev. F. L.
Meares, suggested by Ford's song, Good-night) <p>
Stanley Lucas, Weber and Co., London, 1883 <d> 5p.
Poem fits the tune of Ford's setting, with changes
in Shelley's words, for the sake of Victorian
sensitivity. <g> bm, x

443 Forman, Harry Buxton <t> Tc Stella, from the Greek of
Plato (no. 1 of Epigrams): Thou wert the morning
star <p> Shelley Society's Publications, London,
1886 <d> song for voice and piano in three staves,
one page, printed as a scroll cn the title page of
The Shelley Library, comprising the Shelley
Society's Publication, 4th series, miscellaneous,
no. 1 (printed by Reeves and Turner, with the
title The Shelley Library) <g> x

444 Forrester, J. Cliffe <t> Shelley Album. Nine Songs
Selected from the Poems of Percy Bysshe Shelley
<p> Charles Woolhouse, London, 1888 <d> see below
for separate songs <g> bm, x

445 Forrester, J. Cliffe <t> Ariette for Music: As the
moon's soft splendour <p> 1888 <d> Shelley Album,
pp. 2-5. see first entry.

446 Forrester, J. Cliffe <t> Music: I pant for the music
<p> 1888 <d> Shelley Album, pp. 6-11. see first
entry.

447 Forrester, J. Cliffe <t> The world's wanderers: Tell
    me, thou star <p> 1888 <d> Shelley Album, pp.
    12-13. See first entry.

448 Forrester, J. Cliffe <t> I arise from dreams <p> 1888
    <d> Shelley Album, pp. 14-18. See first entry.

449 Forrester, J. Cliffe <t> Love's philosophy <p> 1888
    <d> Shelley Album, pp. 19-21. see first entry.

450 Forrester, J. Cliffe <t> Arab love song: My faint
    spirit <p> 1888 <d> Shelley Album, pp. 22-27. See
    first entry.

451 Forrester, J. Cliffe <t> Mutability: The flower that
    smiles today <p> 1888 <d> Shelley Album, pp.
    28-30. See first entry.

452 Forrester, J. Cliffe <t> Song: On a faded violet <p>
    1888 <d> Shelley Album, pp. 31-35. See first
    entry.

453 Forrester, J. Cliffe <t> Good night? ah no <p> 1888
    <d> Shelley Album, pp. 36-39. See first entry.

454 Fowler, Keith <t> Indian serenade <p> A. Weekes,
    London, 1925 <d> 5p. <g> bm, x

455 Fowler, Keith <t> Wine of the fairies: I am drunk <p>
    J. Curwen, London, 1925 <d> unison song and piano
    plus sol-fa notation. Curwen Choruses for Equal
    Voices, no. 71665. 3p. <g> bm

456 Fox, Arthur M. <t> The faded violet (On a faded
    violet) <p> Schirmer, New York; Woolhouse, London,
    1888 <d> no. 2 of Three Songs, pp. 5-7. Also no. 6
    in Album of Eight Songs, pub. by E. Asherberg,
    London, n.d., pp. 29-32 (in the Bodleian) <g> ed,
    bm, x

457 Fox, Arthur M. <t> Her voice did quiver (On Fanny
    Godwin) <p> Schirmer, New York; Woolhouse, London,
    1888 <d> no. 1 in Three Songs, pp. 2-4 <g> ed, bm,
    x

458 Fox, Arthur M. <t> I arise from dreams <p> Schirmer
    New York; Woolhouse, London, 1888 <d> no. 3 of
    Three Songs, pp. 8-11 <g> ed, bm, x

459 Frain, M. Theodore <t> I arise from dreams. op. 24
    <p> Frain Publishing Co., New York, 1906 <d> MS,
    with violin, flute, cello, or viola obligato, plus
    piano, by M. T. Frain, "composer of Violet Gate
    and Heigh Baby Ho Baby." 6p. (only voice and piano
    part furnished) <g> bm, x

460 Freer, Eleanor Everett <t> I fear thy kisses. op. 24,
    no. 2 bis. <p> Henry Lemoine, Paris, 1920 <d>
    translated into French by E. E. Freer, as Je
    crains tes baisers, douce femme. two forms, for
    high and low voice. 2p. <g> bn, x, French

461 Fritzsche, Charles <t> Serenata Hindustani (Indian
    serenade)--A song of love's deliquium: I arise
    from dreams <p> Harding, Los Angeles, 1917 <d> 5p.
    <g> lc, x

462 Fry, W. H. <t> To the queen of my heart (Shelly--sic;
    false attribution to Shelley) <p> F. D. Benteen,
    Baltimore, n.d. <d> 2p. <g> Harvard Library, x

463 Fryer, Herbert <t> Music, when soft voices die <p> G.
    Schirmer, New York and London, 1916 <d> no. 5 in
    Five Songs, for high or medium voice. 3p. <g> bm,
    lc

464 Fuller, A. F. <t> I arise from dreams <p> Solar
    Literary and Musical Bureau, Ft. Worth, Texas,
    1909 <d> 4p. <g> lc, x

465 Furbeck, Faya <t> Song: False friend, wilt thou weep
    (The Cenci) <p> unpublished, May, 1926 <d> Music
    was composed for the play as presented by the
    Lenox Hill Players at the Lenox Little Theatre,
    New York, beginning May 19, 1926, directed by
    Wladimir Nelidoff, not seen or available

466 Gade, Felix <t> Good night <p> John Church,
    Cincinnati, 1906 <d> for low and for high voice.
    3p. <g> Harvard Library, x

467 Galliera, Arnaldo <t> Canzone: Music, when soft
    voices die <p> A. and G. Carisch, Milan, 1939 <d>
    Italian by E. M. Avanzi. 2p. <g> lc, x, Italian

468 Galloway, Tod B. F. <t> I arise from dreams <p>
    Presser, Philadelphia, 1904 <d> in Seven Memory

Songs, op. 30, pp. 23-25 <g> lc

469 Gambogi, F. Elvira <t> O world, o life <p> Robert
    Cocks, London, 1895 <d> no. 1 of "Series of
    Artistic Songs." two forms, in C and E flat. 5p.
    <g> bm, x

470 Gardiner, H. Balfour <t> Music, when soft voices die
    <p> Goodwin and Tabb, London, 1908 <d> first of
    Two Lyrics. 2p. <g> ed, x

471 Gardner, John <t> A widow bird <p> unpublished, 1939
    <d> performed 1951 <g> q, x

472 Gatty, Nicholas Comyn <t> Away, away: Away, away,
    away, from men and towns <p> Cary and Co., London,
    1915 <d> 3p. <g> bm, x

473 Gatty, Nicholas Comyn <t> Ode, Unfathomable sea (for
    Shelley's Time): Unfathomable sea! whose waves are
    years <p> Novello, London, 1920 <d> no. 2 in Three
    Short Odes for Chorus and Orchestra. 7p. <g> bm,
    gr, x

474 Gatty, Nicholas Comyn <t> Ode, To suffer woes (from
    Prometheus Unbound) <p> Novello, London, 1920 <d>
    no. 3 in Three Short Odes for Chorus and
    Orchestra. 8p. <g> bm, gr, x

475 Gaul, Harvey Bartlett <t> Ozymandias, king of kings
    <p> Oliver Ditson, Boston, 1935 <d> chorus for
    men's voices with four-hand piano accompaniment.
    Part-songs for men's voices, no. 14748. 9p. <g> lc

476 Gazzotti, Luigi <t> Se mai . . . . Romanza (When
    passion's trance is overpast) <p> "Euterpe
    Alpina," di Paolino Bonavia, Turin, n.d. <d> 4p.
    translated by G. Faccioli <g> Rome, Academy of St.
    Cecilia, x, Italian

477 Geddes, Paul Rossbrugh <t> Love's philosophy <p>
    EU226281, 12 February 1910, and EU68011, 24 May
    1934. 3p. <g> lc

478 Geier, Louise <t> Music, when soft voices die <p>
    John Church, Cincinnati, 1899 <d> no. 3 of Three
    Songs, pp. 2-3 <g> lc, x

479 George, Christian <t> Indian seranade (for Indian
      serenade). op. 10, no. 1 <p> EU147511, 1 July 1937
      <d> for baritone. 5 leaves <g> lc

480 Ghedini, Giorgio Federico <t> Tre canti di Shelley;
      per voce e pianoforte (see below for songs) <p>
      Suvini Zerboni, Milan, 1947 <d> translation by
      Augusta Giudetti. for high voice. 8p. <g> nn, nuc,
      Italian

481 Ghedini, Giorgio Federico <t> The world's wanderers
      (I pellegrini del mondo) <p> 1947 <d> see first
      entry. 3p. <g> Italian, nn

482 Ghedini, Giorgio Federico <t> Rough wind (Vento rude)
      <p> 1947 <d> See the first entry. 2p. <g> Italian,
      nn

483 Ghedini, Giorgio Federico <t> Mutability: The flower
      that smiles (3rd stanza used) (Mentre azzurri
      splendono di cieli) <p> 1947 <d> See first entry.
      1p. <g> Italian, nn

484 Giannini, B. V. <t> Love's philosophy <p> Clementino
      de Macchi, New York, 1899 <d> 4p. <g> nn

485 Gilbert, Florence <t> Whispering waves (To Jane: The
      recollection) <p> Robert Cocks, London, 1895 <d>
      3p. <g> bm, x

486 Gilbertson, Arthur <t> A widow bird <p> Weekes,
      London, 1898 <d> no. 2 cf Three Songs, pp. 4-5 <g>
      bm, x

487 Ginastera, Alberto <t> Beatrix Cenci. Opera based on
      The Cenci <p> Boosey and Hawkes, New York, 1971
      <d> opera commissioned by the Washington Opera
      Society for the opening of the J. F. K. music
      center, September, 1971. English libretto by
      William Shand translated from Spanish text by
      Alberto Girri. Text and musical effects show
      awareness of Artaud's 1935 version of Shelley's
      play. <g> copy of libretto in collection, Spanish

488 Giuffrida, Robert T. <t> A widow bird <p> EU56780, 13
      June 1960 <d> 4p.

489 Glazer, Frank <t> I fear thy kisses <p> EMI, New
York, 1941 <d> 4p. <g> amc, x

490 Gledhill, John <t> A faded flower: The colour from
the flower is gone <p> Stanley Lucas, Weber and
Co., London, 1878; J. and W. Chester, Brighton,
1883 <d> no. 4 in Seven Songs in Two Books, the
Words by Shelley and Burns. 2p. <g> bm, x

491 Gledhill, John <t> To Mary Shelley (song called To
Mary): The world is dreary <p> J. and W. Chester,
Brighton, 1888 <d> 5p. <g> bm, x

492 Glendenning, R. Rashleigh <t> To the queen of my
heart (falsely attributed to Shelley) <p> Novello,
London, n.d. <d> in Four Lyrics <g> listed in
Schirmer's music store

493 Gliere, Reinhold <t> An islet set in the sea (A
little lawny isle). op. 55, no. 2 <p> P.
Jorgenson, Leipzig, n.d. <d> for SSAA, 3p.
Translated by Lina Esbeer into German, probably
from Balmont's translation of Shelley's lyrics. a
capella. <g> East Berlin, x, Russian

494 Glover, Howard <t> Indian serenade <p> Chappell,
London, 1856 <d> 6p. Given as published by Hill
and Co., n.d., 5p, in the Bodleian <g> bm, x

495 Glover, Howard <t> Mary dear: Oh Mary dear, that you
were here <p> Duncan Davison, London, 1863 <d> 5p.
<g> bm, x

496 Glover, Howard <t> Love's philosophy <p> Duncan
Davison, London, 1861 <d> 5p. <g> and, ed, bm, x

497 Glover, Howard <t> Music. A song: I pant for the
music <p> Musical World, London, 1846 <d> Vol. 21,
no. 52 of The Musical World. 3p. Presented to the
Susbcribers of the Musical World, composed
expressly <g> bm, x

498 Gluck, C. W. von <t> The flower that smiles <p>
Leader and Cock, London, 1857 (and 1859; see
below) <d> Adapted by Elizabeth Masson to
Shelley's words using an air from Gluck's
'pilgrimme auf Mecca' (Pelerins de la Mecque.
Opera-comique): La rencontre imprevue. Un

ruisselet bien clair. Also in Songs for the
Classical Vocalist, nc. 13, poem of Dancourt of
1764 (same publisher, 1859) <g> bm

499 Gnessin, Mikhail Fabianovich <t> Prometheus Unbound,
III, iv: Suddenly a change tcok place (on the
cover of the score). After Shelley, a Symphonic
Fragment. op. 4. (D'apres Shelley) <p> P.
Jurgenson, Moscow and Leipzig, 1910 <d> orchestral
score, pp. 3-27. Composed 1906, orchestrated 1908,
published 1910. <g> Berlin, x

500 Gnessin, Mikhail Fabianovich <t> The Cenci,
Beatrice's song. op. 18 <p> probably unpublished
<d> declamation with piano, according to Grove.
not seen

501 Godfery, M. van Sommeren <t> Ozymandias <p> Augener,
London, 1957 <d> p. <g> ed, bm

502 Godfrey, Arthur Eugene <t> A lament: A widow bird sat
<p> Robert Cocks, London, 1893 <d> no. 1 of Songs.
two forms, in C and C minor. 2p. <g> bm, x

503 Gold, Ernest (Goldner in Boston Public Library
catalogue) <t> Music, when soft voices die <p>
Schirmer, New York, 1963 and 1967 <d> no. 7 of
Songs of Love and Parting. also in Twentieth
Century Art Songs. 5p. <g> lc, bm, nn

504 Goldschmidt, Berthold <t> Beatrice Cenci, opera.
Libretto by Martin Esslin <p> unpublished.
composed 1951 <d> Excerpts performed, 13-14 April,
1953 on BBC. See BBC Radio Times, April 13, 1953.
London Philharmonic and four singers <g> grove

505 Goodhart, Arthur Murray <t> Arethusa. Ballad for
Chorus and Crchestra. <p> Novello, London, 1891
<d> The music composed for the 450th anniversary
of the founding of Eton College. SATB plus piano.
24p. <g> bm, x

506 Goossen, Frederic <t> The world's wanderers <p> 1950
to 1955. unpublished. registered in library of
American Composers Alliance <g> q

507 Gounod, Charles Francois <t> The fountains mingle <p>
Weekes, London; also Ditson, Boston, 1850;

Chappell, London, 1871 <d> nc. 12334.4 (1850). 6p.
<g> and, ed, lc, bm, x, Harvard (1871 ed.)

508 Gounod, Charles Francois <t> Gocd night <p> Chappell,
London, 18711 (in Anderson); 1874 (British Museum)
<d> no. 4416 of the Musical Bouquet, pub. by C.
Sheard. 5p. <g> and, bm, ed, paz, x

509 Grace, Harvey <t> A widow bird. op. 8, no. 2 <p>
Richards, London, 1912 <d> nc. 13 of the Encore
Series. 2p. <g> bm, x

510 Graham, Edward Fergus <t> Scng: How stern are the
wces of the desolate mourner <p> unpublished, 1810
<d> written by Shelley for St. Irvyne, ch. 9 and
sent to Graham for musical setting. See Jones,
Letters of Shelley, 1.16 <g> nct found

511 Graham, Edward Fergus <t> Song: How swiftly through
Heaven's wide expanse <p> unpublished, 1810 <d>
written by Shelley for St. Irvyne, ch. 7 and sent
to Graham for musical setting. See Jones, Letters
of Shelley, 1.7 <g> not found

512 Graham Edward Fergus <t> Stanza for the Marseillaise
hymn <p> unpublished, 1811 <d> translation written
by Shelley and sent to Graham for musical setting.
See Jones, Letters of Shelley, 1.106 <g> not found

513 Graham, W. H. J. <t> I arise frcm dreams cf thee <p>
William A. Pond, New York, ca. 1866 <d> 4p. <g>
nn, Harvard

514 Grattann, W. H. <t> Dirge: Rough wind <p> Campbell,
Ransford, London, 1852 <d> nc. 1 of Two Songs. 2p.
<g> and, bm, x

515 Grattann, W. H. <t> I arise from dreams <p> Cramer,
Beale and Co., London, 1855; reprinted by Stanley
Lucas, Weber and Co., London, 1881 <d> 5p. <g> bm,
and, paz, x

516 Grattann, W. H. <t> Musical Thoughts Suggested by
English Poets: As one eramoured is upbcrne in
dream--O'er lily-paven lakes 'mid silver mist <p>
D'Almaine, London, 1850 <d> piano piece inspired
by the two lines of verse. pp. 5-6 in Musical

Thoughts <g> bm, x

517 Grattann, W. H. <t> The world's wanderers: Tell me,
    thou star <p> Campbell, Ransford, London, 1852 <d>
    no. 2 of Two Songs. 4p. <g> and, bm, x

518 Graves, R. (Ralph Greaves?) <t> I arise from dreams
    <p> Oxford University Press <d> probably misprint
    for Greaves, q.v. <g> in bbc list

519 Gray, Alan <t> Arethusa <p> Novello, London, 1892 <d>
    for baritone, chorus, and orchestra. 30p. <g> lc,
    bpl, nn

520 Greaves, Ralph <t> I arise from dreams <p> Oxford
    University Press, London, 1931 <d> 5p. <g> bm, x

521 Greaves, Ralph <t> Music, when soft voices die <p>
    Oxford University Press, London, 1931 <d> for
    SATB. no. 736 of Oxford Choral Songs. 4p. <g> bbc,
    bm

522 Green, Howard Sylvester <t> O world! O life <p> H. S.
    Green, Butler, Pennsylvania, 1925 <d> 3p. <g> lc,
    x

523 Gregory, E. C. <t> A widow bird <p> Novello and Ewer,
    London, 1883 <d> no. 5 cf Six Vocal Sketches, pp.
    15-16 <g> bm, x

524 Groninger, Alma (Chambers) <t> Music, when soft
    voices die <p> ms. <d> SATB, a capella. 1p. <g> q,
    x

525 Groninger, Alma (Chambers) <t> Widow bird <p> ms. <d>
    unison song with piano accompaniment. 1p. <g> q, x

526 Gross, David <t> Forever in a nightmare <p> EU104711,
    19 March 1969 <d> Shelley's words revised and
    others added.

527 Grossmann, Gertrude <t> Ozymandias <p> Edward W.
    Boker, Baltimore, 1908 <d> for low voice. 4p. <g>
    lc, x

528 Grosvenor, Norman <t> Music, when soft voices die <p>
    Novello, London, 1899; also 1902. <d> no. 4 of

Thirteen Vocal Trios for MS, C, and Baritone, pp. 8-9. with rehearsal piano. composition dated 1883 <g> bm, x, ed

529 Grosvenor, Norman <t> Love's philosophy <p> Novello, London, ca. 1899 <d> listed only in the Edinburgh National Library, but not seen. perhaps one of the vocal trios (see above) <g> ed, not seen

530 Groton, Frederic Locksley <t> A faded violet (On a faded violet). op. 2 <p> E. F. Wood, Boston, 1909 <d> three forms, in B flat and F. 3p. <g> bm, x

531 Guerini, R. (Rosa?) nee Wilberforce <t> A widow bird <p> Augener, London, 1879 (?) <d> 2p. <g> East Berlin, ed, x

532 Guerrini, Guido <t> Time: Unfathomable sea (Tempo: Insondabile mare) <p> F. Bongiovanni, Bologna, 1948 <d> no. 1 in Canti della mia prigionia, pp. 9-12. voice and piano. translated by Guerrini <g> nn, Italian

533 Guerrini, Guido <t> Music, when soft voices die (Quando si spegne il canto la musica risuona) <p> F. Bongiovanni, Bologna, 1948 <d> no. 2 in Canti della mia prigionia, pp. 13-15. voice and piano. translated by Guerrini <g> nn, Italian

534 Hadley, Henry Kimball <t> I arise from dreams. op. 4, no. 6 <p> Boston Music Co., Boston, 1894 <d> one of Eight Songs by H. K. Hadley. 5p. <g> nn

535 Hadley, Patrick <t> The Cenci: Come, I will sing for you some low, sleepy tune <p> ms., 1951 <d> 10p. Performed at Norwich and Cambridge Festivals in the 1950's. Broadcast from Birmingham and performed at The Hague. Arrangements lost. For voice and orchestra <g> bl, gr

536 Hadley, Patrick <t> The world's great age begins (Hellas) <p> Oxford University Press, London, 1925 and 1931 <d> Songs of Praise, no. 180. 1p. Set to the hymn tune: Pembroke, 86.86.88 (1931 ed., p.375) <g> bm, x

537 Hadley, Patrick <t> Life of life <p> Oxford, 1912 <d> not seen. given by Blume

538 Hadow, William Henry <t> Life of life <p> Sydney
     Acott, Oxford, 1912 <d> no. 4 in Fourth Album of
     Songs, pp. 12-18 <g> bm, x

539 Hadow, William Henry <t> Music, when soft voices die
     <p> Novello and Ewer, London and New York, 1884
     <d> 4p. <g> mn, bm, x

540 Ham, Albert <t> Music, when soft voices die <p>
     Novello, London, 1922 <d> Part-songs for mixed
     voices, SSATB and rehearsal piano. <p> 3p. <g> bm

541 Hamilton, E. W. <t> Swifter far <p> Lamborn Cock,
     London, 1870 <d> 6p. <g> and, bm, x

542 Harding, Joseph R. W. <t> Love's philosophy <p>
     Metzler and Co., London, 1859 <d> no. 2 of
     Mirthful Moments. 2p. <g> and, bm, x

543 Harper, Robert Sargent <t> Dirge: Rough wind; <p>
     EU270732, 24 September 1941

544 Harper, Robert Sargent <t> Dirge: Rough Wind; Lament:
     Oh world; Fragment: when soft winds; On Fanny
     Godwin; Music, when soft voices die; To--: I fear
     thy kisses; A widow bird; The waning moon <p> ms.,
     September 1941 <d> performed in recitals <g> q

545 Harris, Crafton <t> Dirge: Rough wind <p> ms., 1929
     <d> 3p. <g> q, sent from England

546 Harris, Crafton <t> Fragment: When soft winds and
     sunny skies <p> ms., 1927 <d> 3p. <g> q, sent from
     England

547 Harris, Crafton <t> To --: I fear thy kisses <p> ms.,
     1929 <d> 2p. <g> q, sent from England

548 Harris, Crafton <t> Indian serenade <p> ms., 1948 <d>
     8p. <g> q, sent from England

549 Harris, Crafton <t> Lament: O world! O life! O time!
     <p> ms., 1929 <d> 3p. <g> q, sent from England

550 Harris, Crafton <t> Music, when soft voices die <p>
     ms., 1929 <d> 3p. <g> q, sent from England

551 Harris, Crafton <t> On Fanry Godwin: Her voice did
     quiver <p> ms., 1929 <d> 3p. <g> q, sent from
     England

552 Harris, Crafton <t> The waning moon <p> ms., 1929 <d>
     2p. <g> q, sent from England

553 Harris, Crafton <t> A widow bird <p> ms., 1929 <d>
     2p. <g> q, sent from England

554 Harris, Cuthbert <t> Music, when soft voices die <p>
     Schmidt, Boston, 1921 <d> For women's trio, SSA,
     no. 794 of Schmidt's octavo edition choruses, pp.
     2-4 <g> lc

555 Harris, Floyd O. <t> Music, when soft voices die <p>
     Frederick Wick, Minneapolis, 1949 <d> SSA. no.
     327. 4p. <g> lc

556 Harris, J. Thorne <t> Swifter far than summer's
     flight. op. 60 <p> Wessel, London, 1855 <d> 6p.
     <g> bm, and, x

557 Harris, Victor <t> The fountains mingle with the
     river <p> William A. Pond, New York, 1890 <d> in
     Two Love Songs. 5p. <g> nn

558 Harris, Victor <t> Music, when soft voices die. op.
     13, no. 2 <p> Arthur P. Schmidt, Eoston, 1895 <d>
     voice and piano. 2p. melody different from the
     cthers <g> lc, x

559 Harris, Victor <t> Music, when soft voices die. op.
     25, no. 1 <p> G. Schirmer, New York, 1904 <d> duet
     fcr CT with piano part. 4p. in Two Duets.
     different melody from the others <g> lc, x

560 Harris, Victor <t> Music, when soft voices die. op.
     14, no. 4 <p> Luckhardt and Eelder, New York, 1895
     <d> for chorus, TTEE. 2p. a capella <g> bpl, x

561 Harrison, Julius Allen Greenway <t> Music, when soft
     voices die <p> Novello, London, 1913 <d> SSSSAA
     and rehearsal piano. 6p. no. 446 of Novello's
     Octavo Edition of Trios fcr Female Voices. <g> bm,
     x

562 Hart, Fritz <t> To night <p> 1905 <d> Chorus and

orchestra <g> grove, not seen or found

563 Hartmann, Emil <t> World's wanderers (Vandrerne:
    Klare Stjerne) <p> W. Hansen, Copenhagen, 1898 <d>
    pp. 16-17 in Osterlandske Sange. op. 14 <g> East
    Berlin, x, Danish

564 Hartmann, Thomas Alexandrovitch <t> Hymn of Pan: from
    the forests <p> 1936 <d> in Poems by Shelley for
    voice and orchestra. op. 52. item not found <g>
    grove

565 Hartmann, Thomas Alexandrovitch <t> Indian serenade
    <p> 1936 <d> in Poems by Shelley for voice and
    orchestra. op. 52. item not found <g> grove

566 Hartmann, Thomas Alexandrovitch <t> Time:
    Unfathomable sea! <p> 1936 <d> in Poems by Shelley
    for voice and orchestra. op. 52. item not found.
    <g> grove

567 Hasler, John <t> My faint spirit <p> Breitkopf and
    Hartel, London, 1910 <d> no. 4 of Seven Songs, pp.
    12-14 <g> Berlin, x

568 Hatch, Homer Barnes <t> The Indian serenade (for
    Indian serenade) <p> Schirmer, New York, 1930 <d>
    TTBB and piano. no. 7451 of Schirmer's Secular
    Choruses. 10p. <g> lc

569 Hatten, Geoffrey <t> Music and moonlight: As the
    moon's soft splendour <p> Boosey, London, 1913 <d>
    song of 5p. <g> bm

570 Hatton, John Liptrot <t> The world's wanderers: Tell
    me, thou star <p> Ashdown, London, 1877 (in
    Anderson); Augener, London, 1879 (in British
    Museum) <d> SATB) Augener no. 4955. 4p. <g> and,
    paz, bm, x

571 Hawley, Stanley <t> A widow bird (Das verlassene
    Vogelein) <p> Bosworth, Leipzig, 1898 <d> German
    by L. Osterried. 3p. <g> East Berlin, x, German

572 Hazlehurst, C. <t> Love's philosophy. op. 22, no. 1
    <p> Novello, London, 1921 <d> 4p. <g> bm, x

573 Head, Michael <t> I arise from dreams of thee <p>

Boosey, London, 1921 <d> voice and 'cello plus
piano. 9p. including one of 'cello score phrased
by George M. Jeffreys <g> bm, x

574 Head, Robert L. <t> A lament <p> EU609409, January
    1960

575 Headlam, Else (see Morley)

576 Heale, Helene <t> Lament: Swifter far <p> Monthly
    Musical Record, London, 1889 <d> vol. 19, pp.
    59-62. March 1, 1889 <g> bm, x

577 Heale, Helene <t> The storm: The waters are flashing
    <p> E. Ashdown, London, 1899 <d> no. 9 of
    Twenty-Four Easy Rounds. 1p. <g> bm, x

578 Hecht, Ed. <t> The flight of love: When the lamp is
    shattered. op. 16 <p> Stanley Lucas, Weber and
    Co., London, 1876 <d> SSA with piano. 9p. <g> bm,
    and, x

579 Heffner, Carl <t> Music, when soft voices die <p>
    Weekes, London, 1891 <d> no. 5 in Six Vocal Duets
    (the other texts by George Meredith), pp. 16-17.
    dedicated to George Meredith <g> bpl, x

580 Heise, Peter <t> World's wanderers (Vandrerne) <p>
    Wilhelm Hansen, Copenhagen, n.d. <d> pp. 4-5 in
    Romancer og Sange. translated by Caralis. <g>
    Berlin, x, Danish

581 Heise, Peter <t> Love's philosophy (kjaerlighedens
    Philosophi) <p> Wilhelm Hansen, Copenhagen, n.d.
    <d> pp. 130-132 in Romancer og Sange. translated
    by Caralis <g> Berlin, x, Danish

582 Heninger, Robert E. <t> Serenade (for Indian
    serenade) <p> R. E. Heninger, San Diego, 1960's
    <d> For tenor or soprano. Performed in Los Angeles
    and San Diego area. Presumably published in
    facsimile. <g> q

583 Heninger, Robert E. <t> Dirge: Rough wind, that
    moanest loud <p> R. E. Heninger, San Diego,
    California, 1960's <d> soprano and 'cello.
    presumably published in facsimile <g> q

584 Henry, Bertram C. <t> A widow bird <p> Schmidt,
    Boston, 1889 <d> no. 2 of Three Songs. 2p. <g>
    Harvard Library, x

585 Henze, Hans Werner <t> Ode to the west wind <p>
    Schott, Mainz, 1955 <d> for violoncello and
    orchestra. 88p. in 5 sections for the 5 sections
    of the poem, printed as preface. <g> Grove, bm, x

586 Herbert, Ivy <t> A widow bird <p> Oxford University
    Press, London, 1947 <d> no. 2 of Two Songs. 2p.
    <g> ed, bm, x

587 Hermann, Hans <t> The fountains mingle. op. 37, no. 1
    <p> Ries and Erler, Berlin, 1896 <d> 3p. <g> East
    Berlin, x

588 Herts, Charles Lee <t> Music, when soft voices die
    <p> Gamble Hinged Music Co., Chicago, 1932 <d>
    four-part chorus SATE. rehearsal piano part.
    Gamble's collection of a capella choruses, no.
    1025 <g> lc

589 Herz, H. <t> Thee and only thee: The colour from the
    flow'r is gone (sic for On a faded violet) <p> The
    Musical Bijou, London, 1844 <d> p. 13 in the
    Musical Bijou of 1844 <g> Bodleian, x

590 Higgin, Clifford <t> To a faded violet (On a faded
    violet) <p> Ashdown, London, 1925 <d> SATB and
    rehearsal piano part. no. 35548 of Ashdown
    Festival Music. 8p. <g> bm

591 Hill, Alfred <t> A lament: O world <p> Chappell,
    Sydney, 1948 <d> SATB chorus. 3p. <g> lc

592 Hill, Clarence S. <t> Good night? ah no <p> Novello,
    London, 1909 <d> no. 2 of Five Songs by Shelley
    (only two published). 4p. <g> bm, x

593 Hill, Clarence S. <t> Indian serenade <p> Novello,
    London, 1908 <d> no. 1 of Five Songs by Shelley.
    5p. <g> bm, x

594 Hill, John <t> Music, when soft voices die <p>
    Metzler, London, 1898 <d> no. 2 in Songs, Book I.
    2p. <g> Bodleian, x

595 Hill, Sarah Henrietta <t> A farewell <p> EU108496, 14
     November, 1947

596 Hindemith, Paul <t> The moon: And like a dying lady
     <p> Schott, London; Associated Music Publishers,
     New York, 1942 and 1944 <d> no. 3 of Nine English
     Songs, for soprano or mezzo-soprano. 4p.
     separately published <g> Yale, lc, nn

597 Hine, Mary <t> Out of the day and night (O world) <p>
     B. F. Grist, London, 1867 <d> 2p. <g> and, bm, x

598 Hoch, Madoline Bertha <t> I arise from dreams <p>
     EU163542, 26 March 1938

599 Hoch, Madoline Bertha <t> When soft voices die (for
     Music, when soft voices die) <p> EU263543, 26
     March 1938

600 Holderness, Herbert O. <t> I arise from dreams <p>
     EU397658, 26 February 1917

601 Holesco, Mona <t> Threnos: O world <p> Arthur P.
     Schmidt, Boston, 1916 <d> no. 3 of Changing Moods,
     Seven Songs, pp. 9-11. two forms: middle and low
     voice. <g> lc, x

602 Holland, Theodore Samuel <t> Chant funebre:
     (Sterbenlied): Rough wind that moanest. op. 6, no.
     2 <p> Rouart, Paris, 1908 <d> no. 2 of Deux
     Melodies. French and German translation by D.
     Calvocoressi. 3p. <g> lc, bm, French, German

603 Holland, Theodore Samuel <t> Lamento: O monde (O
     world) <p> Rouart, Paris, 1908 <d> no. 1 of Deux
     Melodies. French and German translation by D.
     Calvocoressi. 3p. Lamento on cover; A Lament, on
     the music <g> lc, French, German

604 Hollander, Benoit <t> To a skylark <p> Phillips and
     Page, London, 1897 <d> no. 2 of Two Songs, the
     first by Browning. 8p. <g> bm, x

605 Holmval, Robert <t> Music, when soft voices die <p>
     Bach and Co., London, 1910 <d> two forms: bass and
     tenor. 2p. <g> bm, x

606 Hopkins, Anthony <t> The Cenci. Music for the play

<p> ms. score, 1947 <d> score in the BBC for
strings and harp (no. 3C065) <g> bbc

607 Hopkins, Franklin <t> The Indian serenade (for Indian
serenade) <p> Cecil Mackie, New York, 1913 <d> in
Thirty Songs for Medium and High Voice; Great
English Poets Series, pp. 8-11 <g> nn

608 Hopkins, Franklin <t> On a poet's lips I slept <p>
Cecil Mackie, New York, 1913 <d> in Thirty Songs
for Medium and High Voice; Great English Poets
Series, pp. 38-40 <g> nn

609 Hopkins, Franklin <t> One word is too often profaned
<p> Cecil Mackie, New York, 1913 <d> in Thirty
Songs for Medium and High Voice; Great English
Poets Series, pp. 103-1C5 <g> nn

610 Hornbeck, Louis <t> To the queen of my heart (false
attribution to Shelley) <p> Horneman and Erslev,
Copenhagen, n.d. <d> no. 1 of Four Songs,
Kjaerlighedssange, op. 2. translation by Caralis:
Til mit Hjertes Dronning. 2p. <g> Berlin, x,
Danish

611 Horne, Marie <t> When the lamp is shattered <p>
Boosey, London, 1925 <d> no. 1 in Three Shelley
Songs. 11p. <g> lc

612 Horne, Marie <t> Madonna, wherefore? <p> Boosey,
London, 1925 <d> no. 2 in Three Shelley Songs.
11p. <g> lc

613 Horne, Marie <t> To Jane, with a guitar <p> Boosey,
London, 1925 <d> no. 3 in Three Shelley Songs.
11p. <g> lc

614 Horowitz, Richard S. <t> Music, when soft voices die
<p> EU225494, 3 July 1940

615 Horrocks, Ami Elise <t> A dirge for the year: Orphan
hours. op. 15, no. 8 <p> Joseph Williams, London,
1893 <d> no. 8 of fifth series of St. Cecilia
two-part songs. 6p. with piano part. <g> bm, x

616 Horrocks, Ami Elise <t> A garden: The spring arose on
the garden fair (The sensitive plant). op. 15, no.
3 <p> Joseph Williams, London, 1906 <d> no. 3 of

Fifth series of St. Cecilia two-part songs, with
piano part. 6p. <g> bm, x

617 Hovhaness, Alan <t> Lament: O world. op. 20 <p>
    Whitney Blake Music Publishers, New York, 1938 <d>
    for medium voice and piano. Also arranged for
    trombone and piano. 4p. <g> bpl, bmi, lc

618 Howard, John Tasker <t> I fear thy kisses <p>
    Fischer, New York, 1937 <d> 3p. <g> lc

619 Howe, Mary (Carlisle) <t> Music, when soft voices die
    <p> ms., 19-- <d> for baritone and soprano and
    string quartet. Gift to lc in 1959. 3p. <g> lc

620 Howell, T. Francis <t> I arise from dreams <p>
    Weekes, London, 1914 <d> no. 1 of Two Songs, pp.
    2-5. <g> bm, lc, x

621 Howells, Herbert <t> The widow bird. op. 22, no. 3
    <p> W. Rogers, London, 1919 <d> in Four Songs, pp.
    10-12 <g> bbc, bm

622 Hoyt, Richard <t> The keen stars were twinkling <p>
    EU975976, 1 February 1967 <d> 11p.

623 Hoyt, Richard <t> Music, when soft voices die <p>
    EU961695, 14 October 1966 <d> 4p.

624 Hoyt, Richard <t> Song of Proserpine <p> EU974848, 13
    January 1967 <d> 7p.

625 Hoyt, Richard <t> Dirge: Rough wind that moanest <p>
    EU961696, 14 October 1966 <d> 6p. <g> bmi

626 Hruby, Dolores <t> Song: False friend, wilt thou
    smile (The Cenci) <p> unpublished, 1958 <d> song
    written by Dolores Hruby for productions of the
    play in The Court Theatre of the University of
    Chicago, July and August, 1958, under the
    direction of Norbert Hruby and Otto Preminger,
    with William Mathieu as Musical Director. Choral
    selections from Palestrina were sung by the
    University Choir, under the direction of Richard
    Vikstrom. <g> music unavailable

627 Hudson, Henry <t> Night: How beautiful is night <p>
    Joseph Williams, London, 1906 <d> no. 8 of St.

Cecilia fourth series of three-part songs. 6p.
text not by Shelley, but it may be a free
adaptation of Queen Mab, IV <g> bm, x

628 Hudson, R. Bertram <t> Enchanted boat (Asia's song
from Prometheus Unbound): My soul is an enchanted
boat <p> Vincent Music Co., London, 1911 <d>
two-part song, with piano part. Vocal Music for
Schools and Classes, ed. by Dr. Charles Vincent.
6p. <g> bm, x

629 Hughes, Elwyn Kent <t> Lines from Shelley: Yet look
on me (To ----) <p> ms., 1955 <d> one of five
songs in opus 14. for high voice. 3p. performed
<g> q

630 Hughes, Elwyn Kent <t> On a faded violet. op. 16 <p>
ms., 1957 <d> one of four songs in a commissioned
cycle. Two forms: low and medium voice. 8p.
performed <g> q

631 Hughes, Elwyn Kent <t> Prometheus Unbound, Earth-moon
dialogue, Act IV <p> ms. <d> bass, tenor and
prepared tape "electronic" music. performed
September, 1969 <g> q

632 Huhn, Bruno <t> I arise from dreams <p> Schirmer, New
York, 1906 <d> 3p. <g> rn

633 Huhn, Bruno <t> Love's philosophy <p> Schirmer, New
York, 1905 <d> no. 2 of Three Songs. 4p. <g> bbc,
bm, x

634 Hullah, John Pyke <t> I arise from dreams <p>
Addison, Hollier, and Lucas, London, 1859; also
Hutchings and Romer, London, 1888 <d> 6p. (Addison
ed.) <g> and, bm, x

635 Hullah, John Pyke <t> Music, when soft voices die <p>
Hutchings and Romer, London, 1861 <d> part-song in
Hullah's Part Music, vol. 1, pp. 25-27, no. 6.
catalogued by Boston Public Library under Hullah
and Carl Maria von Weber. song missing from
shelves and found no place else. apparently a
"shoe-horned" piece (see my introduction). <g> bpl
(lost)

636 Hullah, John Pyke <t> Rarely, rarely, comest thou <p>

Lamborn Cock, Addison and Co., London, 1868; also
Hutchings and Romer, London, 1888 <d> 7p. (Lamborn
Cock ed.) <g> bm, and, bbc, x

637 Hulton, F. Everard W. <t> The flower that smiles
to-day <p> Schott, London, 1908 <d> no. 1 of Seven
Selected Songs, pp. 3-7 <g> bm, x

638 Hulton, F. Everard W. <t> Ode to Night: Swiftly walk
over <p> Schott, London, 1908 <d> no. 4 of Seven
Selected Songs, pp. 17-24 <g> bm, x

639 Humphreys, H. S. (Henry Rauscher, name used as
composer) <t> Tell me, thou star <p> ms. <d>
baritone and orchestra. performed, 1950 <g> q

640 Humphreys, H. S. (Henry Rauscher, name used as
composer) <t> Music, fountain of tears <p> ms. <d>
male chorus, a capella. performed, 1950 <g> q

641 Hunkins, Arthur B. <t> Memories: Music, when soft
voices die <p> Composers Forum, New York, 1966 <d>
also in "Five Short Songs of Gladness (revised
version)," pp. 4-6 in facsimile ed. in NYPL. dated
at the end 1960 <g> q, nn

642 Hunneman, Ida <t> A widow bird <p> C. W. Thompson,
Boston, 1899 <d> 3p. <g> lc, x

643 Hurlstone, William Y. <t> That time is dead forever
<p> Curwen, London, 1939 <d> Curwen edition 2554,
pp. 3-7. solo voice <g> lc, bm, x

644 Hurst, George <t> Music, when soft voices die <p>
BMI, Toronto, 1947 and Associated Music
Publishers, New York <d> 3p. <g> lc

645 Huss, Henry Holden <t> Music, when soft voices die.
op. 28 <p> G. Schirmer, New York, 1917 <d> no. 2
of Two Songs, with piano part. 3p. <g> lc

646 Huston, Thomas Scott, Jr. <t> Indian serenade <p>
ms., 1938 <d> 7p. performed several times <g> q, x

647 Hutchens, Frank <t> The cloud <p> Chappell, London,
1964 <d> SSA and piano. 10p. <g> bm

648 Hutchins, Morris <t> Music, when soft voices die <p>
    Hall and McCreary, Chicago, 1942 <d> SATB, Hall
    and McCreary choral octavos, no. 1090. LC, E107975
    <g> lc

649 Ibberson, William Henry <t> Autumn: a dirge <p>
    Stainer and Bell, London, 1936 <d> four-part song
    with rehearsal piano part. Tonic sol-fa
    translation by H. J. Timothy. 5p. no. 4682, choral
    library no. 301 <g> lc

650 Ibberson, William Henry <t> Spirit of delight:
    Rarely, rarely, comest thou <p> Stainer and Bell,
    London, 1936 <d> trio for ladies' voices. no.
    4681, part-song no. 261. Tonic sol-fa translation
    by H. J. Timothy, 8p. <g> lc

651 Ilgenfritz, McNair <t> Imploration ("song after
    Love's philosophy") <p> Edward Schuberth, New
    York, 1930 <d> 6p. no. 4601 <g> lc

652 Indicator, Lloyd <t> Indian serenade <p> EU313577, 29
    October 1942

653 Ingleby, C. Mansfield <t> I pant for music (for I
    pant for the music), title on cover; Romance on
    the score <p> Lamborn Cock, Addison and Co.,
    London, 1867 <d> 9p. <g> bm, x

654 Ingleby, Ellis <t> Mutability: The flower that smiles
    to-day <p> J. Hopkinson, London, 1887 <d> no. 3 of
    Album of Six Songs, pp. 9-11 <g> bm, x

655 Ingraham, George <t> I arise from dreams <p>
    Schirmer, New York, 1883 <d> for A or S or T
    voice. 6p. <g> nn

656 Ives, Charles E. <t> Rough wind <p> New Music Society
    Publisher, New York, 1933 <d> song in New Music, A
    Quarterly of Modern Composition: Thirty-Four Songs
    by Charles E. Ives, this being no. 27, pp. 55-57.
    Notation at end: From a Symphony, 1898; arranged
    for voice and piano, 1902 <g> bbc, nn, x

657 Ives, Charles E. <t> The world's wanderers <p>
    Redding, Conn., 1922, dated 1895, and 1953 <d> in
    Fifty Songs by Charles E. Ives, p. 253, for voice
    and piano. also no. 4 in Ten Songs (1953)

published by Peer, New York <g> bbc, nn, x

658 Jacob, Gordon <t> Evening: The sun is set, the
swallows are asleep <p> Joseph Williams, London,
1925 <d> no. 11 of A Goodly Heritage: Twelve Songs
of the Countryside for women's voices with
accompaniment of string orchestra and piano, pp.
54-60. SA and piano score, Williams no. 5864 <g>
bm, x

659 Jacob, Gordon <t> Music, when soft voices die <p>
Novello, London, 1937 <d> for SSATTB chorus. no.
1502. rehearsal piano part. 4p. <g> bm, x

660 Jacob, Gordon <t> A widow bird <p> Novello, London,
1938 <d> no. 1811 in Novello's School Songs.
unison song. published also for mixed voices <g>
bm

661 James, Dorothy <t> Mutability: We are as clouds that
veil the midnight moon <p> ms., 1967 <d> women's
chorus and two flutes, two clarinets, and piano.
10p. Recorded by Crest Records. performance, April
13, 1967 commissioned by North Central Division of
MENC, Detroit <g> q

662 James, Eldridge Durand <t> I arise from dreams <p>
EU38830, 18 September 1946

663 Jarrett, Jack Marius <t> To night: Swiftly walk <p>
ms. <g> q

664 Jenkins, D. Cyril <t> As the moon's soft splendour
<p> Paxton, London, 1925 <d> Paxton no. 40350, in
D flat. 4p. <g> bbc, bm

665 Jenkins, D. Cyril <t> Death, the Leveller: The
glories of our blood and state are shadows (By
Shirley. False attribution to Shelley on cover)
<p> W. Paxton, London, 1925 <d> Paxton no. 80054.
8p. <g> bm

666 Jenkins, D. Cyril <t> Music, when soft voices die <p>
W. Paxton, London, 1925 <d> part-song for mixed
voices, SATB, with rehearsal piano part. 5p. <g>
bm, x

667 Jenkins, D. Cyril <t> Ode to the west wind <p> J.

Curwen, London, 1921; also Godwin and Tabb,
London, 1922 <d> SATB and piano (orchestral score
available). 21p. Curwen choral handbook no. 1126.
ed. of G. and T, 27p. <g> bm, x, bpl

668 Jenkins, D. Cyril <t> Storm-Song (Storm-Gan) : The
waters are flashing <p> J. Curwen, London, 1954
<d> SSA and piano, 11p. Welsh words by T. H.
Parry-Williams <g> bm, x, Welsh

669 Jennings, Mabel <t> A widow bird sat <p> Weekes,
London; C. F. Summy, Chicago, 1902 <d> no. 8 of
Twelve Short Songs, pp. 9-11 <g> bm, x

670 Jensen, Adolf <t> To night (An die Nacht): Gottin der
Nacht, schweb uber die Flut <p> Julius Hainauer,
Breslau, n.d. <d> no. 6 of Sechs Leider, pp. 26-30
<g> Hamburg City Library, x, German

671 Jervis-Read, Harold Vincent <t> Day dream: while
skies are blue (not by Shelley) <p> Winthrop
Rogers, London, 1920 <d> 3p. <g> lc

672 John, Louis Edgar <t> Dirge: Rough wind <p> Arthur P.
Schmidt, Boston, 1921 <d> for medium voice. 3p.
<g> nn

673 John, Noel <t> Music, when soft voices die <p> no
information <d> no information <g> listed in
Schirmer's music store. perhaps William Noel
Johnson, q.v.

674 Johnson, Horace <t> Dirge: Rough wind <p> Schirmer,
New York, 1921 <d> 3p. <g> nn

675 Johnson, Mildred <t> Autumn <p> EU8847, 13 July 1929

676 Johnson, William Noel <t> I fear thy kisses <p>
Sheard, London (Woolhouse in Pazdirek), 1889 <d>
no. 4 in Four Songs, pp. 9-10 <g> bm, bbc, ed, x

677 Johnson, William Noel <t> Music, when soft voices die
<p> Schirmer, Boston; Woolhouse, London, 1892 <d>
no. 1 of Two Songs. 2p. <g> bm, ed, x

678 Johnson, William Spencer <t> Good night? ah no <p> T.
Presser, Philadelphia, 1909 <d> 3p. <g> lc, x, bm

679 Jones, J. Owen <t> Rarely, rarely, comest thou <p>
    Rowlands, London, 1929 <d> for tenor and SATB
    chorus and orchestra <d> 20p. <g> bbc, lc

680 Jones, John <t> Men of England: Men of England, heirs
    of glory (The Mask of Anarchy, stanzas 37-40 and
    50-51) <p> Swan Sonnenschein, London, 1888, 1892,
    1897 <d> no. 54 in Chants of Labour: A Song Book
    of the People with Music, pp. 96-97, ed. by Edward
    Carpenter. SATB a capella for S and MS. 3p. <g>
    nn, bm, x

681 Jordan, Jules <t> Love's philosophy <p> Schirmer, New
    York, 1886 <d> 5p. <g> and, bm

682 Josephs, Wilfred <t> Ozymandias <p> ms., ca. 1970 <d>
    second movement of Mortales, op. 62, for SATB,
    Children's chorus, double chorus, and orchestra.
    premiere at 1970 May Festival, Cincinnati, which
    commissioned it. First and third movements:
    Renaissance and Passacaglia. Total is 79p. of ms.,
    intended for publication <g> q

683 Josten, Werner E. <t> Dedication: I fear thy kisses
    <p> Oliver Ditson Co., Boston, 1921 <d> 2p. <g>
    copy in collection

684 Josten, Werner E. <t> The Indian serenade (for Indian
    serenade) <p> EU279398, 24 June 1952

685 Judd, Percy <t> I arise from dreams <p> Augener,
    London, 1922 <d> 5p. <g> bbc, lc, bm, x

686 Judd, Percy <t> Song of autumn: The warm sun is
    failing <p> Boosey, New York, 1924 <d> 4p. <g> bm,
    x

687 Justis, Edgar L. <t> Indian serenade. op. 3, no. 1
    <p> Breitkopf and Hartel, Leipzig, 1903 <d> no. 1
    of Two Songs for soprano or tenor plus piano. 6p.
    <g> lc, bm, x

688 Kantor, Joseph <t> To the moon: Art thou pale <p>
    ms., facsimile copy in American Music Center, New
    York, n.d. <d> SATB plus strings. 8p. <g> amc, x

689 Kappey, Jacob Adam <t> Good night? ah no <p> Addison,
    Hollier and Lucas, London, 1859 <d> 5p. <g> and,
    nn, bm, x

690 Karnavicius (Karnovitch), George <t> Song: A widow
    bird <p> State Publishing House, Moscow, 1924 <d>
    2p. xerox copy sent by Moscow Tchaikovsky
    Conservatory. 2p. This and the next entry are
    presumably part of section two of Remembrances of
    the House of Usher, "Chamber-music Concert"
    published by Universal Edition, Vienna, 1928,
    called "Six Romances by Shelley for middle voice
    with piano accompaniment." Only the cover is
    preserved in the East Berlin music library. <g> x,
    Russian

691 Karnavicius (Karnovitch), George <t> To---: Music,
    when soft voices die <p> State Publishing House,
    Moscow, 1924 <d> viola and soprano. 2p. copy sent
    from Moscow, as above, q.v. Only these two songs
    seem extant. <g> x, Russian

692 Kasassoglou, George B. <t> Hellas, incidental music
    <p> ms., 1947 <d> prelude and lyric parts.
    three-voice chorus plus orchestra. 86p. Translated
    into Greek by Anastasion-Milanos Stratigopoulos
    (published 1932). Sponsored by the British Council
    in Athens, performed often since 1947 by the
    National Broadcasting Station Orchestra <g> grove,
    q, Greek

693 Katims, Herman <t> Threnos <p> ms., 1936 <d> 2 leaves
    <g> lc

694 Kaufer, Joseph <t> Music, when soft voices die <p>
    Lyric-Art, Waukegan, Illinois, 1951 <d> in Dover
    Beach and Other Songs, no. 1 of the volume, pp.
    1-2 <g> nn

695 Keel, Frederick <t> Music, when soft voices die <p>
    J. B. Cramer and Co., London, 1948; New York
    edition: Schuberth and Co. <d> for voice and
    flute. 8p. <g> bm, x

696 Keighley, Thomas <t> Music, when soft voices die <p>
    Bayley and Ferguson, London, 1915 <d> SSC with
    rehearsal piano part. no. 242 of Collegiate Choir
    Part-songs. 4p. <g> bm, x

697 Keighley, Thomas <t> Evening rhapsody: How beautiful
    this night <p> Banks and Son, York, 1928 <d> no.
    984 Series of Anthems and Glees with rehearsal
    piano part. 8p. <g> bm

698 Keil, Julius <t> I fear thy kisses <p> New York,
    193-; reprinted from ms. copy <d> for one voice.
    1p <g> bm

699 Keil, Julius <t> Love's philosophy <p> New York,
    193-, ms. <d> 2 leaves <g> nn

700 Kellie, Lawrence <t> The fountains mingle <p>
    Metzler, London, 1887 <d> no. 9 of Ten Songs, pp.
    34-39. also separately published, 7p. <g> ed, bm,
    x

701 Kelly, F. S. <t> Music, when soft voices die. op. 6,
    no. 4 <p> Schott, London, 1913 <d> no. 4 of Six
    Songs, pp. 22-24 <g> bm, ed, x

702 Kelly, F. S. <t> When the lamp is shattered. op. 6,
    no. 3 <p> Schott, London, 1913 <d> no. 3 of Six
    Songs, pp. 14-21 <g> bm, ed, x

703 Kennedy, Marie Walters <t> Indian serenade <p> Edward
    Schuberth, New York and London, 1912 <d> 4p. <g>
    bm, x

704 Kilpatrick, Jack Frederick <t> The world's wanderers
    <p> American Composers Alliance, New York, 1951
    <g> bmi

705 King, Alfred <t> Music, when soft voices die <p>
    Novello, London, 1886 <d> Novello's Part-Song
    Book, second series, no. 534. SSATBB, called
    Madrigal for Six Voices. 9p. <g> bm, x

706 King, Harold C. <t> Fragment: Ode to the west wind
    <p> Donemus, Amsterdam, 1963 <d> 4p. English
    words: Make me thy lyre...can spring be far behind
    <g> copy in collection

707 Kitnor, Phyllis Enid de <t> Lines: The cold earth
    slept below <p> Weekes, London, 1913 <d> no. 3 of
    Three Songs. 2p. <g> bm, x

708 Kitnor, Phyllis Enid de <t> To music: Silver key of

the fountain <p> Weekes, London, 1913 <d> no. 1 of
Three Songs. 2p. <g> bm, x

709 Kitson, Charles Herbert <t> Music, when soft voices
die <p> Stainer and Bell, London, 1924 <d>
Part-Songs, no. 141. SC and piano. S. and B. no.
3091. 4p. <g> bm, x

710 Klaus, Kenneth Blanchard <t> Dirge: Rough wind <p>
ms., 1953 <d> SATB with rehearsal piano part. 2p.
performed in California, 1953 <g> q

711 Klaus, Kenneth Blanchard <t> Music, when soft voices
die <p> ms. <g> q

712 Klaus, Kenneth Blanchard <t> Recollection: Now the
last day <p> ms., 1967 <d> 4p. performed in Baton
Rouge, 1966 <g> q

713 Klaus, Kenneth Blanchard <t> Widow bird <p> ms., 1946
<d> SATB with rehearsal piano part. performed 1946
at Drake University and 1953 in California. 2p.
<g> q, x

714 Klein, Ivy Frances (Born Salaman) <t> Music, when
soft voices die <p> Murdoch, London, 1928 <d> 3p.
<g> bbc, bm

715 Knautch girls <t> I arise from dreams <p> 1822 <d>
Indian serenade was published in The Liberal as
"Song Written for an Indian Air, Sung by the
Knautch girls: Tazee be tazee no be no." See
Cambridge Shelley, p. 370. Original not found, but
see H. B. Forman, Works (1877), IV, 11.

716 Knott, Thomas B. <t> I arise from dreams <p> Stanley
Lucas, Weber and Co., London, ca. 1887 <d> 5p. two
forms, in G and E. undated but listed on program
of Shelley Song Evening of 11 May 1887 <g> bm, x

717 Korn, Peter Jona <t> To Jane: The keen stars. op. 20
<p> ms., 1953 <d> for sopranc, clarinet in A, and
harp. 6p. <g> amc, x

718 Korn, Peter Jona <t> To the moon: Art thou pale. op.
20 <p> ms., 1952 <d> for soprano, clarinet in A,
and harp. 12p. <g> amc, x

719 Kortkamp, Ivan Otwell <t> The hour of night (adapted
from To the moon) <p> Gamble Hinged Music Co.,
Chicago, 1938 <d> the words in part by Wordsworth
and Shelley. SSAATBB chorus. 6p. <g> lc

720 Kortkamp, Ivan Otwell <t> I arise from dreams <p>
Gamble Hinged Music Co, Chicago, 1943 <d> SATB
plus rehearsal piano. 3p. <g> nn

721 Kozinski, David Boleslaw <t> Time: Unfathomable sea
<p> EU138300, 21 June 1948

722 Kozinski, David Boleslaw <t> Music, when soft voices
die <p> EU114186, 28 January 1948

723 Kraft, Leo <t> To night: Swiftly walk over <p> ms.,
1965 <d> chorus and four-hand piano. 18p. <g> copy
in nn, q

724 Kramer, A. Walter <t> Indian serenade. op. 25, no. 2
<p> Huntzinger and Dilworth, New York, 1916; G.
Ricordi, New York, 1926 <d> 3p. <g> bm, lc, x,
copy (1926) in collection

725 Kramer, A. Walter <t> Music, when soft voices die.
op. 25, no. 2 <p> C. C. Birchard, Boston, 1917; G.
Ricordi, New York, 1926; Mills Music, New York,
1947 and 1961 <d> ed. of 1917 is for two voices a
capella; Mills Choral ed. 681 for SSA plus piano:
3p. 1926 song has 5p. <g> lc, bm

726 Kramer, A. Walter <t> Heart's devotion: I fear thy
kisses. op. 18, no. 2 <p> Oliver Ditson, Boston,
1919 <d> low voice in F; very low voice in D <g>
lc

727 Krejn, Grig <t> Mir tumanny ugejum (The foggy world
grows sad). op. 7, no. 4 <p> Tzimmerman, Moscow
and St. Petersburg, pre-revolution <d> Balmont
translation. 3p. <g> East Berlin, x, Russian

728 Krenkel, Gustav <t> Nevermore: A widow bird <p> Cary
and Co., London, 1909 <d> two forms: E flat minor
and C minor. 4p. <g> bm, x

729 Kreuz, Emil <t> A widow bird. op. 15, no. 4 <p>
Augener, London, 1891 <d> no. 4 of Five Songs for
Soprano Voice, pp. 14-15. Also in Monthly Musical

Record, vol. 22, 1 August 1892, pp. 179-181 <g>
bm

730 Kroeger, Ernest Richard <t> Life of life: Life of
life, thy lips enkindle. op. 34, no. 3 <p>
Schmidt, Boston, 1896 <d> 4p. <g> lc, x

731 Kursteiner, Jean Paul <t> The soul's victory (a
setting of part of the last canto of Prometheus
Unbound): To suffer woes. op. 24, no. 3 <p>
Kursteiner, New York, 1916 <d> 3p. <g> listed in
Schirmer's music store, nn

732 Lambert, Agnes E. <t> The whispering waves that were
half asleep (from The "Pine Forest" <p> Boosey,
London, 1907 <d> 4p. in two forms: E flat and F
<g> bm, x

733 Lambert, Frank <t> The fountains mingle <p> Chappell,
London, 1902 <d> three forms: in E, F, and G. 5p.
<g> ed, bm, x

734 Lambert, John <t> The Cenci; incidental and
background music <p> unpublished, 1959 <d> the
music composed for the play, revived at the Old
Vic theatre, April 29, 1959, under the direction
of Michael Benthall, with Hugh Griffith and
Barbara Jefford in the cast. One critic speaks of
the background music as consisting mostly of
chords; several speak of the song, False Friend,
as appealingly sung by Miss Jefford. <g> music
unavailable

735 Lapo, Cecil Elwyn <t> Music, when soft voices die <p>
Edwin H. Morris, New York, 1948 <d> SSAATTBB and
piano reduction. 4p. <g> nn

736 Larchet, John F. <t> The philosophy of love (for
Love's philosophy) <p> Boosey, London, 1908 <d> in
three forms: D flat, E flat, and F. 5p. <g> lc,
bm, x

737 Larsson, Lars-Erik <t> Prometheus Unbound. various
scenes and choruses, with orchestra <p> Sweden,
ca. 1942 <d> the music composed in 1941 for a
performance by the Radic Theatre, 1 January 1942
comprising one-third the whole text of Shelley.
music is mainly orchestral: interludes and

background. Voice scores consist of II, v, Life of
life (soprano, harp, strings); IV, The pale stars
are gone (soprano, flute, clarinet, harp, strings)
and Here, oh here (female chorus); Weave the dance
(female chorus, harp, strings); female chorus of
spirits, a capella, We join the throng; female
chorus and string quartet, We come from the mind;
female chorus a capella And our singing shall
build. Translation by Anders Osterling. Date is
unspecified in information supplied by Sveriges
Radio, Music library. <g> Swedish Radio Music
Library, Swedish

738 Larsson, Lars-Erik <t> Prometheus Unbound, IV: Weave
the dance <p> Sweden, ca. 1942 <d> female chorus
with piano, under title of "Luftandarnas kor"
(Chorus of the air spirits), taken from the radio
theatre performance described above <g> Swedish
Radio Music Library information, Swedish

739 Lawner, Morris <t> Music, when soft voices die <p>
ms., ca. 1945 <d> 2p. <g> q, x

740 Lawrence, Charles <t> Music, when soft voices die <p>
Hutchings and Romer, London, 1872 <d> four-part
song in Chorister's Album no. 12, SATB, a capella.
4p. <g> bpl, x

741 Lawrence, E. M. <t> Time long past: Like the ghost of
a friend long dead <p> Novello and Ewer, London,
1879 <d> SATB a capella. 4p. <g> bm, x

742 Le Bas, Gertrude <t> A lament: Swifter far <p> G.
Ricordi, London (printed in Milan), 1910 <d> 2p.
<g> lc, x

743 Lee, Arthur (see B. Dunstan)

744 Lee, Norman <t> From dreams of thee (Indian serenade)
<p> EU132976, 5 October 1936 <d> song with piano.
7 leaves <g> lc

745 Leeds, Geoffrey Norman <t> Music, when soft voices
die <p> H. F. Deane, London, 1929 <d> four-part
song. Year Book Press Series of Unison and
Part-Songs no. 328. SATB and rehearsal piano part.
sol-fa notation. 5p. <g> bm, x

746 Leggatt, Susie <t> Good-Night: ah no (for Good
    night?) <p> George White, London, n.d. <d> 4p. <g>
    Bodleian, x

747 Lehmann, Liza <t> The fountains mingle <p> Boosey,
    London, 1895 <d> 7p. <g> bm, x

748 Lehmann, Liza <t> Music, when soft voices die <p>
    Boosey, London, 1895 <d> for middle voice. Album
    of Nine English Songs, pp. 20-21 (by L. L.) <g> nn

749 Lehmann, Liza <t> A widow bird sat <p> Boosey,
    London, 1895 <d> for middle voice, Album of Nine
    English Songs (by L. L.), pp. 8-9 <g> nn

750 Lenox, F. (Esq.) <t> I arise from dreams <p> Duff and
    Hodgson, London, 1844 <d> 5p. <g> and, bm, x

751 Lester, William <t> To music: Silver key of the
    fountain <p> Studio Publishing Co., Chicago, 1913
    <d> no. 1 of Two Short Songs. 1p. <g> Harvard
    Library, x

752 Lester, William <t> Song of Proserpine <p> Studio
    Publishing Co., Chicago, 1913 <d> no. 2 of Two
    Short Songs. 3p. <g> Harvard Library, x

753 Levy, Eduard <t> Annabel Lee (ascribed to Shelley,
    not Poe) <p> Albert Stahl, Berlin, n.d. <d> op.
    33. Shelley on song. 5p. <g> East Berlin, x

754 Lewis, Janet <t> Indian serenade <p> EU845026,
    September 1964 <d> 9 leaves

755 Ley, Henry George <t> As the moon's soft splendour.
    op. 6, no. 4 <p> Sydney Acott, Oxford, 1913; rev.
    ed., Joseph Williams, London, 1932 <d> no. 4 in
    First Album of Songs, pp. 13-15 <g> bm, x

756 Ley, Henry George <t> Music, when soft voices die.
    op. 6, no. 1 <p> Sydney Acott, Oxford, 1913; rev.
    ed., Joseph Williams, London, 1932 <d> no. 1 in
    First Album of Songs, pp. 4-6. <g> bm, x

757 Ley, Henry George <t> Dirge: Rough wind <p> Novello,
    London, 1913 <d> SATB. 3p. <g> bm

758 Liddle, Samuel <t> Arabic love song: My faint spirit
    <p> Forsyth Brothers, London, 1899 <d> two forms:
    in E and D. 6p. <g> bm, x

759 Liddle, Samuel <t> Love's philosophy <p> Boosey and
    Co., London, 1902 <d> no. 2 in Two Love Songs. two
    forms: F and A flat. 5p. <g> bm, x

760 Lidgey, C. A. <t> I arise from dreams <p> Pitt and
    Hatzfeld, London, 1888; H. B. Stevens, Boston, n.d
    <d> also in Album of Ten Songs. op. 2, no. 3, pp.
    32-39. <g> nn, bm

761 Lidgey, C. A. <t> Music, when soft voices die <p>
    Stanley Lucas, Weber, Pitt and Hatzfeld, London,
    1888 <d> Pazdirek gives Cary. also in Strand
    Musical Magazine, Vol. 5, 286-288, June, 1897,
    with 1892 copyright by H. B. Stevens Co. in Album
    of Ten Songs, pp. 40-43 <g> paz, magazine is in nn

762 Lidgey, C. A. <t> One word is too often profaned <p>
    Pitt and Hatzfeld, London, 1888 <d> 5p. given by
    Pazdirek as Cramer's publication. in Album of Ten
    Songs, pp. 27-31 <g> ed, bm, x

763 Lidgey, C. A. <t> A widow bird <p> Pitt and Hatzfeld,
    London, 1888; Chappell, London, 1892 and 1908;
    also 1896, reprint in Strand Musical Magazine of
    July, 1896, pp. 86-88 <d> Chappell ed. is in E
    minor and F minor in 1908 <g> nn, ed, bbc, paz

764 Liebling, Georg <t> The Indian serenade (Abends). op.
    37 <p> Novello, London, 1899 <d> 4p. German words
    by Gottfried Kinkel <g> bm, x German

765 Liebling, Georg <t> Time long past: Like the ghost of
    a dear friend dead <p> Novello, London, 1899 <d>
    5p. German words by Wolfgang Muller <g> bm, x,
    German

766 Lincoln, Henry John <t> Ariette: As the moon's soft
    splendour <p> 1833 <d> See the ref. to the song in
    the Athenaeum, no. 273, 19 January 1833, p. 747.
    Set to music by Lincoln, according to Medwin; see
    The Shelley Papers (Forman, Shelley's Poetry, IV,
    144)

767 Lind, L. S. <t> Love's philosophy <p> EU98641, 26
      January 1935

768 Linley, George <t> Swifter far than summer's flight.
      Ballad <p> Campbell, Ransford and Co., London,
      1852 <d> 5p. <g> and, bm, x

769 Lipkin, Malcolm <t> Lament <p> ms., 1963 <g> q

770 Lipkin, Malcolm <t> To---- (poem of 1821): Music,
      when soft voices die <p> ms., 1963 <g> q

771 Lipkin, Malcolm <t> World's wanderers <p> ms., 1963
      <g> q

772 Lipkin, Malcolm <t> Time <p> ms., 1963 <g> q

773 Lissmann, Kurt <t> Time: Unfathomable sea (Unendlich
      Meer) from the cycle "Vom Leben" <p> P. J. Tonger,
      Cologne, 1953 <d> 4p. SATB, a capella <g> East
      Berlin, x, German

774 Little, Edgar <t> I arise from dreams <p> Schirmer,
      New York, 1898 <d> TTBB <g> lc, paz

775 Lloyd, Charles Harford <t> The cloud <p> The Year
      Book Press, of Swan Sonnenschein, London, 1909 <d>
      Year Book Press Series of Unison and Part-Songs,
      no. 36, for SSC. 5p. <g> bm, x

776 Lloyd, Charles Harford <t> To a skylark <p> Novello,
      London, 1885 <d> SSA, Novello's Collection of
      Trios, vol. 7, no. 167. 5p. Tonic sol-fa series,
      no. 997 <g> bm, x

777 Lloyd, David John de <t> Music, when soft voices die
      <p> Hughes and Son, Wrexham, 1930 <d> part-song
      for male voices. sol-fa notation. 3p. <g> bm

778 Loder, Edward J. <t> The colour from the flower is
      flown, Canzonet (for On a faded violet) <p> E.
      Wessel and Co., 1876 <d> no. 19 of The British
      Vocal Album, ed. by J. W. Davison. 4p. the words
      adapted from Shelley <g> bm, x

779 Loder, Edward J. <t> Dirge: Rough wind <p> John
      Limbird, London, 1841 <d> pp. 124-125 in The
      Harmonist; a Collection of Classical and Popular

Music, vol. 2. "The music (from a collection of airs published at Bonn) by Edward James Loder" <g> bm, x

780 Loder, George <t> The faded violet (for Cn a faded violet) <p> Henry G. Langley, New York, 1844; Silas Andrus, Hartford, 1848 <d> for four male voices and piano, in New York Glee Bock, pub. by Langley, pp. 200-201 <g> New York Historical Society, nn

781 Loder, George <t> Spirit of delight: Rarely, rarely, comest thou <p> Henry G. Langley, New York, 1844; Silas Andrus, Hartford, 1848 <d> New York Glee Book (pub. by Langley), pp. 248-249. <g> New York Historical Society, nn

782 Loder, Kate Fanny (Afterwards Lady Thompson) <t> My faint spirit <p> Leader and Cock, London, 1854 <d> 5p. <g> and, bm, x

783 Lcewensohn, B. <t> Music, when soft voices die. op. 6 <p> P. Jorgenson, Moscow, pre-1914 <d> no. 1 of four songs, pp. 2-5 German by Swiridoff (Wohl kann verklingen das Lied) and Russian by Balmont <g> Berlin, x, German, Russian

784 Lcewensohn, B. <t> To the moon. op. 6 <p> P. Jorgenson, Moscow, pre-1914 <d> no. 2 of Four Songs, pp. 2-5. German by Swiridoff (An den Mond) and Russian by Balmont <g> Berlin, x, German, Russian

785 Locwensohn, B. <t> A widow bird. op. 6 <p> P. Jorgenson, Moscow, pre-1914 <d> no. 3 of Four Songs, pp. 2-5 German by Swiridoff (Das Voglein klagt) and Russian by Balmont <g> Berlin, x, German, Russian

786 Lcewensohn, B. <t> World wanderers. op. 6 (for The world's wanderers) <p> P. Jorgenson, Moscow, pre-1914 <d> no. 4 of Four Scngs, pp. 2-7. German by Swiridoff (Die Weltwanderer) and Russian by Balmont <g> Berlin, German, Russian, x

787 Lcudon, M. J. <t> World's wanderers <p> EU518129, 6 August 1921

788 Lousada, A. Percy <t> Love's philosophy <p> Moutrie
    and Son, London, 1882 <d> 5p. "Dedicated to
    Moo-Moo" <g> bm, x

789 Lovatt, S. E. <t> As the moon's soft splendour <p>
    Boosey and Hawkes, London, 1930 <d> Boosey's
    Festival Series, no. 336 with sol-fa notations.
    8p. <g> bm

790 Lovatt, S. E. <t> Music, when soft voices die <p>
    Bayley and Ferguson, London, 1912 <d> SATB chorus,
    with rehearsal piano part. Choral Album no. 1108.
    7p. available also in tonic sol-fa ed. <g> bm, x,
    bbc

791 Luard-Selby, Bertram (see Selby)

792 Lubin, Ernest <t> A widow bird <p> ms., ca. 1940 <d>
    1p. song for middle voice with piano <g> q, copy
    in collection

793 Lucas, Clarence <t> Love's philosophy <p> Oliver
    Ditson, Boston, 1891 <d> called "Malaguena (A
    Spanish Dance of African Origin)" with "Music in
    the Moorish style of Southern Spain" for MS or B
    in B flat minor. 3p. <g> Harvard Library, x

794 Lucas, Clarence <t> Love's philosophy (different from
    above) <p> John Church, Cincinnati, 1904 <d> no. 2
    of Five Songs for Medium Voice. 8p. Entirely
    different melody <g> bm, x

795 Lucas, Clarence <t> The world's wanderers. op. 8 <p>
    Ashdown, London, 1889 <d> no. 1 of Two Lyrics. 4p.
    <g> bm, x, nn

796 Lucas, Leighton <t> Music, when soft voices die <p>
    Ascherberg, Hopwood and Crew, London, 1953 <d>
    Mortimer Series of Modern Part-Songs, no. 352,
    SATB a capella, with piano rehearsal part. 3p.
    sol-fa notation <g> bm, x

797 Luening, Otto <t> Good night? ah no <p> Highgate, New
    York, facsimile printing from ms., composed 1929
    <d> 1p. <g> q

798 Luening, Otto <t> I faint, I perish with my love <p>
    Highgate, New York, facsimile printing from ms.,

composed 1929 <d> 1p. <g> q

799 Luening, Otto <t> A Roman's chamber: In the cave
     which wild weeds cover <p> Highgate, New York,
     facsimile printing from ms., composed 1928 <d> 1p.
     <g> q

800 Luening, Otto <t> Wake the serpent not <p> Highgate,
     New York, facsimile printing from ms., composed
     1928 <d> 1p. <g> q

801 Lumby, Herbert Horace <t> To the moon: Art thou pale
     <p> unpublished <d> in G sharp minor. no. 1. of
     Two Shelley Songs, op. 17, no. 1. 4p. <g> Grove,
     ms. copy in collection

802 Lumby, Herbert Horace <t> Love's philosophy <p>
     unpublished <d> in E major. no. 2 of Two Shelley
     Songs, op. 17, no. 2. 8p. <g> Grove, ms. copy in
     collection

803 Lustgarten, S. <t> Dirge (Probably Time long past)
     <p> Max Staegemann, Berlin, n.d. <d> no. 5 of
     Lieder-Album of 15 songs, pp. 14-15 <g> Berlin, x,
     German

804 Lustgarten, S. <t> Indian serenade <p> Max
     Staegemann, Berlin, n.d. <d> no. 15 of
     Lieder-Album of 15 songs, pp. 48-51 <g> Berlin, x,
     German

805 Lynas, Frank <t> A widow bird <p> Augener, London,
     1951 <d> SATB chorus with rehearsal piano part.
     3p. <g> bbc, x

806 MacDowell, Edward <t> Winter, a poem for pianoforte
     (after Shelley's Widow bird) <p> Breitkopf and
     Hartel, Leipzig, 1888 (in Grove), 1894, 1906
     (revised) <d> op. 32, no. 4 in Four Little Poems,
     pp. 8-9 (1906), for piano only, with epigraph "A
     widow bird" (8 lines) <g> Grove, nn

807 Maccunn, Hamish <t> Autumn song: The warm sun is
     failing <p> Joseph Williams, London, 1892 <d> no.
     6 in Album of Ten Songs (Album no. 49), pp. 31-35
     <g> bm, x

808 Maccunn, Hamish <t> I arise from dreams <p> Augener,

London, 1895 <d> 6p. <g> ed, paz, bm, x

809 Maccunn, Hamish <t> On a faded violet <p> Augener,
    London, 1893; Novello, London, 1914 <d> Augener
    ed. for solo voice, 4p. Novello ed. for SSA and
    piano, no. 450 of Novello's octavo ed. of Trios
    for Female Voices. 7p. no. 2254 of Novello's tonic
    sol-fa Series (1916) <g> ed, bm, x

810 Macfarren, George Alexander <t> I arise from dreams
    of thee <p> Cramer, Beale, London, 1850 to 1876 in
    British Museum <d> no. 3 of "Lyrics composed for
    Clarina Thalia Macfarren". 7p. Date inferred from
    the rest of set. copy found only in the Bodleian
    <g> Bodleian, x

811 Macfarren, George Alexander <t> Music, when soft
    voices die <p> Edwin Ashdown, London, n.d. <d> no.
    1 of Two Songs. 3p. W and S no. 5755. "Wessel and
    Co.," at the end. <g> bm, x

812 Macfarren, George Alexander <t> My faint spirit (From
    the Arabic) <p> Lamborn Cock, London, 1850 to 1876
    in British Museum; Cramer, Beale, London, n.d. in
    Royal Academy <d> no. 7 of "Lyrics, composed for
    Clarina Thalia Macfarren". 7p. <g> bm, x, Royal
    Academy

813 Macfarren, George Alexander <t> O world! O life! O
    time! <p> Edwin Ashdown, London, n.d. <d> no. 2 of
    Two Songs <g> not found

814 Macfarren, George Alexander <t> One word is too often
    profaned <p> Cramer, Beale, London, 1850 to 1876
    in British Museum <d> no. 1 of "Lyrics composed
    for Clarina Thalia Macfarren". 5p. <g> bm, x

815 Macfarren, George Alexander <t> A widow bird, song
    <p> Chappell and Co., London, 1867 in Anderson;
    1857 and 1858 in British Museum <d> for voice
    (4p.) including piano accompaniment, plus clarinet
    or harmonium score (5p.) <g> bm, x

816 Macfarren, George Alexander <t> A widow bird (title:
    Song. Poem of Shelley) <p> Hallbergerische
    Verlagshandlung, Stuttgart, 1847 <d> in
    Beethoven-Album. Ein Gedenkbuch dankbarer Liebe
    und Verehrung fur den grossen Todten gestiftet und

beschrieben von einem Verein von Kunstlein und
Kunstfreunden aus Frankreich, England, etc., pp.
160-62. totally different melody from the other
"widow bird" by Macfarren <g> bn, x

817 Macirone, Clara Angela <t> One word is too often
    profaned <p> Joseph Williams, London, 1900? <d>
    SATB. no. 8 of A Collection of Glees, part-songs,
    etc. for Male and Mixed Voices. 6p. <g> bm, x

818 Maconchy, Elizabeth <t> Nocturnal. To the night (for
    To night): Soon, soon, too soon, Death will come
    (adapted from stanza 5) <p> Oxford University
    Press, London, 1966 <d> no. 3 of Nocturnal, the
    other two by William Barnes and Edward Thomas,
    poets. SATB chorus, a capella. 3p. <g> lc, bm, x

819 Maddison, Adela <t> A lament: That time is dead
    forever. op. 9, no. 10 <p> Metzler, London, 1895
    <d> no. 10 of Twelve Songs, pp. 43-47 <g> bm, x

820 Malewinsky, W. <t> Ostrovok (The Islet) <p> State
    Publishing Co, Moscow, 1924 <d> 3p. <g> bn, x,
    Russian

821 Malotte, Albert Hay <t> To a skylark <p> G. Schirmer,
    New York, 1940 <d> for medium voice. 9p. <g> lc,
    copy in collection

822 Mancinelli, Luigi <t> Serenata indiana (Indian
    serenade) <p> G. Ricordi, Milan, 1914 <d> no. 5 of
    Sei melodie. Words by Lodovico Giordano <g> lc,
    Italian

823 Manhire, Wilson <t> A widow bird <p> W. Paxton
    London; Edward B. Marks Music Co., New York, 1929
    <d> no. 40433 (Marks ed.). 3p. <g> lc

824 Mann, Adolph <t> To Mary <p> J. B. Cramer and Co.,
    London, 1923 <d> song <g> lc

825 Mann, Richard <t> I arise from dreams <p> Addison and
    Lucas, London, n.d. <d> 5p. no. 1167 x. <g>
    Bodleian, x

826 Mansfield, Purcell James <t> Music, when soft voices
    die. op. 28 <p> Cary, London, 1932 <d> no. 2764.
    three-part song for female voices. 8p. <g> bm, lc,

x

827 Marshall, Charles <t> The sensitive plant <p> Boosey
    and Co., London (Willcocks in Pazdirek), 1908 <d>
    in two forms: F and A flat. 5p. <g> bm, x

828 Marshall, Florence A. <t> I arise from dreams of thee
    <p> Novello, Ewer and Co., London, 1877 <d> 6p.
    <g> and, paz, bm, x

829 Marshall, Florence A. <t> Mutability: The flow'r that
    blooms today <p> Lamborn Cock, London, 1874 <d>
    6p. L. C. 105 <g> bm, x

830 Marshall, John P. <t> I arise from dreams of thee <p>
    Oliver Ditson, Boston, 1903 <d> medium voice in C.
    no. 1 of Songs. 4p. <g> bm, x

831 Marston, C. W. <t> I arise from dreams <p> G. D.
    Russell, Boston, 1875 <d> 4p. <g> Harvard Library,
    x

832 Marston, C. W. <t> If I had but two little wings
    (falsely ascribed to Shelley) <p> Oliver Ditson,
    Boston, 1868 <d> 3p. <g> Harvard Library, x

833 Marvin, Edwin Russell <t> When passion's trance. op.
    17 <p> Composer's Press, Brooklyn, 1892 <d> 5p.
    <g> bm, x

834 Masson, Elizabeth <t> The flower that smiles <p>
    Leader and Cock, London, 1857 <d> adapted to an
    air from Gluck's Pilgrimme auf Mecca (sic). 5p.
    also in Ein Bach der fliesst. Songs for Classical
    Vocalist, II, 23, of 1859, 5p. in separate
    numbers. see Gluck <g> bm, x

835 Matthews, Edith M. <t> Indian serenade <p> E. M.
    Matthews, Merthyr Tydfil, 1905 <d> Welsh
    translation by "Pelidros". for TTBB chorus. 11p.
    <g> bm, x, Welsh

836 Matthews, Ewart E. <t> If I walk in autumn's evening
    <p> Oxford University Press, London, 1928 <d> no.
    2 of Two Songs by Shelley, 2p. <g> bm, x

837 Matthews, Ewart E. <t> Music, when soft voices die
    <p> Oxford University Press, London, 1928 <d> no.

1 of Two Songs by Shelley. 2p. <g> bm, x

838 Matthews, Harry Alexander <t> Music, when soft voices
    die <p> Schirmer, New York, 1932; also Oxford
    University Press <d> four-part men's chorus, with
    rehearsal piano part. no. 35898, Schirmer's
    secular choruses, no. 7669. 4p. <g> lc

839 Maury, Lowndes <t> Nocturne: The keen stars <p>
    Theodore Presser, Bryn Mawr, Pennsylvania, 1950
    <d> for high voice and piano. 4p. <g> amc, x

840 McAlpin, Colin <t> A faded violet (for On a faded
    violet) <p> Cary and Co., London, 1903 <d> no. 4
    of Ten Songs, pp. 6-7 <g> bm, x

841 McAlpin, Colin <t> Music, when soft voices die <p>
    Cary and Co., London, 1903 <d> no. 6 of Ten Songs,
    p. 9. <g> bm, x

842 McAlpin, Colin <t> A widow bird <p> Cary and Co.,
    London, 1903 <d> no. 8 of Ten Songs, pp. 10-11 <g>
    bm, x

843 McAlpin, Colin <t> A lament: O world <p> Cary and
    Co., London, 1903 <d> no. 9 in Ten Songs, pp.
    13-15 <g> bm, x

844 McAlpin, Colin <t> A lament: Swifter than the
    summer's flight (for Swifter far than summer's
    flight) <p> Cary and Co., London, 1903 <d> no. 9b
    in Ten Songs, pp. 16-19 <g> bm, x

845 McDaniel, Williams J. <t> Stanzas written in
    dejection: The sun is warm <p> 17 October 1969,
    EU143747 <d> 6 leaves <g> q

846 McDermott, T. H. <t> Music, when soft voices die <p>
    J. J. Ewer and Co., London, 1854 <d> no. 5 in Six
    Songs for Voice and Piano, pp. 22-28 <g> and, bm

847 McDonald, Harl <t> He is gone: He came like a dream
    in the dawn of life <p> Elkan-Vogel Co.,
    Philadelphia, 1945 <d> 5p. <g> lc

848 McEwan, J. <t> Music, when soft voices die. Ballad
    <p> Coventry, London, 1850 <d> 3p. <g> ed, bm, x

849 McEwen, John Blackwood <t> Hellas, Scene <p>
    privately printed, 1894 <d> for soprano solo,
    female chorus (SSA) and orchestra. 19p. for voice
    part. choral score donated by Royal Academy of
    Music <g> Grove, copy of chorus in collection

850 Meares, Rev. F. L. (see Ernest Ford) <t> Song,
    "Fare-Well," words suggested by Shelley's Good
    night? ah no <p> Stanley Lucas, Weber, London,
    1883 <d> 5p. For Victorian sensitivity, changes
    Shelley's words and uses Ford's melody <g> bm, x

851 Melartin, Erkki <t> Indian serenade (Indisk Sang in
    Finnish). op. 19, no. 1 <p> K. G. Fazer,
    Helsingfors; Breitkopf and Hartel, Leipzig, n.d.
    <d> 6p. <g> Berlin, x, Finnish, German

852 Mendes, Raoul <t> Song, from the Arabic <p> ms., 1887
    <d> sung at Shelley Society Shelley Song Evening,
    11 May 1887. program in Pforzheimer Library

853 Mendl, S. F. <t> Say not good night: Good night! ah
    love (for Good night) <p> Chappell, London, 1888
    <d> 5p. very slight adaptation of Shelley's words
    <g> ed, bm, x

854 Mengel, Albert <t> I arise from dreams <p> Oliver
    Shattinger Piano and Music Co., St. Louis, 1907
    <d> no. 1 of Three Songs. 3p. <g> lc, x

855 Merrick, Frank <t> Prometheus Unbound: (Chorus of
    echoes--Child of ocean) <p> Stainer and Bell,
    London, 1934 <d> no. 4499, choral library no. 288.
    mixed chorus, with rehearsal piano part. 8p. <g>
    lc

856 Metcalfe, W. <t> A widow bird <p> Joseph Williams,
    London, 1889 <d> no. 5 in Six Songs, pp. 16-17.
    German version by Willy Kastner <g> bm, x, German

857 Metcalfe, W. <t> On a faded violet <p> Joseph
    Williams, London, 1899 <d> no. 6 in Six Songs, pp.
    18-19. German version by Willy Kastner <g> bm, x,
    German

858 Michell, Guy <t> The Indian serenade (for Indian
    serenade) <p> Vincent Music Co., London, 1909 <d>

6p. <g> bm, x

859 Miller, H. Thomas <t> Music, when soft voices die <p>
    26 August 1964, EU841862 <d> 3p.

860 Miller, Lewis M. <t> To the moon: Art thou pale <p>
    Elkan-Vogel, Philadelphia, 1969 <d> SATB, a
    capella <g> q

861 Mills, Charles <t> On a faded violet. op. 92 <p> ACA,
    New York, 1950 (composer's facsimile ed.) <d> MS
    and piano <g> q

862 Mittler, Franz <t> From dreams of thee: I arise from
    dreams <p> Associated Music Publishers, New York,
    1946 <d> for high voice. 6p. <g> Yale

863 Morgan, R. Orlando <t> Indian serenade. op. 34 <p>
    1903 <g> lc, not seen

864 Morgan, Wilford <t> I arise from dreams <p> W.
    Morgan, also Cramer and Co., London, n.d. <d> 6p.
    <g> Bodleian, x

865 Mori, Frank <t> Prometheus Unbound: My soul is an
    enchanted boat (Asia's song) <p> Ascherberg,
    London (Pazdirek) ; Cramer, London, 1865 (British
    Museum) <d> no. 4 of (9) New Songs. 4p. <g> ed,
    paz, bm, x

866 Moritt, Fred G. <t> Love's philosophy <p> EU356014,
    23 November 1943

867 Morley, Edith (afterwards Lady Headlam) <t> Song of
    Proserpine <p> J. B. Cramer, 1906; W. Paxton,
    London, 1925 <d> 4p. (1906 ed.) <g> bm, x

868 Mosely, B. L. <t> Song: False friend, wilt thou smile
    (The Cenci) <p> unpublished, 1886 <d> According to
    the program note the music was specially composed
    for the production at the Grand Theatre,
    Islington, sponsored by The Shelley Society, with
    Alma Murray as Beatrice. Other music, played by
    the orchestra under the direction of W. H.
    Brinkworth, was taken from Auber, Parker,
    Donizetti, Meyerbeer, Sullivan, and Kottaun and
    was used, in part, for the scenes and for a dance
    <g> not available

869 Mounsey, Ann Sheppard (afterwards Bartholomew) <t>
    Mutability: The flower that smiles. op. 30 <p>
    Ewer and Co., London, 1855 <d> four-part song. no.
    4 of six four-part songs. 4p. a capella. given as
    1882? by British Museum and 1855 by Anderson <g>
    and, bm, x

870 Mount, Julian (William M. Hutchinson) <t> Arabian
    love song: My faint spirit <p> W. Marshall and
    Co., London, 1878 <d> 2p. <g> and, bm, x

871 Mourant, Walter <t> The Indian serenade (for Indian
    serenade) <p> ms., Composers' facsimile ed., 1963
    <d> 3p. <g> q, x

872 Moysey, H. L. <t> Cold: The cold earth slept below
    <p> Weekes, London, 1872 <d> 7p. <g> bm, x, and

873 Moysey, H. L. <t> Good night? ah no <p> Weekes,
    London, 1872 <d> no. 2 cf Four Songlets, pp. 5-7
    <g> and, bm, x

874 Mozart, Wolfgang Amadeus <t> Ah Perdona from La
    Clemenza di Tito (music adapted to Indian
    serenade) <p> 1819 (for the composition of the
    poem) <d> Shelley's derivation of the meter from
    Mozart's song is expounded by H. Buxton Forman in
    The Athenaeum of August 31 and November 2, 1907,
    and in his edition of Medwin's Shelley of 1913, p.
    317, a claim accepted by Neville Rogers, Shelley
    at Work, p. 204. See also the Knautch girls entry,
    above. <g> bm, etc.

875 Muller, Helene <t> The world's wanderer: Tell me,
    thou star (for The world's wanderers) <p> C.
    Lonsdale, London, 1875 <d> no. 2 in Two Songs, pp.
    4-5 <g> bm, x, ed

876 Muller, Helene <t> To the moon: Art thou pale <p> C.
    Lonsdale, London, 1875 <d> no. 1 of Two Songs, pp.
    2-3 <g> bm, x, ed

877 Mullins, Hugh English <t> Music, when soft voices die
    <p> ms., 1947 <d> performed at UCLA and in
    Decatur, Illinois and on Los Angeles radio <g> q

878 Munns, Eric V. Stuart <t> I fear thy kisses <p>
    Joseph Williams, London, 1914 <d> in two forms: C

and F. 3p. <g> bm, x

879 Murchison, Louise <t> To night <p> Raymond A.
     Hoffmann Co., Chicago, 1940 <d> SSA <g> lc

880 Musgrove, Thomas W. <t> A lament: O world. op. 25,
     no. 1 <p> Willis Music co., Cincinnati, 1912 <d>
     4p. <g> lc, x

881 Musgrove, Thomas W. <t> A widow bird. op. 25, no. 2
     <p> Willis Music Co., Cincinnati, 1912 <d> 4p. <g>
     lc, x

882 Myaskovsky, Nikolai <t> Alastor. Poem for orchestra.
     op. 14 <p> State Publishing Co., Moscow, 1922;
     also 1931 <d> orchestral score, 84p. reprint 82p.
     no words used <g> grove, nn, bm

883 Neidlinger, W. H. <t> Indian serenade <p> William
     Maxwell Music Co., New York, 1904 <d> SSAA. 6p.
     <g> nn

884 Neidlinger, W. H. <t> O world! O life! <p> William
     Maxwell Music Co., New York, 1907 <d> no. 3 in Six
     Songs, pp. 8-10. <g> bm, x, lc

885 Netchaev, Vasily Vasilyevich <t> Ed eza mnu (Follow
     me, for Fragment: Follow to the deep wood's weeds
     <p> State Publishing House, Moscow, 1922 <d> op.
     1. no. 7 in Songs for the Young, pp. 22-23. dated
     July 29, 1918. <g> bn, x, Russian

886 Nevin, Ethelbert <t> I fear thy kisses <p> Boston
     Music Co., Boston, 1913 <d> p. 245 in Vance
     Thompson, The Life of Ethelbert Nevin. given in
     text as B. M. Co. 3823, but found nowhere else.
     <g> East Berlin, x

887 Niccolini, Giuseppe <t> Les Cenci. Opera <p>
     Florence, 1860? <d> given only by G. E. Woodberry
     in the appendix to his edition of The Cenci
     (Boston, 1907). The attribution should probably be
     to Giuseppe Rota, for 1862 (q.v.) since Niccolini
     died in 1842 and composed only six operas after
     1819 when he became chapel master of Piacenza
     Cathedral. Woodberry may allude to I Cenci, a play
     by G. B. Niccolini of 1844, q. v. in A. Zanco,
     Rivista Italiana del Dramma of 15 May 1939,

257-274 and N. I. White, PMLA, of December, 1922.
<g> not found

888 Nicholls, Frederick <t> A widow bird <p> J. H.
Larway, London, 1910 <d> in two forms: E minor and
G minor. 3p. <g> Bodleian, x

889 Nikolaev, Leonid <t> Ostrovok (The islet) <p> A.
Gutheil, Moscow, 1902 <d> in two forms: MS and S.
2p. Balmont translation. <g> East Berlin, x,
Russian

890 Norris, Homer A. <t> To thy chamber sweet (for Indian
serenade) <p> Cliver Ditson, Boston, 1901 <d> 5p.
<g> bm, x

891 Nosse, Carl E. <t> O thou immortal deity <p> Sam Fox
Publishing Co., New York, 1969 <d> SATB and organ.
New York Choral Art Publications. Second Choral
Series. 10p. <g> lc

892 Nunn, E. Cuthbert <t> Love's philosophy <p> Charles
Avison, London, 1907 <d> no. 1 of Four Songs <g>
lc

893 O'Neill, Norman <t> The Indian serenade (for Indian
serenade?) <p> Ricordi, Milan (given by Pazdireck
as Normann O'Neill), 1900 <g> bl, grove, paz, not
found, listed in Schirmer's music store

894 Oakeley, Herbert Stanley <t> Love's philosophy. op.
17, no. 4 <p> Novello, London, 188- <d> no. 4 in
Six Part-Songs, pp. 12-15. TTBB, a capella <g>
bpl, x

895 Oakley, Harold <t> Love's philosophy <p> Samuel
Weekes, London, 1903 <d> 5p. <g> bm, x

896 Ogdon, Wilbur <t> Moon song: Art thou pale <p>
unpublished, Master copy held by Cameo, Hollywood,
California, 1959 <d> performed Paris, 1953 and
Bloomington, Indiana, 1957 and 1961 <g> q

897 Ogilvy, Frederick Allsworth <t> Rarely, rarely,
comest thou <p> Patterson, London, 1933 <d> no.
1618 Lyric Collection of Choral Music. with staff
and sol-fa notation. 6p. <g> bm, lc, x

898 Oldenburg, Elizabeth L. <t> Enchantment <p> EU86484,
    23 July 1947

899 Olmstead, Clarence <t> Thy sweet singing: My soul is
    an enchanted boat (from Prometheus Unbound) <p> G.
    Schirmer, New York, 1939 <d> 7p. <g> lc

900 Omsoc <t> Gentle maiden: I fear thy kisses <p> R.
    Mills, London, 1888 <d> 4p. <g> bm, x, ed

901 Orchard, W. Arundel <t> When passion's trance is
    overpast <p> Novello, London, 1940 <d> SSATB, a
    capella, Novello's Part-Song Book, no. 1517 <g>
    bm, lc

902 Osborne, George Alexander <t> The cloud <p> Chappell,
    London, 1867 <d> 7p. Sung by Mme. Rudersdorff at
    the Norwich Festival <g> bm, x, and, ed

903 Osborne, George Alexander <t> The wish of my heart
    (for Good night): good night? ah no <p> Ashdown
    and Parry, London, 1861 <d> 5p. <g> and, bm, x

904 Owen, Harold John <t> To---- (for Music, when soft
    voices die) <p> ms. <g> q

905 Parker, Alfred T. <t> The philosophy of love (for
    Love's philosophy) <p> George Withers and Sons,
    London, 1909 <d> 4p. <g> bm, x

906 Parker, Dorothy Davis (Mrs. Joseph W. Parker) <t>
    Love's philosophy <p> EU725613, 15 June 1962

907 Parker, Elizabeth <t> A widow bird <p> Weekes,
    London, 1907 <d> 4p. <g> bm, x

908 Parker, Henry <t> My soul is an enchanted boat (from
    Prometheus Unbound) <p> J. B. Cramer, London, 1887
    <d> 9p. <g> bm, x, ed

909 Parker, Louis Napoleon <t> Ginevra: Wild, pale, and
    wonder-stricken <p> ms., 1886 and 1893 <d> 14p.
    ms. dated April 1, 1893 is in Pforzheimer Library.
    Sung or recited by Miss Alma Murray on April 25,
    1893. Also on program for Dramatic Readings for
    the United Richard Wagner Society (London Branch),
    July 6, 1886.

910 Parker, Louis Napoleon <t> Indian serenade <p> Weekes, London, 1888 <d> 7p. <g> bm, paz, x

911 Parker, Louis Napoleon <t> A widow bird <p> Ashdown, London (in Pazdirek); Lamborn Cock, London, 1874 <d> 3p. SSAA with rehearsal piano <g> paz, bm, x

912 Parkhurst, H. E. <t> Longing <p> ms., 1912 <d> 6p. unpaged facsimile in lc <g> lc

913 Parry, Charles Hubert H. <t> Good night? <p> Stanley Lucas, Weber, London, 1885; Year Book Press, London, 1913; Novello, ca. 1923 <d> no. 2 of English Lyrics, set to Music (1885), Set I, pp. 4-7 <g> bbc, bl, bm, x

914 Parry, Charles Hubert H. <t> Music, when soft voices die. op. 12, no. 3 <p> Lamborn Cock, London, 1873; also Novello, 1897, etc.; also Ashdown, 1927 <d> ed. of 1873 for solo voice, 4p. Novello's 1897 ed. for SATB, with sol-fa notation, 2p. Also four-part song for SATB. Also in Six Modern Lyrics (of Novello), pp. 22-24 and in Novello's Part-Song Book, vol. 18, no. 766. Ashdown's Vocal Duets, no. 103, for SA with piano, 5p. called Music <g> bm, and, bbc, bl, paz, x

915 Parry, Charles Hubert H. <t> O world, O life, O time <p> Novello, London, 1920 (written ca. 1870) <d> no. 6 of English Lyrics, Set XII, pp. 24-25 <g> bm, bbc, x, bl

916 Parry, Charles Hubert H. <t> Prometheus Unbound, Scenes <p> Novello, Ewer and Co., London, 1880 <d> SATB and piano. 80p. includes these scenes: Part I, Monarch of Gods and Demons; Thrice three hundred thousand years; Chorus of Furies; Chorus of Spirits (From unremembered ages); Life of life. Part II: Ye congregated powers of heaven (Scene I) and Unseen Spirits--The pale stars are gone (Scene 2); The pine boughs are singing; semichorus of hours, Weave the dance; and, finally, Then weave the web of the mystic measure. A few solo voices are included (Prometheus, Jupiter, Demogorgon). <g> bl, ed, grove, paz, bm, x

917 Pascal, Florian (pseudonym of Joseph Williams, q.v.)

918 Pascoe-Williams, Leonard (see Williams, L. P.)

919 Pearce, Leonard <t> Song to the men of England,
    wherefore plough <p> Lansbury's Labour Weekly,
    London, 1926 <d> vol. 2, no. 81, 25 September
    1926, p. 16 (back cover). SATB, a capella. also
    advertised for sale separately, in 1 May 1926
    issue. <g> bm, x, nn

920 Pearson, Albert <t> I arise from dreams of thee <p>
    Boosey and Co., London, n.d. <d> pp. 28-29 in The
    Cavendish Music Books, no. 114 (1878-1911) <g> bm,
    x

921 Pearson, Henry Hugh <t> Arethusa: Arethusa arose <p>
    J. Alfred Novello, London, ca. 1836 <d> (Hugo
    Pierson in German) no. 2 of the Characteristic
    Songs of Shelley, 5p. For all the H. Pearson
    entries see discussion in A. and B. Pollin, "In
    Pursuit of Pearson's Shelley Songs," Music and
    Letters, 46 (1965), 322-331. Missing is no. 3 of
    the six songs. <g> Novello archives, x

922 Pearson, Henry Hugh <t> Dirge: Rough wind (Ein
    Herbst-Grablied) <p> Breitkopf and Hartel,
    Leipzig, 1839-1841 <d> possibly the one of the six
    Characteristic Songs unfound, here republished as
    no. 2 of Zwei Lieder, pp. 8-11. B and H no. 6516.
    In 1906 Breitkopf catalogue as Windsbraut, du
    Klagerin. translation by Wahl <g> Berlin, x,
    German

923 Pearson, Henry Hugh <t> Hymn of Proserpine <p> J.
    Alfred Novello, London, ca. 1836 <d> no. 5 of the
    Characteristic Songs. 5p. voice with flute
    obligato and piano. see first Pearson entry. <g>
    Novello archives, x

924 Pearson, Henry Hugh <t> Invocation to night: Swiftly
    walk over the western wave <p> J. Alfred Novello,
    London, ca. 1836 <d> no. 6 of the Characteristic
    Songs, 3p. see first Pearson entry. <g> Novello
    archives, x

925 Pearson, Henry Hugh <t> On a faded violet <p>
    Novello, Ewer and Co., London, ca. 1836 <d> no. 1
    of the Characteristic Songs. 5p. See the first H.
    Pearson entry. <g> Novello archives, x

926 Pearson, Henry Hugh <t> Serenade (Indisches
    Standchen): I arise from dreams (Dein Bild im
    Traum) <p> Breitkopf and Hartel, Leipzig,
    1839-1841 <d> possibly the one of the
    Characteristic Songs unfound; no. 1 of Zwei
    Lieder, pp. 3-11. no. 6516. Translation by Wahl
    <g> Berlin, x, German

927 Pearson, Henry Hugh <t> Song of Beatrice Cenci: False
    friend, wilt thou smile <p> J. Alfred Novello,
    London, ca. 1836 <d> no. 4 of the Characteristic
    Songs. 4p. <g> bbc, x

928 Pease, Jessie L. <t> I arise from dreams of thee <p>
    Withe Smith Publications, New York, 1894 (?) <d>
    seen only in Vienna State Library which had this
    as 5 pages inserted, unpaged from The Song
    Journal, Whitney-Marvin Music Co., Detroit, XV,
    no. 6 (May, 1894), Vienna MS 26103. The Song
    Journal not found in USA <g> Vienna

929 Peele, Dudley <t> The Indian serenade (for Indian
    serenade) <p> H. T. FitzSimons, Chicago, 1930 <d>
    four-part chorus, TTBB. 10p. Aeolian Series of
    Choral Music, Male Voices, no. 4028. First prize
    of Swift and Co., Male Chorus Competition, 1930
    <g> lc

930 Peery, Rob Roy <t> Indian serenade <p> H. W. Gray,
    New York, 1932 <g> lc

931 Perkins, Charles Callahan <t> Indian serenade <p>
    Brandus, Paris, 1849 <d> one of Eight Melodies,
    French text by Ch. Monselet. 4p. including
    separate voice sheets in English and in French
    plus piano accompaniment. two staves with slight
    variation in melody for differences in
    syllabication <g> bm, x, French

932 Perkins, Charles Callahan <t> Asia's song: My soul is
    an enchanted boat (Prometheus Unbound) <p>
    Brandus, Paris, 1849 <d> one of Eight Melodies,
    French text by Ch. Monselet. 4p. including
    separate voice sheets in English and in French
    plus piano accompaniment. two staves with slight
    variation in melody for difference in
    syllabication. <g> bm, x, French

933 Perkins, Henry Samuel <t> I arise from dreams of thee
    <p> Enoch, London, 1880 <d> 5p. <g> and, ed, bm, x

934 Peters, J. V. <t> Music, when soft voices die <p>
    Elkin and Co., London, 1949 <d> SATB with
    rehearsal piano part and sol-fa notation. Elkin
    2149. 3p. <g> bm, x

935 Pfautsch, Lloyd <t> Music, when soft voices die <p>
    Chappell, London; Lawson-Gould, New York, 1959 <d>
    four-part mixed chorus with soprano solo and
    rehearsal piano part. Lloyd Pfautsch Choral
    Series, no. 793. 7p. <g> bm, lc, copy in
    collection

936 Phelps, Mona Holesco (see Mona Holesco)

937 Phillips, Harold D. <t> Rarely, rarely, comest thou
    <p> Oxford University Press, London, 1930 <d> SATB
    chorus with rehearsal piano part. Oxford Choral
    Songs, no. 734. 19p. <g> bbc, bm

938 Phillips, Montague F. <t> The whispering waves <p>
    Chappell and Co., London, 1912 <d> part-song for
    SATB. 4p. <g> bm, lc

939 Piatti, Alfredo <t> The colour from the flow'r is
    gone (On a faded violet) <p> Chappell, London,
    1867 <d> 5p. <g> and, bm, x

940 Pierik, Marie <t> The cloud <p> facsimile publication
    by the composer, 1943 <d> no. 1 of Two Songs, pp.
    1-4 <g> lc

941 Piket, Frederick <t> Indian serenade <p> Associated
    Music Publishers, New York, 1955 <d> for SATB
    chorus with rehearsal piano. no. 3 of Six about
    Love. 7p. <g> copy in collection

942 Piket, Frederick <t> When the lamp is shattered <p>
    Associated Music Publishers, New York, 1957 <d>
    For SSAA chorus with rehearsal piano. 9p. <g> copy
    in collection

943 Pimsleur, Solomon <t> Dirge <p> facsimile <g> amc

944 Pimsleur, Solomon <t> I fear thy kisses. op. 17, no.

16 <p> facsimile publication, 1942 <d> song for
medium voice. LC no. E109822, 1 October 1942 <g>
amc, lc, x

945 Pimsleur, Solomon <t> I pant for the music <p> AMC,
New York, 1924. facsimile reproduction <d> op. 17,
no. 7 <g> amc

946 Pimsleur, Solomon <t> Music, when soft voices die.
op. 17, no. 5 <p> facsimile reproduction, 1941 <d>
one double leaf <g> nn

947 Pimsleur, Solomon <t> My faint spirit <p> American
Composers Alliance, New York, 1957 <d> facsimile
reproduction <g> amc, bmi

948 Pimsleur, Solomon <t> One word is too often profaned
<p> American Composers Alliance, New York, 1957
<d> facsimile reproduction <g> bmi

949 Pimsleur, Solomon <t> The rude wind is singing <p>
AMC, New York, 1924. facsimile reproduction, 1941
<d> op. 17, no. 2. 1p. <g> amc, x

950 Pimsleur, Solomon <t> Threnos. <p> AMC, New York,
1924. facsimile reproduction <d> op. 17, no. 1 <g>
amc

951 Pimsleur, Solomon <t> Time <p> AMC, New York, 1924
<d> op. 17, no. 2 <g> amc

952 Pimsleur, Solomon <t> Unsatisfied desire <p> AMC, New
York, 1924 <d> op. 17, no. 5 <g> amc

953 Pimsleur, Solomon <t> The waning moon <p> AMC, New
York, 1924 <d> op. 17, no. 3 <g> amc

954 Pizzetti, Ildebrando <t> Lamento <p> ms., Rome, 1920
<d> for tenor and chorus a capella <g> bl, grove

955 Pointer, John <t> Love's philosophy. op. 10, no. 3
<p> Novello, London, 1907; reprinted 1908 <d> in
two forms: A flat and E. 5p. <g> ed, lc, bm, x

956 Pointer, John <t> Rough wind that moanest loud. op.
21, no. 3 <p> Novello, London, 1922 <d> Novello's
Part-Song Book, Series 2, no. 1406 for SATB with
rehearsal piano part. 4p. <g> bm, x

957 Porter, Quincy <t> Music, when soft voices die <p>
    Music Press, New York, 1947 <d> for medium voice.
    2p. <g> bbc, Yale, x

958 Powell, Laurence <t> Ozymandias. op. 21, no. 3 <p> C.
    C. Birchard, Boston, 1924 <d> Laurel octavo no.
    480. SATB with piano. 12p. <g> bm, x

959 Pratten, W. S. <t> Swifter far than summer's flight
    <p> T. Prowse, London, 1848 <d> no. 1 of Three
    Songs. 5p. <g> bm, and, x

960 Pratten, W. S. <t> Oh! there are spirits in the air
    (sic) <p> T. Prowse, London, 1848 <d> no. 2 of
    Three Songs. 6p. <g> and, bm, x

961 Pratten, W. S. <t> Spirit cf night: Swiftly walk over
    <p> T. Prowse, London, 1848 <d> no. 3 cf Three
    Songs. 6p. <g> and, bm, x

962 Pyke, Dorothy <t> To night <p> Stainer and Bell,
    London, 1911 <d> Stainer and Bell's Modern Songs,
    no. 47 <g> lc

963 Quilter, Roger <t> Arab love song: My faint spirit.
    op. 25, no. 4 <p> Winthrop Rogers, London, 1927
    <d> 5p. <g> bm, x

964 Quilter, Roger <t> I arise from dreams. op. 29 <p>
    Boosey, London, 1931 <d> 8p. <g> bbc, bl, bm, x

965 Quilter, Roger <t> Music: I pant for the music which
    is divine <p> J. Curwen and Sons, London, 1948 <d>
    7p. <g> bl, ed, x

966 Quilter, Roger <t> Love's philosophy <p> Boosey,
    London and New York, 1905; also 1923 and 1924. op.
    3, no. 1 <d> also in Standard Vocal Repertoire,
    published by R. D. Row, vol. 2, and in Fifty
    Modern English Scngs (Boosey, 1923), pp. 6-9 and
    in Englische Lyrik. Funf Lieder mit
    Klavierbegleitung, no. 2 (Schott, Mainz, 1924),
    German translation by Gcldschmidt-Livingston <g>
    bbc, bl, bm, nn, German

967 Quilter, Roger <t> Music and mocnlight: The keen
    stars were twinkling <p> J. Curwen and Sons,
    London; G. Schirmer, New York, 1948 <d> 6p. <g>

bbc, ed, x

968 Quilter, Roger <t> Music, when soft voices die. op.
     25, no. 5 <p> Winthrop Rogers, London; Boston
     Music Co., Boston, 1927 <d> 3p. <g> bl, bm, nn

969 Quilter, Roger <t> One word is too often profaned <p>
     J. Curwen, London, 1947 <d> 5p. <g> bm, bbc, ed, x

970 Raalte, Charles van <t> Good night <p> Chappell,
     London, 1889 <d> 5p. <g> ed, bm, x

971 Rachmaninov, Serge <t> Ostrovok (The isle). op. 14,
     no. 2 <p> 1896, 1922, 1939, 1947, 1955 <d> First
     published in Twelve Songs, translation by
     Constantine Balmont, A. Gutheil, Moscow, Paris,
     etc., 1896, vol. 1, pp. 44-45, and reprinted 1947
     by Boosey and Hawkes, New York. Words in French
     (by M. D. Calvocoressi), German (by Lina Esbeer)
     and English (translated by Edward Agate from the
     Russian: A little island set in sea, etc.).
     Translated by Geraldine Farrar as "The Mirage" and
     published 1922. Published in Polish in Piesni
     wybrane, Polskie Wydawnictwo Muzyczne, Cracow,
     1955. also in Fifty Art Songs (Schirmer, 1939),
     pp. 188-190, in an English version by Carl Engel.
     <g> bn, bm, x, German, French, Russian, Polish

972 Radecki, Olga von <t> A widow bird <p> Schmidt,
     Boston, 1886 <d> no. 3 of Four New Songs. 3p. <g>
     Harvard Library, x

973 Ranken, C. A. <t> Song of Beatrice Cenci: False
     friend (The Cenci) <p> Stanley Lucas, Weber and
     Co., London, 1876 <d> 5p. <g> bm, x

974 Raphael, Juliet <t> Music, when soft voices die <p>
     Boni, New York, 1927 <d> in Madrigal and
     Minstrelsy, p. 41 <g> lc, nn

975 Raphling, Sam <t> Lover's logic (The fountains
     mingle) <p> General Music Publishing Co., Hastings
     on the Hudson, 1968 <d> no. 1 of New Songs on Four
     Romantic Poems <g> lc

976 Ratcliffe, Desmond <t> A widow bird <p> Elkin,
     London; Galaxy Music, New York, 1951 <d> no. 1 in

Two Shelley Songs, for S or T. 2p. <g> x, bbc, ed, bm

977 Ratcliffe, Desmond <t> Wine of the fairies <p> Elkin, London, 1951 <d> no. 2 in Two Shelley Songs, for S or T. 3p. <g> bbc, ed, bm

978 Rathaus, Karol <t> Winter: A widow bird <p> M. Witmark, New York, 1949 <d> four-part chorus, SATB, a capella, with rehearsal piano part. 5p. <g> nn

979 Rathbone, George <t> Music: I pant for the music <p> Novello, London, 1929 <d> SATB chorus with rehearsal piano part. nc. 1440 of Novello's part-song book. 4p. <g> bbc, bm, x

980 Rauscher, Henry, pseudonym of H. S. Humphreys, q.v.

981 Raymond, John <t> Music, when soft voices die <p> Plymouth Music Co., New York, 1964 <d> SSA chorus. 4p. John Raymond Choral Series no. 200 <g> lc

982 Rea, William <t> I arise from dreams <p> Augener, London, 1868 <d> no. 1 cf Four Songs. 6p. <g> and, ed, paz, bm, x

983 Read, Gardner <t> To a skylark. op. 51 <p> Associated Music Publishers, New York, 1939 <d> SATB, a capella. 10p. <g> nn, x

984 Reed, Alfred <t> To music: Music, when soft voices die <p> EU57121-26, 26 November 1946 <d> one of suite, Six Songs from the Golden Treasury. also arranged for SSAA. performed <g> lc, q

985 Reed, Alfred <t> Winter: A widow bird <p> EU57121-26, 26 November 1946 <d> one of suite, Six Songs from the Golden Treasury <g> lc, q

986 Reed, Francis A. <t> As the moon's soft splendour <p> Stanley Lucas, Weber, London, 1887 <d> 5p. <g> ed, bm, x

987 Reeves, Boleyne <t> The cold earth slept <p> London <d> advertised on the back of sheet music <g> unfound

988 Reeves, Boleyne <t> The fugitives: The waters are
     flashing <p> Addison, Hollier and Lucas, London,
     1861 <d> 13p. <g> bm, x

989 Reeves, Boleyne <t> I arise from dreams <p> R. Mills,
     London, 1845 <d> for voice with harp or piano <g>
     bm, x

990 Reeves, Boleyne <t> Swifter far than summer's flight
     <p> London <d> advertised on the back of sheet
     music <g> unfound

991 Reeves, Boleyne <t> When the star of the morning
     (sic, from The cloud ?) <p> London <d> advertised
     on the back of sheet music <g> unfound

992 Reimann, Aribert <t> Epitaf auf texte von Percy
     Bysshe Shelley <p> Schott, Mainz, 1965 <d> Four
     texts of Shelley set to seven instruments: flute,
     cor anglais, celesta, harp, viola, cello, double
     bass, and tenor solo <g> Schott catalogue and
     correspondence with the company

993 Reimann, Aribert <t> Autumn: A dirge (The warm sun is
     failing) <p> Schott, Mainz, 1965 <d> see Epitaf of
     Reimann <g> German

994 Reimann, Aribert <t> A lament: O world <p> Schott,
     Mainz, 1965 <d> see Epitaf of Reimann <g> German

995 Reimann, Aribert <t> The past: Wilt thou forget the
     happy hours <p> Schott, Mainz, 1965 <d> see Epitaf
     of Reimann <g> German

996 Reimann, Aribert <t> Song: A widow bird <p> Schott,
     Mainz, 1965 <d> see Epitaf of Reimann <g> German

997 Reinhardt, Carl <t> I arise from dreams (called The
     Indian's Lament) <p> Musical Bouquet Office and J.
     Allen, London, 1856 <d> nc. 1026, Musical Bouquet.
     3p. <g> bm, x

998 Reitz, Edward E. <t> Good night <p> unpublished,
     despite the number; E683426, 24 February 1928;
     renewed 15 February 1956

999 Reiz <t> The Cenci <p> 1950 <d> background music
     composed by Reiz for a production in the Walt

Whitman School, New York, February, 1950,
according to a review in the New Yorker
Staats-Zeitung of February 10, 1950, which speaks
of the Buhnenpartitur by Reiz <g> not seen

1000 Reizenstein, Franz <t> Voices of Night, a cantata
     (includes Serenade: I arise from dreams) <p>
     Novello, London, 1952 <d> for baritone, chorus and
     orchestra (137 p. in voice and piano reduction
     score). Words arranged by Christopher Hassall from
     eight poets, Shelley's Indian Serenade being no. 6
     and the whole of Part 3 (12 nos. in 5 Parts), pp.
     57-61. <g> bbc, gr, bm, copy in collection

1001 Respighi, Ottorino <t> I tempi assai lontani: come
     l'ombra (for Time long past: Like the ghost of a
     dear friend) <p> Ricordi, Milan, 1918 <d> pp. 1-5
     of Cinque lirichi. Translation by Roberto Ascoli
     <g> bm, bn, x, Italian

1002 Respighi, Ottorino <t> Arethusa <p> Ricordi, Milan,
     1911; also Universal, Vienna, 1923 <d> song with
     orchestra. Translated by Roberto Ascoli. German by
     R. S. Hoffmann <g> bl, nn, Italian, German

1003 Respighi, Ottorino <t> Canto funebre: Rude vento
     (Rough wind) <p> Ricordi, Milan, 1918 <d> pp. 6-10
     in Cinque lirichi. translated by Roberto Ascoli
     <g> bn, x, Italian

1004 Respighi, Ottorino <t> Il tramonto: Gia v'ebbe un
     uomo, nel cui tenue spirto (The sunset: There late
     was one) <p> F. Bongiovanni, Bologna, 1912;
     Ricordi, Milan, 1918 (1929 in BN copy) <d> scored
     for 1st and 2nd violins, viola, cello. 20p. no.
     117087 (Bologna), 20p. Subtitled lyric poem for
     voice and string quartet. no. 118089 (Milan).
     translated by Roberto Ascoli. <g> bn, nn, bm,
     Italian

1005 Respighi, Ottorino <t> Serenade Indiana: el sonno tra
     i fantasimi di te sognavo (Indian serenade) <p> F.
     Bongiovanni, Bologna, 1912 <d> 5p. <g> bm, x,
     Italian

1006 Respighi, Ottorino <t> La sensitiva. (The sensitive
     plant) <p> Universal ed.; Vienna and New York,
     1924 <d> for MS and orchestra. 36 p. voice plus

piano reduction. German (Die Mimosa) by R. S.
Hoffmann <g> bm, x, Italian, German

1007 Respighi, Ottorino <t> Su una violetta morta (On a
faded violet) <p> F. Bongiovanni, Bologna, 1919
<d> for MS and piano. 4p. translated by F. Rocchi.
no. 3 of Sei Melodie <g> bm, x, Italian

1008 Reynvaan, Marie C. C. <t> A widow bird (Liedje) <p>
G. Alsbach, Amsterdam, 1907 <d> pp. 3-5 of
Shelley-Liederen. words in Dutch and English <g>
Berlin, x, Dutch

1009 Reynvaan, Marie C. C. <t> On Fanny Godwin: Her voice
did quiver (Op Fanny Godwin) <p> G. Alsbach,
Amsterdam, 1907 <d> pp. 6-11 of Shelley-Liederen.
words in Dutch and English <g> Berlin, x, Dutch

1010 Reynvaan, Marie C. C <t> A dirge: Rough wind (Ein
klaagzang) <p> G. Alsbach, Amsterdam, 1907 <d> pp.
12-13 of Shelley-Liederen. words in Dutch and
English <g> Berlin, x, Dutch

1011 Reynvaan, Marie C. C. <t> To Mary Shelley: The world
is dreary (Aan Mary Shelley) <p> G. Alsbach,
Amsterdam, 1907 <d> pp. 14-15 of Shelley-Liederen.
words in Dutch and English <g> Berlin, x, Dutch

1012 Rhoads, Kenneth Warren <t> Indian serenade <p>
EU344962, 26 August 1943

1013 Rhodes, Harold W. <t> The widow bird <p> Year Book
Press, London, 1909 <d> four-part song for SSAA.
no. 32 of the Year Book Press Series of Unison and
Part-Songs. 6p <g> bm, x

1014 Richards, F. Dewey <t> I arise from dreams of thee. A
serenade (for Indian serenade) <p> F. Dewey
Richards, n. p., 1902 <d> 7p. <g> lc, x

1015 Richards, K. L. <t> Indian serenade <p> EU607794, 6
March 1925

1016 Rickman, F. R. <t> Good night <p> Boosey and Co.,
London, 1912 <d> for voice and piano with violin
and 'cello obligato. 6p., including one for each
stringed instrument <g> lc, x

1017 Robbins, Reginald C. <t> Fragment (Solitude): The sun
     is warm, the sky is clear <p> Maurice Senart,
     Paris, 1928 (also 1941) <d> no. 131 in Songs of
     ...Robbins. for middle voice. 3p. issued 1941 for
     high voice <g> lc, Columbia University

1018 Robbins, Reginald C. <t> The Invitation (To Jane):
     Best and brightest <p> Maurice Senart, Paris, 1928
     <d> no. 63 of Songs. 3p. <g> Columbia University

1019 Robbins, Reginald C. <t> Ode to the west wind <p>
     Maurice Senart, Paris, 1928 <d> for bass. 10p. <g>
     Columbia University

1020 Robbins, Reginald C. <t> Ozymandias <p> Maurice
     Senart, Paris, 1928 <d> for bass or baritone. 3p.
     <g> Columbia University

1021 Robbins, Reginald C. <t> The poet's dream: On a
     poet's lips I slept <p> Maurice Senart, Paris,
     1928 <d> nos. 66 and 66a of Songs, for high voice
     and for bass <g> Columbia University

1022 Robbins, Reginald C. <t> To Jane: The moon's soft
     splendour <p> Maurice Senart, Paris, 1928 <d> nos.
     61 and 61a of Songs. for high voice and for tenor
     <g> Columbia University

1023 Roberton, Hugh S. <t> Music, when soft voices die <p>
     Paterson's, Glasgow, 1927 <d> female voices. no.
     1574 of The Lyric Collection of Part-Songs
     (Paterson's Publications). 2p. <g> bm, x

1024 Robinson, Aletha Mae <t> Indian serenade: I arise
     from dreams <p> facsimile publication, Harrison,
     Godwin, Smith, n. p., 1952 <d> 3p. <g> lc, bmi

1025 Robinson, Barbara Lemon <t> Music, when soft voices
     die <p> EU260498, 6 June 1941

1026 Robinson, Dora <t> Love's philosophy <p> Chappell,
     London, 1899 <d> 5p. <g> bm, x

1027 Rochberg, George <t> Dirge: Rough wind <p> ms., 1969
     <d> for voice and piano. for a Book of Songs <g> q

1028 Rochberg, George <t> Song of day (from Allegory): The

deathless stars (from The two spirits, stanza 2)
<p> ms., 1969 <d> for Book of Songs <g> q

1029 Roeder, Martin <t> Apollo, a Cantata. op. 62 (for
Hymn of Apollo) <p> C. Dieckmann, Leipzig; Edward
Schuberth, New York, 1890 <d> for soloists (SAT)
chorus, and orchestra. pp. 3-50 in piano score.
Free metrical translation into German by Raro
Miedtner <g> Berlin, bpl, x, German

1030 Roeder, Martin <t> A lament: oh world. op. 53, no. 2
(for o world) <p> Novello, London, 1899 <d>
Novello's collection of trios, no. 222. 5p. <g>
bm, x

1031 Roeder, Martin <t> Love's philosophy <p> Novello,
London, 1892 <d> no. 221 in Novello's Collection
of Trios, Quartets, etc. for female voices. a
two-part song, op. 53, no. 1 <g> bm, x

1032 Roeder, Martin <t> One word is too often profaned <p>
Ditson, Boston, 1892 <d> for medium voice in F
minor. 9p. also in Oliver Ditson Song Album, pp.
42-48 (1892) with German translation by Roeder <g>
paz, bm, x, German

1033 Roeder, Martin <t> Pan, a Cantata: From the forests
and the highlands we come. op. 63 <p> C.
Dieckmann, Leipzig; Edward Schuberth, New York,
1890 <d> for baritone, chorus and orchestra. pp.
3-48 in piano version. free metrical translation
into German by Raro Meidtner <g> bpl, Berlin, x,
German

1034 Roeder, Martin <t> Shall we roam, my love (To the
queen of my heart, falsely attributed to Shelley)
<p> A. P. Schmidt, Boston and London, 1892 <d> 6p.
<g> bm, x

1035 Roff, Joseph <t> A dirge <p> Hal Leonard Music,
Winona, Minnesota, 1967 <d> Hal Leonard Choral
Library, Select series, octavo, no. R3-101. 6p.
SATB <g> lc

1036 Rogers, Bernard <t> Adonais, a symphony, no. 1 <p>
presumably unpublished, 1925 <g> grove

1037 Rogers, W. B. <t> A song: A widow bird <p> Robert

Cocks, London, 1851 <d> no. 7 of A Set of Seven
Songs, pp. 24-26. <g> bm, x

1038 Rogers, W. B. <t> Love's philosophy <p> Robert Cocks,
London, 1851 <d> no. 1 of A Set of Seven Songs,
pp. 1-5 <g> Harvard Library, bm, x

1039 Rohland, Cora <t> Indian serenade <p> Thiebes
Stierling Music Co., St. Louis, 1895 <d> 5p. <g>
nn

1040 Ronald, Landon <t> Adonais, an Elegy. a Dramatic
scene <p> Enoch, London, 1903 <d> for voice and
orchestra. text selected by Vernor Blackburn. 11p.
<g> bbc, ed, bm, x

1041 Ronald, Landon <t> Good night <p> Enoch, London, 1911
<d> 4p. <g> bm, x, lc

1042 Ronald, Landon <t> Love's philosophy <p> Metzler,
London, 1898; Keith Prowse, London, 1900; Enoch,
London, 1911 <d> 5p. in Metzler ed. no. 10 of
"Famous Lyrics" in Enoch edition <g> bm, x

1043 Rorem, Ned <t> A dirge: Rough wind <p> Theodore
Presser, Bryn Mawr, Penn., 1956 <d> no. 2 in Five
Prayers for the Young. SSA a capella, with
rehearsal piano part, pp. 6-7. <g> usi, lc, copy
in collection

1044 Rorem, Ned <t> Now I lay me down to sleep (falsely
ascribed to Shelley) <p> Theodore Presser, Bryn
Mawr, Penn., 1956 <d> no. 3 in Five Prayers for
the Young. SSA with rehearsal piano, p. 8. <g>
usi, lc, copy in collection

1045 Rorem, Ned <t> Fragment: Wine of the fairies (Wine of
eglantine) <p> Theodore Presser, Bryn Mawr, Penn.,
1956 <d> no. 4 in Five Prayers for the Young. pp.
9-11 SSA a capella. <g> usi, copy in collection

1046 Rorem, Ned <t> Gentle visitations: Ye gentle
visitations <p> Elkan-Vogel Co., Philadelphia,
1961 <d> SSA a capella with rehearsal piano. 5p.
<g> usi, copy in collection

1047 Rosenfeld, Leopold <t> World's wanderers (Vandrerne)
<p> Wilhelm Hansen, Copenhagen, n.d. <d> 3p. <g>

Berlin, x, Danish

1048 Rosenhoff, Orla <t> Love's philosophy (Kjaerlighedens philosophi) <p> Horneman and Erslev, Copenhagen, n.d. <d> in Digte efter det Engelske ved Caralis. no. 2, op. 4. 1p. <g> Berlin, x, Danish

1049 Rosenhoff, Orla <t> To the queen of my heart (Til mit hjertes dronning), wrong attribution to Shelley <p> Horneman and Erslev, Copenhagen, n.d. <d> in Digte efter det Engelske ved Caralis. op. 4, no. 1. 1p. <g> Berlin, x, Danish

1050 Rota, Giuseppe II <t> Beatrice Cenci (for The Cenci?) <p> Parma, 1862 <d> opera performed, if not published, in Parma, according to Alberto Basso, La Musica (Turin, 1971). According to Clement and Larousse, Dictionnaire des Operas (Paris, 1905), an opera in three acts, performed in 1863. libretto by D. Ralbino. There is no reference to Shelley, but the literary nature of other Rota operas suggests the use of the 1833 French translation by Astolphe Marquis de Custine. See also Niccolini. <g> no score or libretto available.

1051 Rozycki, Ludomir <t> Beatrix Cenci. opera. op. 48 or 53 (for The Cenci?) <p> Warsaw, 1927; Poznan, 1936 <d> given by Grove as op. 53, with a libretto after a drama by Juliusz Slowacki, written by the composer and his wife and produced in Warsaw 10 January 1927 (but probably derived from Shelley's play). However, a suite by Rozycki, entitled Italie, pour piano, op. 50, contains as its fourth number a four-page piano piece entitled La Mort de Beatrice Cenci (Gebethner and Wolff, Warsaw, 1925) and lists, on the back cover, Beatrice Cenci. Opera, op. 48. Blume, Die Musik in Geschichte und Gegenwart, lists for Rozycki a four-act opera, Beatrice Cenci, presented or produced 30 January 1937, and also an aria from act 3 for voice and piano, published in the monthly Muzyka of 1927. <g> op. 50, no. 4 in nn

1052 Rubbra, Edmund Duncan <t> A widow bird. op. 28 <p> Oxford University Press, London, 1931; Alfred Lengnick, London, 1953 <d> 3p. in Lengnick ed. <g> bm, bbc, bl, ed

1053 Rubinstein, Anton Gregorievich (adaptation by D. Rhys
     Ford) <t> Elegy to the moon <p> Melrose Music Co.,
     Warren, Ohio, 1937 <d> four-part chorus of mixed
     voices, in Kamennoi Ostroi sketches. adapted to
     Rubinstein's melody. 6p. <g> lc, not seen

1054 Rubstein, Ariel Alfred <t> Threnos <p> EU182213, 18
     November 1938

1055 Russell, John <t> I fear thy kisses <p> Walton Music
     Corp., California, 1969 <d> SATB <g> lc

1056 Rutland, Harold <t> Art thou pale for weariness <p>
     J. Curwen, London, 1923 <d> 3p. <g> bm, x

1057 Sahnow, Will <t> Men of England <p> Workers Music
     Association, London, n.d. <d> for unison or SATB
     chorus <g> bbc, unseen

1058 Salaman, Charles Kensington <t> I arise from dreams
     of thee <p> Schirmer, New York; Ashdown, London;
     Church, Cincinnati; Ditson, Boston, 1866; also
     republished 1868, 1902, 1905, 1910, 1920 <d> also
     pub. by D'Almaine of London (6p.) published by
     Ashdown, 1868, arranged by C. Salaman solely for
     the piano, 10p. also Bayley and Ferguson, London,
     n.d.: Standard Vocal Albums, Tenor Songs, pp. 3-7.
     See Fletcher for choral arrangement of 1909.
     included in Duncan, The Ministrelsy of England,
     Augener, 1905-1909, and in Krehbiel, Famous Songs,
     published by Church of Philadelphia (1902), vol.
     3, and in Francis Day's Standard Folio of 100 Best
     Songs, pp. 70-73 (1910). Arranged by Victor Harris
     for women's voices, Oliver Ditson, Boston, 1902
     <g> bm, nn, x

1059 Salaman, Charles Kensington <t> Love's philosophy <p>
     Ashdown, London ca. 1866 <d> in two forms: C and A
     flat. 6p. also published by Ashdown, 1866,
     arranged by Salaman solely for the piano. <g>
     Bodleian, x

1060 Salathiel, Lyndon <t> Indian serenade <p> EU213452, 7
     February 1940

1061 Salter, Mary Turner <t> Good night <p> Oliver Ditson,
     Boston, 1910 <d> for low voice in G flat <g> lc

1062 Samazeuilh, Gustave <t> Symphonic Etudes, after "La
     Nef" of Elemir Bourges, poeme dramatique
     (Prometheus Unbound) <p> Durand, Paris, 1906-1909
     <d> The dramatic poem, "La Nef," freely develops
     the myth of Prometheus, based on Aeschylus and
     Shelley. pp. 3-63 in the pocket score text
     examined. orchestral parts indicated. Sole
     reference to Shelley is in the preliminary note.
     <g> bn, copy of pocket score in nn

1063 Sanders, Harlon Wayne <t> A dirge <p> EU414148, 26
     March 1945

1064 Sanderson, Wilfrid <t> Indian serenade <p> Leonard,
     London, 1909 <d> in two forms: D minor and F
     minor. 6p. <g> bm, x

1065 Sartoris, Adelaide <t> Good night. <p> Robert W.
     Ollivier, London, 1860 <d> duet. 5p. <g> and, bm,
     x

1066 Sawyer, Frank E. <t> I fear thy kisses <p> Charles
     Sheard, London; White-Smith Music Pub. Co.,
     Boston; 1894 <d> TTBB with piano part. 4p. <g> bm,
     x

1067 Saxe, George <t> O world, O life <p> EU241747, 8
     January 1941

1068 Saxe, Serge <t> Adonais: The one remains <p> Peer,
     New York, 1955 <d> song with piano. 8p. copyright
     by Peer International Corp., EP89304, 12 April
     1955 <g> lc, copy in collection

1069 Saxe, Serge <t> Wedded souls (fragment: Wedded
     souls): I am as a spirit <p> Southern Music
     Publishing Co., New York, 1952 <d> 3p. <g> usi,
     copy in collection

1070 Schnecker, Peter A <t> Love's philosophy <p> Pond,
     New York, Ditson, Boston, 1893 <d> for alto or
     baritone in G. 3p. <g> Yale, bm, x

1071 Schnecker, Peter A. <t> To the night: Swiftly,
     swiftly walk o'er the western wave <p> 1897 <d>
     for bass. 7p. <g> Yale

1072 Schroeter, Max <t> Canzonetta: I fear thy kisses <p>

Howard and Co., London, 1881 <d> Canzonetta from
the opera "Nausicaa". 3p. <g> bm, x, ed

1073 Schroeter, Max <t> Queen of my heart: Shall we roam,
my love (false attribution to Shelley) <p> Howard
and Co., London, 1879 <d> in two forms: D and F.
6p. <g> ed, bm, x

1074 Schrogin, Orey Yudi <t> Indian serenade <p> EU102939,
19 April 1935 <d> harmonized for the pianoforte by
Pauline Goldberg

1075 Schultheis, W. <t> To the queen of my heart: Shall we
roam, my love (false attribution to Shelley) <p>
Addison, Hollier and Lucas, London, n.d. <d> 7p.
A.h.L.200. <g> Bodleian, x

1076 Schumann, Robert A. <t> The fugitives: The waters are
flashing. op. 122, no. 2 <p> Bartholf Sennf,
Leipzig, 1852 (?); Augner, London, n.d. Breitkoff
and Hartel, n.d. <d> Balladen, pp. 14-17: Die
Fluchtlinge (Breitkoff and Hartel). 4p. in each
edition. composed 1852 <g> Royal Academy of Music,
Yale, bm, Harvard, nn, x, German

1077 Schumann, Robert A. (See Bushell for an adaptation of
op. 28, no. 2)

1078 Schwartz, W. S. <t> World's wanderers <p> EU521104, 1
October 1921

1079 Schwartz, W. S. <t> On a faded violet <p> EU521110, 1
October 1921

1080 Scott, Charles P. <t> Widow bird <p> Arthur P.
Schmidt, Boston, 1899 <d> for high voice. 3p. <g>
lc, x

1081 Scott, Hayward Argyll <t> The skylark: Hail to thee,
blithe spirit <p> Vincent Music Co., London, 1905
<d> no. 1 of Four Songs, pp. 2-3 <g> bm, x

1082 Scrinzi, G. <t> Indian serenade <p> Warren and
Phillips, London, 1908 <d> 6p. <g> bm, x

1083 Scrinzi, G. <t> Sing again: As the moon's soft
splendour <p> Warren and Phillips, London, 1908
<d> 6p. <g> bm, x

1084 Scull, Harold Thomas <t> Music, when soft voices die.
     op. 24 <p> Augener, London, 1952 <d> SSA and
     piano. 4p. <g> bm, x

1085 Seeger, Charles Louis <t> When soft winds and sunny
     skies <p> Schirmer, New York, 1911 <d> no. 6 in
     Seven Songs <g> lc

1086 Segal, Daniel Alan <t> Love's philosophy <p>
     EU834699, July 1964

1087 Selby, Bertram Luard <t> A widow bird <p> Boosey,
     London, 1902, 1923, 1932 <d> 5p. also in Fifty
     Modern English Songs, Eoosey, 1923, pp. 20-23, and
     advertised in Schirmer's Fifty Modern English
     Songs of 1932. <g> lc, bm, x

1088 Selle, William Christian <t> Hellas, choruses <p>
     Reeves and Turner, for the Shelley Society,
     London, 1886 <d> in 16 parts for solo, duets,
     trios, and four-part chorus, with piano
     accompaniment and piano overture. 98p. published
     for the Shelley Society as extra series, no. 1.
     <g> ed, lc, Yale, bm, x, Royal Academy

1089 Selmer, Johann Peter <t> Alastor, orchestral work.
     op. 8 <p> 1872 <d> mentioned by Grove, but not
     found

1090 Selmer, Johann Peter <t> Love's philosophy <p> Carl
     Warmuths Verlag, Christiania, 1890 <d> no. 3 of
     Drei Gedichte von Shelley fur Orchestre, Tenor und
     Bariton Solo, op. 13, pp. 43-55 translated by
     Strodtmann. 55p. for the set <g> East Berlin,
     English, German, Danish, x

1091 Selmer, Johann Peter <t> The lament of Tasso (for
     Tasso): I loved--alas! our life is love <p> Carl
     Warmuths Verlag, Christiania, 1890 <d> no. 1 of
     Drei Gedichte von Shelley fur Orchestre, Tenor und
     Bariton Solo, op. 13, pp. 3-23. translated by P.
     Cornelius. 55p. for the set <g> East Berlin,
     English, German, Danish, x

1092 Selmer, Johann Peter <t> The world's wanderers <p>
     Carl Warmuths Verlag, Christiania, 1890 <d> no. 2
     of Drei Gedichte von Shelley fur Orchestre, Tenor
     und Bariton Solo, op. 13, pp. 25-41. translated by

Strodtmann. 55p. for the set <g> East Berlin,
English, German, Danish, x

1093 Sharman, Cecil <t> A widow bird <p> Oxford University
Press, London, 1936 <d> Oxford Choral Songs no.
560. rehearsal piano part. 5p. <g> lc

1094 Shaw, Martin <t> The rain: I bring fresh showers (The
cloud) <p> J. B. Cramer, London, 1952 <d> no. 235
of Cramer's Library of Unison and Part-Songs.
unison song. 4p. <g> bm

1095 Sheets, Kate Randolph <t> I arise from dreams of thee
<p> printed by Kate Randolph Sheets, Philadelphia,
1899 <d> 7p. <g> lc, x

1096 Shelley, Percy Florence <t> Shelley's Hymn of Pan <p>
Reeves and Turner, London, 1887 (for the Shelley
Society) <d> The Shelley Society's Publications.
Extra Series, no. 3. composed March, 1864. for
voice and keyboard instrument. 9p. <g> ed, bbc,
Pforzheimer Library

1097 Shepherd, H. <t> Music, when soft voices die <p> West
and Co., London, 1915 <d> Song ascribed to Keats
on cover and on by-line. 3p. <g> bm, x

1098 Sherman, Richard Morton <t> Sonnet; poem by Shelley:
Lift not the painted veil <p> Lincoln Music Corp.,
New York, 1948 <d> 3p. <g> lc

1099 Silfverston, Hilding <t> Autumn <p> EU51101, 1 May
1968 <d> 2p.

1100 Simmons, William Glenn <t> Four fragments from
Shelley <p> EU173471, 18 July 1949

1101 Simon, Robert H. M. <t> Indian serenade <p> EU371443,
20 September 1954

1102 Simpson, Frederick James <t> Music, when soft voices
die <p> Novello, Ewer and Co., London, 1888 <d>
op. 1, no. 1. TTB, a capella. 2p. <g> bm, x

1103 Simpson, Frederick James <t> To-morrow: Where art
thou <p> Novello, Ewer and Co., London, 1888 <d>
op. 1, no. 4. TTB, a capella round. 1p. <g> bm, x

1104 Simpson, Frederick James <t> The world's wanderers:
     Tell me, thou star <p> Novello, Ewer and Co.,
     London, 1888 <d> op. 1, no. 3. TTB, a capella. 2p.
     <g> bm, x

1105 Sinjani, Christofor Nikolaievich <t> Love's
     philosophy <p> EU273918, 24 April 1952

1106 Skeete, H. B. <t> The lost Love: She dwelt among the
     untrodden ways (Wordsworth's "Lucy" poem ascribed
     to Shelley on the cover and title page <p>
     Novello, London, 1878 <d> 4p. <g> ed, bm

1107 Slinn, Edgar Beck (or Beck-Slinn) <t> A widow bird
     <p> Augener, London, 1927 <d> 3p. <g> bm, lc, x

1108 Sloan, T. R. <t> Love's philosophy <p> EU137994, 20
     January 1937 <d> 3p. <g> lc

1109 Sloper, Edmund Lindsay <t> Swiftly walk over the
     western wave <p> Wessel and Co., London, 1850 <d>
     5p. given as 1848 in Anderson, 1850 in British
     Museum <g> and, bm, x

1110 Smith, D. S. <t> To night <p> Birchard, Boston, 1901
     <d> in the Laurel Song Book <g> Sears, lc (not
     seen)

1111 Smith, Edwin <t> Music, when soft voices die <p>
     Novello, London, 1952 <d> The Orpheus no. 663.
     TTBB with rehearsal piano part. no. 17591 of
     Novello. 4p. <g> bm

1112 Smith, Eric A. <t> Music, when soft voices die <p> J.
     Curwen, London and Philadelphia, 1935 <d> no.
     61314. SATB, with rehearsal piano part. 4p. <g>
     lc, bm

1113 Smith, Gerrit <t> Music, when soft voices die <p>
     Huntzinger and Dilworth, New York, 1916 <d> for
     middle voice. 2p. <g> nn, bm

1114 Smith, W. E. <t> Music, when soft voices die <p>
     Joseph Williams, London, 1935 <d> SATB, with
     rehearsal piano part. 3p. St. Cecilia series 21,
     no. 60 <g> bm, lc, x

1115 Smith, William Adrian <t> I arise from dreams <p>

William Adrian Smith, New York, 1882 <d> for
middle voice. 3p. <g> nn

1116 Someren-Godfery, M. van (see Godfery)

1117 Somervell, Arthur <t> Music, when soft voices die <p>
Boosey, London, 1903 <d> SATB and piano part. no.
6 in Wind Flowers, Cycle of Quartets, Solos, and
Duets, pp. 28-33 <g> bm, x, bbc, paz

1118 Speelman, John Robert <t> Serenade to Jane <p>
EU227221, 19 January 1951

1119 Spencer, S. Reid <t> Good night <p> Willis Music Co.,
Cincinnati, 1919 <d> SATB. Second Octavo Secular
Series, no. 3674. 6p. <g> lc, x

1120 Spencer, Williametta <t> Music, when soft voices die
<p> ms., ca. 1958 <d> performed at California
concerts and on radio <g> q

1121 Spier, Harry Reginald <t> The Indian serenade <p> G.
Schirmer, New York, 1924 <d> 7p. <g> bm, lc

1122 Spiro. A. <t> Good night? <p> A. Gutheil, Moscow,
1886 <d> translated by N. Minsky. 2p. <g> East
Berlin, x, Russian

1123 Spohr, Ludvig <t> Good night? <p> Novello, London,
1844; also 1848 <d> TTBB. Included in The New York
Glee Book, ed. George Loder, Henry G. Langley,
1844. pp. 198-199, and reprinted by Silas Andrus,
Hartford, 1848. separately published in Germany
but destroyed in Berlin Library <g> New York
Historical Society, nn

1124 Springer, Norman <t> Indian serenade <p> EU131646, 20
May 1948

1125 Springfield, Tom <t> Love's philosophy <p> possibly
published London, 1969 <d> no. 4 in Seven Songs.
recorded in LC in catalogue of assignment of
rights, from Promex, Ltd., to Springfield Music
Ltd., of London <g> lc

1126 Squire, Hope <t> A widow bird <p> Stainer and Bell,
London, 1938 <d> 4p. <g> bm, x, lc

1127 Stanford, Charles Villiers <t> Autumn: The warm sun
     is failing <p> J. Curwen and Sons, London, 1914
     <d> op. 138, no. 3. Curwen's Choruses for Equal
     Voices no. 1419. SA. also no. 3 in Six Two-Part
     Songs of Boosey, 1914 <g> grove, paz, bm, x

1128 Stanford, Charles Villiers <t> Prometheus Unbound.
     Asia's song: My soul is an enchanted boat <p>
     Stainer and Bell, London, 1911 <d> two forms: in F
     and in A. op. 125, no. 2. 8p. <g> bl, grove, bm, x

1129 Stanford, Charles Villiers <t> Prometheus Unbound.
     The song of the spirit of the hour: My coursers
     are fed with the lightning <p> Stainer and Bell,
     London, 1911 <d> op. 125, no. 4. 8p. <g> bl,
     grove, bm, x

1130 Stanford, Charles Villiers (see also Thomas: The Swan
     and the Skylark)

1131 Staton John Fredrick <t> As the moon's soft splendour
     <p> Banks, York, 1935 <d> four-part mixed chorus
     with rehearsal piano part. York Series of Anthems
     and Glees no. 1191. 7p. <g> lc, bm

1132 Stebbins, G. Waring <t> I arise from dreams <p>
     Arthur P. Schmidt, Boston, 1907 <d> S or T. 6p.
     <g> bm, x

1133 Steinert, Alexander Lang <t> Ozymandias <p> Maurice
     Senart, Paris, 1932 <d> no. 2 in Three Poems by
     Shelley, pp. 4-7 <g> lc, bpl, x

1134 Steinert, Alexander Lang <t> To the Nile: month after
     month, the gathered rains descend <p> Maurice
     Senart, Paris, 1932 <d> no. 3 in Three Poems by
     Shelley, pp. 8-14, <g> lc, bpl, x

1135 Steinert, Alexander Lang <t> The waning moon <p>
     Maurice Senart, Paris, 1932 <d> no. 1 in Three
     Poems by Shelley, pp. 2-3 <g> lc, x, bpl

1136 Stephen, David <t> Oh, gentle moon: Oh, gentle moon,
     the voice of thy delight <p> Oxford University
     Press, London, 1929 <d> SATB with piano rehearsal
     part. Oxford Choral Songs no. 728. 6p. <g> bm, x

1137 Stephenson, Thomas Wilkinson <t> Music, when soft
      voices die <p> Boosey, London, 1916 <d> no. 2 in
      Three English Lyrics. 3p. <g> bbc, x

1138 Stevens, Halsey <t> Lines to an Indian air: I arise
      from dreams <p> ms., 1930 <d> performed from ms.
      and then withdrawn <g> q

1139 Stith, Mrs. Townshend <t> Good Night <p> Kretschmar
      and Nunns, Philadelphia, 1835 ; also 1834 <d>
      dated 1835 (?) by the Library of Congress.
      Headnote: "Good Night" Words by Shelley: "Delinea
      gli anima colorisee la vita". Composed and
      respectfully dedicated to Mrs. Shelley by Mrs.
      Townshend Smith. solo voice and unspecified
      keyboard score, presumably piano. 3p. apparently
      first published in Godey's Lady's Book, vol. 8,
      pp. 160-161, March 1834, in the same form as by
      Kretschmar. <g> lc, x, Harvard Library

1140 Stith, Mrs. Townshend <t> Love's philosophy. A
      favourite Ballad <p> George Willig, Philadelphia,
      April 26, 1830 <d> Headnote: Written by Percy
      Bysche Shelly. Composed and Arranged for the Harp
      or Piano Forte And affectionately dedicated to her
      Sister Mrs. Edward George by Mrs. Townshend Stith.
      3p. <g> lc, x

1141 Stocks, H. C. L. <t> I arise from dreams of thee <p>
      Gwynn Pub., Llangollen, 1943 <d> no. 3026 of
      Part-Songs for SATB, a capella, with sol-fa
      notation. Welsh translation by T. Gwynn Jones. 3p.
      <g> bm, x, Welsh

1142 Stone, David <t> To a snowdrop: Lone flower, hemmed
      in with snows (false attribution to Shelley,
      instead of to Wordsworth) <p> Boosey, London, 1960
      <d> no. 5 in Winter: Five Songs for SSA and piano.
      7p. <g> lc, x

1143· Stone, David <t> A widow bird <p> Boosey, London,
      1960 <d> no. 3 in Winter: Five Songs for SSA and
      piano. 4p. <g> lc, x

1144 Storer, John <t> The flower that smiles to day
      (Mutability) <p> Ashdown and Parry, London, 1882
      <d> 6p. <g> bm, x

1145 Storer, John <t> Six Vocal Impromtus (sic). Poetry by
     Shelley. Music by John Storer, Mus. Doc <p>
     National Music Co., London, 1887 <d> The six songs
     (see next entries) occupy pp. 4-19. The Preface
     explains: "They are really Impromtu pieces, the
     music being the spontaneous outcome of the Poetry,
     and not thought out songs either as to rhythmic
     phrasing or stereotype form.... Let the time vary
     as the feelings of the performer are swayed by the
     sentiment in the words."

1146 Storer, John <t> I fear thy kisses, gentle maiden <p>
     1887 <d> no. 1 of Six Vocal Impromtus (q.v.), pp.
     4-5 <g> bm, x

1147 Storer, John <t> Music, when soft voices die <p> 1887
     <d> no. 2 of Six Vocal Impromtus (q.v.), pp. 6-7
     <g> bm, x

1148 Storer, John <t> Time long past <p> 1887 <d> no. 3 of
     Six Vocal Impromtus (q.v.), pp. 9-11 <g> bm, x

1149 Storer, John <t> If I walk in Autumn's even <p> 1887
     <d> no. 4 of Six Vocal Impromtus (q.v.), p. 12 <g>
     bm, x

1150 Storer, John <t> To-morrow: Where art thou <p> 1887
     <d> no. 5 of Six Vocal Impromtus (q.v.), p. 13 <g>
     bm, x

1151 Storer, John <t> Love's philosophy <p> 1887 <d> no. 6
     of Six Vocal Impromtus (q.v.), pp. 14-19 <g> bm, x

1152 Strilko, Anthony <t> Lines from Shelley: The cold
     earth slept below <p> Lawson-Gould Music
     Publishers, New York, 1963 <d> four-part mixed
     chorus a capella. Lawson-Gould Choral Series
     51154. 11p. <g> lc

1153 Sullivan, Arthur S. (with C. H. H. Parry) <t> Arabian
     Love Song: My faint spirit <p> Chappell, London,
     1866, also 1868 <d> Included in Twelve Songs
     (Chappell, 1868) by Jules Benedict and Sullivan
     (this the only one by Sullivan) <g> bm, x

1154 Surette, Tom W. <t> I arise from dreams of thee <p>
     White, Smith and Co., Boston, 1881 <d> 3p. <g>

Harvard Library, x

1155 Sutton, Alfred James <t> Beatrice's Song: False
     friend, wilt thou smile (The Cenci) <p> Wessel,
     London, 1858; John Shepherd, London, 1870 <d> no.
     2 in Six Songs. 5p. <g> bm, and, Yale

1156 Sutton, Alfred James <t> The Indian's lament: I arise
     from dreams of thee <p> Wessel, London, 1858; John
     Shepherd, London, 1870 <d> no. 1 in Six Songs, 5p.
     <g> bm, and, Yale, x

1157 Svedrofsky, Sidney <t> Berceuse. op. 1, no. 1 <p>
     EU283844, 3 February, 1942 <d> Song in E flat
     major

1158 Sweetman, P. W. <t> A widow bird <p> Waterloo Music
     Co., Waterloo, Canada, 1962 <d> SSA. Waterloo
     Festival Series <g> lc

1159 Taneyev, Serge Ivanovitch <t> Ostrovok (The isle) <p>
     State Publishing House, Moscow, 1947 <d> op. 17,
     no. 1, pp. 12-13 of Romances, all translated by
     Balmont <g> bbc, x

1160 Taneyev, Serge Ivanovitch <t> In loneliness dreams
     fade and blossom <p> State Publishing House,
     Moscow, 1947 <d> op. 17, no. 2. pp. 14-15 of
     Romances <g> bbc, x, Russian

1161 Taneyev, Serge Ivanovitch <t> Music, when soft voices
     die <p> State Publishing House, Moscow, 1947 <d>
     op. 17, no. 3. pp. 16-18 of Romances <g> bbc, x,
     Russian

1162 Taneyev, Serge Ivanovitch <t> The star of blessed
     sleep has faded <p> State Publishing House,
     Moscow, 1947 <d> op. 17, no. 4. pp. 19-22 of
     Romances <g> bbc, x, Russian

1163 Taneyev, Serge Ivanovitch <t> Cradle song: The gentle
     wind grows calm <p> State Publishing House,
     Moscow, 1947 <d> pp. 182-183 of Romances <g> bbc,
     x, Russian

1164 Taylor, Francis O. <t> Music, when soft voices die
     <p> Broadcast Music, Inc., New York, 1943 <d> SSA,
     with piano. 7p. <g> lc, x

1165 Tcherepnin, Nikolai <t> An die Musik (To music: Crystalline fount of tears for "Silver key of the fountain of tears") <p> P. Jurgenson, Moscow; R. Forberg, Leipzig, 1896 <d> op. 21, no. 1, translated into Russian by Balmont, into German by Lina Esbeer. no. 1 of 8 Leider, pp. 2-5. Also in Album of Ten Songs by Russian Composers, Boston Music Co., pp. 24-27, 1914, with English translated from the Russian by Nathan Haskell Dole <g> Sears supplement, Hamburg, x, East Berlin, German, Russian

1166 Tcherepnin, Nikolai <t> O Himmelswanderer (The world's wanderers) <p> P. Jurgenson, Moscow; R. Forberg, Leipzig, n.d. <d> op. 21, no. 7, translated into Russian by Balmont, into German by Lina Esbeer. no. 7 of 8 Lieder <g> Hamburg, x, Russian, German

1167 Tcherepnin, Nikolai <t> Im Himmelsraume regt die Nacht sich bebend (Dark night flutters its wings) <p> P. Jurgenson, Moscow; R. Forberg, Leipzig, n.d. <d> op. 21, no. 8, translated into Russian by Balmont, into German by Lina Esbeer. no. 8 of 8 Lieder <g> Hamburg, x, Russian, German

1168 Temmerman, Marcel de <t> La complainte de l'automne (for Autumn: A dirge?) <p> Editions du Magasin Musical (Pierre Schneider), Paris, 1932 <d> SATB, a bouche fermee (humming). no text indicated aside from title. 2p. <g> bn, x

1169 Temmerman, Marcel de <t> Hymne a l'ete: Venez accourez. Jours d'ete <p> Editions du Magasin Musical (Pierre Schneider), Paris, 1932 <d> SSAATTBB and solo, a capella. 4p. <g> bn, x, French

1170 Thatcher, Reginald Sparshott <t> Music, when soft voices die <p> Stainer and Bell, London, 1912 <d> S. and B. Unison Songs no. 2, with sol-fa notation. 2p. <g> bm, x

1171 Theman, Karl George <t> To night: Swiftly walk over <p> EU411057, 5 March 1945 <d> for SSAA chorus

1172 Thiman, Eric <t> Serenade: I arise from dreams <p> Joseph Williams, London, 1950 <d> TTBB chorus,

with rehearsal piano part and with sol-fa
notation. 6p. St. Cecilia Series 28, no. 1 <g> bm,
bbc, x

1173 Thomas, Arthur Goring <t> Serenade: The keen stars
were twinkling (for To Jane) <p> Eoosey, London;
also Metzler, also Cramer; 1882 <d> 6p. <g> bm,
ed, paz, x

1174 Thomas, Arthur Goring <t> The Swan and the Skylark.
Cantata (To a skylark) <p> Boosey and Co., London,
1894 <d> The words by Hemans, Keats, and Shelley,
the excerpt from the poem, "Higher still. . . thou
wingest," on pp. 61-66, for soloist and SATB
chorus, with piano score. 90p. in piano score
version. Also orchestrated from this score of the
composer by C. Villiers Stanford, both versions
being posthumous <g> bbc, bpl, ed, paz, bm, x

1175 Thomas, Mansell <t> The triumph song (Can
Buddugoliaeth) <p> Oxford University Press,
London, 1936 <d> chorus of male voices, with piano
rehearsal part. 4p. translated by J. C. Morgan
(for Tom Parry) <g> bm, lc, Welsh

1176 Thomas, Muriel L. <t> Music, when soft voices die <p>
Snell and Sons, Swansea, 1951 <d> in Welsh and
English, the Welsh by Wil Ifan. 3p. <g> bbc, x,
Welsh

1177 Thompson, Christiana <t> I arise from dreams of thee
<p> Phillips and Page, London, 1885 <d> 8p. <g>
bm, x

1178 Thorne, Edward H. <t> On a faded violet: The colour
from the flow'r is gone <p> Stanley Lucas, Weber,
London, 1876 <d> 4p. <g> and, bm, ed, x

1179 Tiersot, Julien <t> Hellas, Introduction and chorus
<p> 1897 <d> attributed in Grove. for chorus and
orchestra. not found, even in Paris.

1180 Tiltman, Henry Thomas <t> Music, when soft voices die
<p> Stainer and Bell, London, 1922; also 1926 and
1928 <d> song in 1922 ed. four-part song, with
sol-fa notation by H. J. Timothy, S. and B. Choral
Library no. 214, in 1926. two-part song, S. and B.
Part-Songs no. 196, in 1928 <g> bm, lc

1181 Tippett, Michael <t> I pant for the music which is divine <p> Schott, London, 1960 <d> unison song for voices, strings, and piano. Composed for the Jubilee of the East Sussex and West Kent Choral Festival. 5p. <g> bm, ed

1182 Tollefsen, Augusta <t> Winter: A widow bird <p> Composer's Press, New York, 1940 and 1943 <d> in 1940 pub. as vocal solo for medium to high voice, and in 1943 as a three-part women's chorus, SSA. arranged by H. S. Sammond. 3p. <g> lc, nn

1183 Toms, John R. <t> Music, when soft voices die <p> John R. Toms, Wellington, Somerset, n.d. <d> 3p. <g> Bodleian, x

1184 Tourtellot, F. B. <t> I arise from dreams of thee <p> Chamberlain and Harrington, New York, 1900; also 1906 and 1920 <d> in Chamberlain and Harrington, Songs of All the Colleges, p. 93; also in Dann, Song Series, vol. 4, p. 306; also in Songs of Rutgers, Fischer, 1920, 5th ed., for four male voices, a capella as bass solo with TTB, in Hamilton College Song Book (1953), p. 120; Songs of Ohio State (1916), p. 124; Songs of the University of Virginia (1906), p. 82; Songs of Stevens (1930), p. 143, et al. <g> nn

1185 Tovey, Donald Francis <t> I fear thy kisses <p> Joseph Williams, London, 1905 <d> op. 3, no. 2 in Six Songs for a Low Voice, set II. J. W. Album, no. 328, pp. 7-8. German by Willy Kastner <g> bm, x, German

1186 Tovey, Donald Francis <t> Indian serenade <p> Joseph Williams, London, 1905 <d> op. 3, no. 5 in Six Songs for a Low Voice, pp. 24-28, Set II. J. W. Album, no. 328. German by Willy Kastner <g> bm, x, German

1187 Tovey, Donald Francis <t> Music, when soft voices die <p> Joseph Williams, London, 1905 <d> op. 5, no. 24 (in 4 parts) of Twenty-Five Rounds for Equal Voices, p. 25. German by Willy Kastner <g> bm, x, German

1188 Tovey, Donald Francis <t> To the moon: Art thou pale from weariness <p> Joseph Williams, London, 1905

<d> op. 5. no. 16 (in 4 parts) of Twenty-Five
Rounds, p. 20. Also in appendix, for one voice and
piano, Album 329, pp. 12-13. German by Willy
Kastner <g> bm, x, German

1189 Tovey, Donald Francis <t> When the lamp is shattered
<p> Joseph Williams, London, 1905 <d> no. 3 in Six
Songs for a Low Voice, set II. op. 3, no. 3. J. W.
Album no. 328. German by Willy Kastner <g> bm, x,
German

1190 Tovey, Donald Francis <t> A widow bird <p> Joseph
Williams, London, 1905 <d> op. 5, no. 21 (in 5
parts) of Twenty-Five Rounds, p. 29. also in
Appendix, for one voice and piano, Album 329, pp.
18-19. German by Willy Kastner <g> bm, x, German

1191 Towne, Marian Etta <t> A widow bird <p> EU359493, 28
May 1954

1192 Trangas, Andreas Mikhail <t> Good night <p> EU323858,
15 February 1943

1193 Treharne, Bryceson <t> Daughters of Jove, whose voice
is melody (Homer's hymn to the moon) <p> Boston
Music Co., Boston, 1945 <d> SSAA with piano. 9p.
<g> lc

1194 Treharne, Bryceson <t> Ozymandias <p> Boston Music
Co., Boston, 1917 <d> 9p. <g> bm, x

1195 Treharne, Bryceson <t> A widow bird <p> Boston Music
Co., Boston, 1917, 1942 <d> 4p. also in Seven
Centuries of Solo Song (Boston Music Co., Boston,
1942), vol. 6, pp. 34-36 <g> nn

1196 Treutler, Lilian <t> A widow bird <p> Vincent Music
Co., London, 1907 <d> 4p. <g> bm, x

1197 Troup, E. J. <t> On a faded violet <p> Stanley Lucas,
Weber and Co., London, 1884 <g> ed, bm

1198 Tyrer, Andersen <t> Music, when soft voices die <p>
Augener, London, 1939 <d> SATB a capella with
rehearsal piano part. 4p. <g> bm, x

1199 Van Dieren, Bernard <t> The Cenci: Come, I will sing
you some low, sleepy tune <p> Oxford University

Press, London, 1925 <d> op. 3, Two Songs for
Baritone and String Quartet, by Shelley and De
Quincey. Words in French by M. D. Calvocoressi.
6p. <g> bm, ed, Royal Academy, x, French

1200 Vannah, Kate <t> From dreams of thee (Indian
serenade) <p> White Music Publishing Co., Boston,
1908 <d> song for high voice in D flat <g> lc

1201 Vaughan Williams, Ralph <t> Prometheus Unbound:
Prefatory recitation from the work for Sinfonia
Antarctica (To suffer wces) <p> Oxford University
Press, London, 1953 <d> score of the symphony,
145p. first performed on 14 January 1953 by Halle
Orchestra in Manchester under John Barbirolli and
recorded for HMV. full orchestra, soprano solo,
and small SSA chorus. Each of the 5 movements is
preceded by a spoken epigraph, the first, Prelude
(Andante Maestoso), being 7 lines from Prometheus
Unbound. the others are from Psalm 104,
Coleridge's Hymn, Donne, and Captain Scott's
Journal. The material from the music by Vaughan
Williams for the film "Scott of the Antarctic."
The Prelude, pp. 1-37, is scored for soprano
(without words), SSA and orchestra. <g> bm, nn

1202 Vaughan Williams, Ralph <t> On death (stanza 2): O
man! Hold thee on <p> Oxford University Press,
London, 1940 <d> A song of courage in Six Choral
Songs, pp.3-5 <g> bl, ed, grove, bm, nn

1203 Vaughan Williams, Ralph <t> Hellas (Scene 1,
semichorus 1): Life may change <p> Oxford
University Press, London, 1940 <d> A song of
liberty in Six Choral Songs, pp. 6-8 <g> bl, ed,
grove, bm, nn

1204 Vaughan Williams, Ralph <t> Prometheus Unbound (IV,
end): Love, from its awful throne <p> Oxford
University Press, London, 1940 <d> A song of
healing in Six Choral Songs, pp. 9-10 <g> bl, ed,
grove, bm, nn

1205 Vaughan Williams, Ralph <t> Prometheus Unbound (IV,
iv, last stanza): To suffer woes <p> Oxford
University Press, London, 1940 <d> A song of
victory in Six Choral Songs, pp.11-13 <g> bl, ed,
Grove, bm, nn

1206 Vaughan Williams, Ralph <t> The Revolt of Islam (V,
     Song, 2, following 51): O Spirit vast and deep <p>
     Oxford University Press, London, 1940 <d> A song
     of pity, peace, and love in Six Choral Songs, pp.
     14-18 <g> bl, ed, grove, bm, nn

1207 Vaughan Williams, Ralph <t> Hellas (final chorus):
     The world's great age begins anew <p> Oxford
     University Press, London, 1940 <d> A song of the
     new age in Six Choral Songs. pp. 19-23 <g> bl, ed,
     grove, bm, nn

1208 Vene, Ruggero <t> Buona notte: Buona notte, buona
     notte, come mai (Shelley's Italian) <p> G.
     Ricordi, New York, 1949 <d> English text by
     Margaret McKee from Shelley's original. 8p. <g>
     lc, Italian

1209 Verrinder, Charles Garland <t> A lament: Swifter far
     <p> Lamborn Cock, London, 1866; J. B. Cramer,
     London, 1881 <d> no. 2 of Two scenas. 8p. 1881
     reprint uses the same plates and gives only the
     Shelley song. <g> bm, x

1210 Vibbard, Harry <t> Indian serenade <p> Fischer and
     Bro., New York, 1924 and 1952 <d> for organ,
     alone, with solo part carried by English horn or
     clarinet stop. no words given. 6p. <g> bpl, x

1211 Violet (pseudonym) <t> Indian slumber song. (from
     Hellas): We strew these opiate flowers <p>
     Ransford, London, 1867 <d> for SS and piano. 7p.
     Other songs by Violet (on cover): The Household
     robin, Nightwinds, Were I a star, and The rose and
     the nightingale <g> bm, x

1212 Vogrich, Max <t> Indian song: I arise from dreams of
     thee <p> G. Schirmer, New York, 1890 <d> one of
     Six Duets for S and Ms or T and B. G. Schirmer's
     ed., 229. with German translation by Dr. Roman
     Woerner <g> Berlin, x, German

1213 Volkmann, Robert <t> An die nacht: Gottin der nacht
     (To night: Swiftly walk over) <p> B. Schott,
     Mainz, n.d. <d> op. 45. Fantasiestuck for Alto
     with orchestra (score, 30p.). Also with four-hand
     piano score (unseen). Only the orchestral score,
     without solo part, found. translated by Louise von

Ploennies <g> East Berlin, x, German

1214 Voormolen, Alexander <t> From--The recollection: Now
     the last day <p> Donemus, Amsterdam, 1970 <d>
     medium voice, string orchestra, and celesta.
     listed in Sonorum Speculum, no. 46, p. 50 <g> not
     seen, in English

1215 Walker, David <t> The Cenci. special music for a
     version of the play <p> unpublished, 1971 <d>
     music composed by Walker for the January, 1971
     production of Cafe La Mama, New york, under the
     direction of Martin Brenzell, in the translation
     of Simon Watson Taylor from the French of Antonin
     Artaud, originally performed in Paris, 1935. see
     R. Desormiere's version of the play. <g> not
     available

1216 Walker, Ernest <t> Liberty: The fiery mountains
     answer each other < > Stainer and Bell, London,
     1908 <d> op. 26. S. and B. Male Voice Choir
     Library, no. 13, TTBB, with rehearsal piano part.
     8p. <g> bm, x

1217 Walker, Ernest <t> Music, when soft voices die <p> J.
     Williams, London, 1927 <d> no. 6 in Six Two-Part
     Songs, St. Cecilia Series, vol. 18, no. 6. 3p. <g>
     bm, x

1218 Walker, Ernest <t> Song of Proserpine. op. 17, no. 4
     <p> J. Williams, London, 1906 and 1912 <d> St.
     Cecilia Series 11, no. 14, for three voices plus
     piano, 3p. <g> bm, x

1219 Walker, Ernest <t> The world's wanderers <p> Stainer
     and Bell, London, 1908 <d> S. and B. Three-Part
     Songs for Equal Voices, no. 2. op. 25 <g> bm

1220 Wallace, William <t> Prometheus Unbound: My soul is
     an enchanted boat <p> 1896 <d> voice, violin and
     piano, according to Grove <g> bl, Grove, not found

1221 Ward-Stephens, Ida May Pierrepont <t> I rise from
     dreams of thee (Indian serenade) <p> Theodore
     Presser, Philadelphia, 1917 <d> 3p. <g> lc, x

1222 Ward, Robert Eugene <t> Epithalamium: Night! with all

thine eyes look down <p> ms. <g> q

1223 Washburn, Robert <t> A lament <p> 29 December 1969,
     EU160046 <d> no. 2 of Five Songs for Male Voices.
     copyright held by Phi Mu Alpha Sinfonia Fraternity
     of America, Inc. <g> lc

1224 Washburn, Robert <t> Music, when soft voices die <p>
     29 December 1969, EU160046 <d> no. 3 of Five Songs
     for Male Voices. copyright held by Phi Mu Alpha
     Sinfonia Fraternity of America, Inc. <g> lc

1225 Watson, Thomas <t> Music, when soft voices die <p>
     EU65589, 7 August 1968 <d> 2 leaves <g> q, lc

1226 Watzel, Le Roy <t> I arise from dreams of thee <p>
     Gamble Hinged Music Co., Chicago, 1934 <d> TTBB
     and piano. Gamble's collection of secular part
     songs for men's voices, no. 1082. 10p. <g> lc

1227 Webb, Michael <t> A widow bird <p> H. G. Neville, Los
     Angeles, 1933 <d> Associated Composers series no.
     7. 5p. <g> lc

1228 Webb, T. H. <t> World wanderers (for The world's
     wanderers) <p> ms., Leipzig, 1894 <d> 4 leaves,
     signed May, 1894, Leipzig <g> bpl, x

1229 Weber, Carl Maria von <t> air from Der Freischutz
     (see Callcott)

1230 Weber, H. <t> Love's philosophy <p> W. H. Willis,
     Cincinnati, 1907 <d> for medium voice in D flat.
     6p. <g> lc, x

1231 Wellner, G. D. <t> Fountains of love; Song (probably
     Love's philosophy) <p> EU111547, 14 October 1935

1232 Welsing, Hermann S. <t> Love's philosophy <p> Boosey,
     London, 1893 <d> 5p. <g> ed, paz, bm, x

1233 Wesley, Samuel Sebastian <t> Dirge for the year:
     orphan hours, the year is dead <p> Augener,
     London, 1909 <d> in Augener, The Minstrelsy of
     England, pp. 69-71 <g> rn

1234 West, John Ebenezer <t> How eloquent: How eloquent
     are eyes <p> Novello, London, 1912 <d> SATB, with

rehearsal piano part. Novello's Part-Song Book,
Series 2, no. 1253. 12p. <g> bm, x

1235 West, John Ebenezer <t> A lament: O world <p>
Novello, London, 1907 <d> SATB, with rehearsal
piano part. Novello's Part-Song Book, Series 2,
no. 1031. 4p. <g> bm

1236 Westbrook, W. J. <t> Good night! <p> Lamborn Cock,
Addison and Co., London, 1866 <d> 4p. <g> and, bm,
x

1237 Whelpley, Benjamin Lincoln <t> I arise from dreams
<p> Boston Music Co., 1913 <d> op. 17, no. 5 of
Songs. 6p. also in Three Pieces, op. 4, as
Serenade <g> paz, nn, x, bm

1238 Whinfield, W. G. <t> Love's philosophy <p> Augener,
London, 1907 <d> no. 2 of Two Songs. 3p. <g> bm, x

1239 Whinfield, W. G. <t> A widow bird <p> Augener,
London, 1905 <d> no. 5 of Songs, with piano
accompaniment, 4p. <g> bl, bm, x

1240 Whishaw, Frederick <t> Music, when soft voices die
<p> Reid Bros., London, n.d. <d> p. 111 in Reid
Bros.' 101 Standard Songs. 4 lines <g> Central
Music Library of the Boro of Westminster

1241 Whitacre, Cyril V. <t> Indian serenade <p> Weekes,
London, 1910 <d> 5p. <g> bm, x

1242 Whitaker, George <t> From the Arabic: My faint spirit
<p> Elkin, London, 1922 <d> no. 1 of Album of Six
Songs. 4p. <g> bm, x

1243 White, Felix Harold <t> Desolation: A widow bird <p>
J. Curwen, London, 1924 <d> 1 page unaccompanied
song <g> bm

1244 White, Mary Louise <t> Rarely, rarely, comest thou
<p> Joseph Williams, London, 1906 <d> op. 26, no.
4. 6p. <g> bm, x

1245 White, Maude Valerie <t> Prometheus Unbound (II, v):
Thy words are sweeter. . . and My soul is an
enchanted boat <p> Chappell, London, 1883 <d>

recitative and song. 11p. <g> bm, paz, x

1246 White, Maude Valerie <t> To Mary: O Mary dear <p>
     Boosey, London, 1882 <d> 4p. <g> bm, x

1247 White, Maude Valerie <t> When passion's trance is
     overpast <p> Ricordi, London, 1882, also Oliver
     Ditson, Boston, 1888 <d> 6p. 1888 ed. is one of
     the Sparkling Gems, 3p. also pub. 1885 in French
     version (by Paul Solanges) and Italian version (by
     A. Zanardini) together, and in German version (by
     Baron Erwin Ferstel) <g> bm, bbc, x, Italian,
     French, German

1248 White, Maude Valerie <t> A widow bird <p> Pitt and
     Hatzfeld, London, 1888 <d> 4p. <g> bm, ed, paz, x

1249 Whiting, Charles Edward <t> I arise from dreams <p>
     J. R. Miller, Boston, 1858 <d> for tenor voice.
     3p. Cover also gives Oliver Ditson. <g> Harvard
     Library, Yale, x

1250 Whitley, Arthur <t> The cloud: I sift the snow <p>
     Chappell, London, 1877 <d> not found <g> and, paz

1251 Whittaker, W. Gillies <t> Prometheus Unbound. Chorus
     of Spirits: From unremembered ages <p> Banks,
     York, 1931 <d> SATB, with rehearsal piano part.
     no. 1075 York Series of Anthems and Glees. 8p. <g>
     bm

1252 Whyte, Ian <t> Wine of the fairies (Wine of
     Eglantine): I am drunk <p> J. and W. Chester,
     London, 1928 <d> for middle voice. 3p. <g> bn, ed,
     bm, x

1253 Wideen, Ivar <t> The world's wanderers: Tell me, thou
     star <p> 1890 <d> men's chorus. translated into
     Swedish <g> q, Swedish

1254 Wiedmann, Max <t> Ozymandias <p> Richard Kaun, Berlin
     and Milwaukee, 1907 <d> op. 4. versions for high
     and medium voice. German by E. von Griesbach. 7p.
     <g> lc, nn, German

1255 Willan, Healey <t> Music, when soft voices die <p> F.

Harris Co., London, 1926 <d> no. 1 of Healey
Willan Song Album, no. 2 for medium voice, pp. 3-5
<g> bbc, x

1256 Willett, Hilda <t> Music, when soft voices die <p>
Novello, London, 1904 <d> no. 1 of Two Songs. 3p.
<g> bm, copy in collection

1257 Williams, David Christmas <t> Indian serenade <p> J.
Fischer and Bro., New York and Birmingham,
England, 1911; also 1913 <d> SATB with rehearsal
piano part. no. 3675 (and 3675a, sol-fa ed.) of
Fischer's Edition Choruses. Competition Festival
and Eisteddfod Series. 11p. Also with German
translation by F. W. Schneider, in 1913 (12p.) <g>
bm, nn, x, German

1258 Williams, John Gerrard <t> A hate-song: A hater he
came <p> J. Curwen, London, 1924 <d> 4p. <g> bm,
x, lc

1259 Williams, John Gerrard <t> The isle: There was a
little lawny islet <p> Novello, London, 1922 <d>
SSA and piano. Novello's Octavo Edition for Female
Voices, no. 477. 4p. <g> lc, x

1260 Williams, John Gerrard <t> A lament: O world! O life!
<p> Ashdown, London, 1928 <d> 3p. no. 3 of Four
Songs <g> bm

1261 Williams, John Gerrard <t> Reverie: If I walk in
autumn's even <p> Stainer and Bell, London, 1923
<d> no. 2 of Two Songs. 2p. <g> lc, bm

1262 Williams, John Gerrard <t> Three Miniatures on Poems
by P. B. Shelley. Dawn (The point of one white
star;). The isle. and Time (Unfathomable sea) <p>
J. and W. Chester, London, 1919 <d> 17p. no
similarity in melodic line of the last two and the
two songs of the same titles by Williams <g> bm,
East Berlin, x

1263 Williams, John Gerrard <t> Time: Unfathomable sea <p>
Novello, London, 1922 <d> 3p. <g> bm, x

1264 Williams, John Gerrard <t> A widow bird <p> Weekes,
London, 1913; 1922 in British Museum <d> no. 2 of
Two Songs. 3p. <g> bm

1265 Williams, Joseph (under pseudonym of Florian Pascal)
     <t> He came like a dream <p> Jcseph Williams,
     London, 1905 <d> no. 1 in Eight Songs, Fourth Set,
     pp. 1-3. Album no. 320. <g> bm, x

1266 Williams, Leonard Pascoe <t> As the moon's soft
     splendour <p> Ashdown, London, 1930 <d> (sometimes
     Pascoe-Williams) 3p. <g> bm

1267 Williams, Leonard Pascoe <t> How wonderful is death
     (Queen Mab) <p> Ashdown, London, 1928 <d> no. 2 in
     Three Shelley Songs (second set). 3p. <g> lc, bm,
     x

1268 Williams, Leonard Pascoe <t> I arise from dreams <p>
     Ashdown, London, 1928 <d> no. 3 in Three Shelley
     Songs (second set). 5p. <g> lc, bm, x

1269 Williams, Leonard Pascoe <t> The isle <p> Ashdown,
     London, 1927 <d> no. 1 in Three Shelley Songs
     (first set). 3p. <g> lc, bm, x

1270 Williams, Leonard Pascoe <t> Longing: I pant for the
     music which is divine <p> Ashdown, London, 1928
     <d> no. 1 in Three Shelley Scngs (seccnd set). 3p.
     <g> lc, bm, x

1271 Williams, Leonard Pascoe <t> Music, when soft voices
     die <p> Ashdown, London, 1927 <d> no. 3 in Three
     Shelley Songs (first set). 3p. <g> lc, bm, x

1272 Williams, Leonard Pascoe <t> When passion's trance is
     overpast <p> Ashdown, London, 1930 <d> 4p. <g> bm,

1273 Williams, Leonard Pascoe <t> A widow bird <p>
     Ashdown, London, 1927 <d> no. 2 in Three Shelley
     Songs (first set). 3p. <g> lc, bm, x

1274 Williams, Ronald Ray <t> Music, when soft voices die
     <p> ms. <d> no. 6 of Suite of Six Texts for Tenor
     and String Quartet. 2p. <g> q, x

1275 Williams, W. Matthew <t> Indian serenade <p> Gwynn
     Publishing Co., Llangollen, 1943 <d> SATB, a
     capella, with sol-fa notation. no. 3026. 3p. <g>
     bm, Welsh

1276 Williams, W. Matthew <t> Remembrance: Music, when
       soft voices die <p> Gwynn Publishing Co.,
       Llangollen, 1943 <d> SATB a capella, with sol-fa
       notation. Translated into Welsh by T. Gwynn Jones.
       no. 3027. 2p. <g> bm, x, Welsh

1277 Williams, W. S. Gwynn <t> Thou art fair (To Sophia)
       <p> J. Curwen, London, 1926 <d> Curwen no. 2965.
       no. 1 of three pieces, "Penillion in English," pp.
       2-5. Shelley's poem is set to the harp air "Pen
       Rhaw" and is preceded by a foreword by Williams
       explaining the peculiar style of penillion
       singing, the voice chanting the poem to the melody
       on the harp. The song book numbers 16p. <g> copy
       in collection

1278 Wilson, Don C. <t> Music, when soft voices die <p>
       EU53848, 25 May 1922

1279 Wilson, Ira B. <t> Autumn <p> Lorenz Music Co.,
       Dayton, Ohio, 1911 <d> two forms: for men's voices
       and women's voices <g> lc (not found)

1280 Wilson, Mortimer <t> I arise from dreams <p>
       Composers Music Corp., New York, n.d. <g> listed
       in Schirmer's music store

1281 Wilson, Mortimer <t> To the moon <p> Composers Music
       Corp., New York, n.d. <d> not found <g> listed in
       Schirmer's music store

1282 Wilson, Mortimer <t> A widow bird <p> Composers Music
       Corp., New York, n.d. <d> not found <g> listed in
       Schirmer's music store

1283 Winckworth, W. F. <t> When passion's trance <p>
       Weekes, London, 1900 <d> in A flat. no. 28 of An
       English Series of Original Songs. 5p. <g> bm, x

1284 Windt, H. de <t> Good night <p> Stanley Lucas, Weber,
       London, 1885 <d> 4p. <g> ed, bm, x

1285 Wintle, Ogle <t> The world's wanderers: Tell me, thou
       star <p> Lamborn Cock and Cramer, London, 1871 <d>
       no. 5 of Six Songs. 5p. <g> and, bm, x

1286 Wise, Michael (1684) <t> To suffer woes which hope
       thinks infinite <p> Beacon Press, Boston, 1964 <d>

in Hymns for the Celebration of Life, ed. Henry
Leland Clarke. Congleton 10.10.10.10. SATB, a
capella. p. 427 <g> x

1287 Wolff, Arthur Sheldon <t> Dirge: Rough wind <p> ms.
<d> performed 1955, 1956, 1962, 1963, 1966 <g> q

1288 Wood, Charles <t> As the moon's soft splendour <p>
Novello, London 1905; 1911 <d> Musical Times no.
754, SATB. Novello's Tonic Sol-Fa Series no. 1947
(1911). 4p. <g> bbc, bm, x

1289 Wood, Charles <t> Autumn: The warm sun is failing <p>
Stainer and Bell, London, 1924 <d> SATB, with
rehearsal piano part. S. and B. Choral Library no.
193. 7p. <g> bm, x

1290 Wood, Charles <t> The isle: There was a little lawny
islet <p> E. Arnold, London, 1923 <d> Two-part
song for treble voices and piano. 5p. with sol-fa
notation. E. Arnold's Singing Class Music 156 <g>
bm, x

1291 Wood, Charles <t> Music, when soft voices die <p>
Stainer and Bell, London, 1908; Schirmer, New
York, 1913; Year Book Press, London, 1916;
Ascherberg, London, 1961 <d> In 1913, no. 2 of
Three Songs; in 1916, Year Book Press Series no.
501, 8p. SSA. In 1961 arranged for SATB by Denis
Wright <g> bm, copy in collection

1292 Wood, Charles <t> Ode to the west wind <p> Novello,
London, 1869 <d> op. 3. SATB with piano. 37 p.
Novello Part-Song Book, Series 2, no. 740.
Novello's no. 8119. in Pazdirek, chorus and
orchestra <g> bm, East Berlin, x

1293 Wood, Charles <t> When winds that move not (From
Moschus) <p> Stainer and Bell, London, 1913 <d>
no. 39 of S. and B. Male Voice Choral Library.
ATTB, with rehearsal piano part. 10p. <g> bm, x

1294 Wood, Charles <t> The whispering waves <p> Novello,
London, 1905 <d> SATB, with rehearsal piano part.
4p. Novello's Part-Song Book, Series 2, no. 985
<g> bm, x

1295 Wood, Charles <t> The widow bird <p> Novello, Ewer

and Co., London, 1896 <d> SATB with rehearsal
piano part. 3p. <g> bm, x

1296 Wood, Ralph Walter <t> Away! the moor is dark
(Stanzas. April, 1814) <p> ms. <d> female voice
and small orchestra. second movement of "Quiet
Pilgrimage," a Choral Sinfonietta <g> q, copy at
British Music Information Centre, London

1297 Woodman, R. Huntington <t> Good night <p> G.
Schirmer, New York, 1897 <g> lc

1298 Woodman, R. Huntington <t> Music, when soft voices
die <p> Schirmer, New York, 1913 <d> for high
voice. 3p. <g> lc

1299 Woodman, R. Huntington <t> My soul is an enchanted
boat <p> G. Schirmer, New York, 1914 <d> no. 4 in
Five Songs. 3p. <g> bm, lc

1300 Woodville, Alan <t> In the twilight: Shall we roam,
my love (false attribution to Shelley) <p> West
and Co., London, 1917 <d> duet for soprano and
baritone with piano. 4p. <g> bm, x

1301 Wright, Denis (see Charles Wood: Music, when soft
voices die)

1302 Wright, Ellen (afterwards Standing) <t> I arise from
dreams of thee <p> Chappell, London, 1894 <d> no.
6 of a Cycle of Love Songs. 6p. <g> bm, x

1303 Wright, John <t> Adonais, Two stanzas <p> ms. <d>
performed at Wigmore Hall, 1953 <g> q

1304 Wright, William Lyndon <t> Music, when soft voices
die <p> G. Ricordi, New York, 1928 <d> for mixed
voices <g> lc

1305 Yates, Edmund <t> I arise from dreams <p> Boosey,
London, 1914 <d> no. 2 of Six Songs of the Poets.
duet and piano. in two forms. 8p. <g> bm, x

1306 Yetts, Ethel Frances <t> Rarely, rarely, comest thou
<p> Bach and Co., London, 1913 <d> 4p. <g> bm, x

1307 Zay, W. Henri <t> Love's philosophy <p> Chappell,
London, 1906 <d> 2 forms: in F and A flat. 4p. <g>

bm, x

1308 Zeleznova, A. V. <t> The fountains mingle (Love's
     philosophy) <p> Tzimmerman, St. Petersburg, n.d.
     <d> op. 3. no. 4 of Romances. 3p. <g> Berlin, x,
     Russian

1309 Zeuner, Charles <t> The glories of our mortal state
     (by Shirley. False attribution to Shelley) <p>
     Boston, C. Bradlee, 1833 <d> 2p. Printed headnote,
     under the title: "A Sacred Song Written by
     Shelly". Footnote: "Entered according to Act of
     Congress in the year 1833 by C. Bradlee in the
     Clerk's office of the District Court of
     Massachusetts." On the second page are printed
     stanzas 2 and 3 of Shirley's poem. <g> lc, x

PART II

The Indices

Glendenning, R. Rashleigh	492
Gliere, Reinhold	493
Glover, Howard	494-497
Gluck, C. W. von	498
Gnessin, Mikhail Fabianovich	499-500
Godfery, M. van Sommeren	501
Godfrey, Arthur Eugene	502
Gold, Ernest (Goldner in Boston Public Library catalogue)	503
Goldschmidt, Berthold	504
Goodhart, Arthur Murray	505
Goossen, Frederic	506
Gounod, Charles Francois	507-508
Grace, Harvey	509
Graham, Edward Fergus	510-511
Graham Edward Fergus	512
Graham, W. H. J.	513
Grattann, W. H.	514-517
Graves, R. (Ralph Greaves?)	518
Gray, Alan	519
Greaves, Ralph	520-521
Green, Howard Sylvester	522
Gregory, E. C.	523
Groninger, Alma (Chambers)	524-525
Gross, David	526
Grossmann, Gertrude	527
Grosvenor, Norman	528-529
Groton, Frederic Locksley	530
Guerini, R. (Rosa?) nee Wilberforce	531
Guerrini, Guido	532-533
Hadley, Henry Kimball	534
Hadley, Patrick	535-537
Hadow, William Henry	538-539
Ham, Albert	540
Hamilton, E. W.	541
Harding, Joseph R. W.	542
Harper, Robert Sargent	543-544
Harris, Crafton	545-553
Harris, Cuthbert	554
Harris, Floyd O.	555
Harris, J. Thorne	556
Harris, Victor	557-560
Harrison, Julius Allen Greenway	561
Hart, Fritz	562
Hartmann, Emil	563
Hartmann, Thomas Alexandrovitch	564-566
Hasler, John	567
Hatch, Homer Barnes	568

Raphael, Juliet   974
Raphling, Sam   975
Ratcliffe, Desmond   976-977
Rathaus, Karol   978
Rathbone, George   979
Rauscher, Henry, pseudonym of H.   980
     S. Humphreys, q.v.
Raymond, John   981
Rea, William   982
Read, Gardner   983
Reed, Alfred   984-985
Reed, Francis A.   986
Reeves, Boleyne   987-991
Reimann, Aribert   992-996
Reinhardt, Carl   997
Reitz, Edward E.   998
Reiz   999-1000
Respighi, Ottorino   1001-1007
Reynvaan, Marie C. C.   1008-1011
Rhoads, Kenneth Warren   1012
Rhodes, Harold W.   1013
Richards, F. Dewey   1014
Richards, K. L.   1015
Rickman, F. R.   1016
Robbins, Reginald C.   1017-1022
Roberton, Hugh S.   1023
Robinson, Aletha Mae   1024
Robinson, Barbara Lemon   1025
Robinson, Dora   1026
Rochberg, George   1027-1028
Roeder, Martin   1029-1034
Roff, Joseph   1035
Rogers, Bernard   1036
Rogers, W. B.   1037-1038
Rohland, Cora   1039
Ronald, Landon   1040-1042
Rorem, Ned   1043-1046
Rosenfeld, Leopold   1047
Rosenhoff, Orla   1048-1049
Rota, Giuseppe II   1050
Rozycki, Ludomir   1051
Rubbra, Edmund Duncan   1052
Rubinstein, Anton Gregorievich   1053
     (adaptation by D. Rhys Ford)
Rubstein, Ariel Alfred   1054
Russell, John   1055
Rutland, Harold   1056
Sahnow, Will   1057

Speelman, John Robert	1118
Spencer, S. Reid	1119
Spencer, Williametta	1120
Spier, Harry Reginald	1121
Spiro. A.	1122
Spohr, Ludvig	1123
Springer, Norman	1124
Springfield, Tom	1125
Squire, Hope	1126
Stanford, Charles Villiers	1127–1130
Staton John Fredrick	1131
Stebbins, G. Waring	1132
Steinert, Alexander Lang	1133–1135
Stephen, David	1136
Stephenson, Thomas Wilkinson	1137
Stevens, Halsey	1138
Stith, Mrs. Townshend	1139–1140
Stocks, H. C. L.	1141
Stone, David	1142–1143
Storer, John	1144–1151
Strilko, Anthony	1152
Sullivan, Arthur S. (with C. H. H. Parry)	1153
Surette, Tom W.	1154
Sutton, Alfred James	1155–1156
Svedrofsky, Sidney	1157
Sweetman, P. W.	1158
Taneyev, Serge Ivanovitch	1159–1163
Taylor, Francis O.	1164
Tcherepnin, Nikolai	1165–1167
Temmerman, Marcel de	1168–1169
Thatcher, Reginald Sparshott	1170
Theman, Karl George	1171
Thiman, Eric	1172
Thomas, Arthur Goring	1173–1174
Thomas, Mansell	1175
Thomas, Muriel L.	1176
Thompson, Christiana	1177
Thorne, Edward H.	1178
Tiersot, Julien	1179
Tiltman, Henry Thomas	1180
Tippett, Michael	1181
Tollefsen, Augusta	1182
Toms, John R.	1183
Tourtellot, F. B.	1184
Tovey, Donald Francis	1185–1190
Towne, Marian Etta	1191
Trangas, Andreas Mikhail	1192

A Roman's chamber: In the cave which wild weeds cover
       799
A bridal song: The golden gates of Sleep unbar
      395   436
A dirge: Rough wind, that moanest loud
        2   148   162   174   205   315   345   357   386   399
      482   514   543   544   545   583   602   615   625   649
      656   672   674   710   757   779   803   922   943   956
      993 1003 1010 1027 1035 1043 1063 1168 1233 1287
A hate-song: A Hater he came and sat by a ditch
      1258
A lament: O world! O life! O time! (often Dirge)
        6   56   117   150   189   202   232   238   251   339
      423   469   502   522   544   549   574   591   597   601
      603   617   693   742   769   813   819   843   844   880
      884   915   950   954   994   997 1030 1054 1067 1209
     1223 1235 1260
A new national anthem: God prosper, speed, and save
       31
A sensitive plant: A Sensitive Plant in a garden grew
      616   827 1006
A widow bird: A widow bird sate mourning
       11   53   57   59   67   76   124   144   165   188
      196   306   361   366   409   431   471   486   488   502
      509   523   525   531   553   571   584   586   621   642
      660   669   690   713   728   729   749   763   785   805
      806   815   816   823   842   856   881   888   907   911
      972   976   978   985   996 1008 1013 1037 1052 1080
     1087 1093 1107 1126 1143 1158 1182 1190 1191 1195
     1196 1227 1239 1243 1248 1264 1273 1282 1295
Adonais
      260   311   405 1036 1040 1068 1303
Alastor
      350   882 1089
Arethusa: Arethusa arose
       77   177   298   341   505   519   921 1002
Autumn (A dirge): The warm sun is failing
       13   174   649   675   686   807   993 1099 1127 1149
     1168 1279 1289
Buona notte: 'Buona notte, buona notte!'--Come mai
      1208
Death: Death is here and death is there
      325
Dirge for the year: Orphan Hours, the Year is dead
       52   318   615
Epigrams (To Stella, from the Greek of Plato): Thou
      wert the morning star among the living

909
Good-night? ah! no; the hour is ill
```
      22    113    145    172    290    295    299    310    334    422
     438    453    466    508    592    595    678    689    746    797
     850    853    873    903    913    970    998   1016   1041   1061
    1065   1119   1122   1123   1139   1192   1236   1284   1297
```
Hellas
```
     129    277    536    692    849   1088   1179   1203   1207   1211
```
Homer's hymn to the moon: Daughters of Jove, whose
    voice is melody
    1193
Hymn of Apollo: The sleepless Hours who watch me as
    I lie
    60 1029
Hymn of Pan: From the forests and highlands
```
      79    216    331    564   1033   1096
```
Indian serenade: I arise from dreams of thee
```
       1     24     46     71     96     99    103    110    120    128
     133    152    156    161    178    185    209    215    235    240
     242    245    250    267    278    286    289    320    328    367
     381    389    394    419    432    448    454    458    459    461
     464    468    479    494    513    515    518    520    534    548
     565    568    573    582    593    598    600    607    620    632
     634    646    652    655    662    684    685    687    703    715
     716    720    724    750    754    760    764    774    804    808
     810    822    825    828    830    831    835    851    854    858
     862    863    864    871    874    883    890    893    910    920
     926    928    929    930    931    933    941    964    982    989
     997   1000   1005   1012   1014   1015   1024   1039   1058   1060
    1064   1074   1082   1095   1101   1115   1121   1124   1132   1138
    1141   1154   1156   1172   1177   1184   1186   1200   1210   1212
    1221   1226   1237   1241   1249   1257   1268   1275   1280   1305
```
Laon and Cythna: It seemed that in the dreary night
    (VII, 23)
    342
Liberty: The fiery mountains answer each other
    1216
Lines: That time is dead for ever, child!
    643   819
Lines: The cold earth slept below
```
     207    707    872    987   1152
```
Lines: When the lamp is shattered
```
      34    109    206    212    255    282    296    578    611    702
     942   1189
```
Love's philosophy: The fountains mingle with the river
```
       3     23     55     62     75     90    114    125    137    164
     175    179    191    194    227    234    241    249    265    273
     283    288    293    321    323    329    333    358    368    382
```

```
404   412   424   433   437   449   477   484   496   507
529   542   557   572   581   587   633   651   681   699
700   733   736   747   759   767   788   793   794   802
866   892   894   895   905   906   955   966   975  1026
1031  1038  1042  1048  1059  1070  1086  1090  1105  1108
1125  1140  1151  1230  1231  1232  1238  1307  1308
```

Matilda gathering flowers: And earnest to explore
    within--around
    380
Music: I pant for the music which is divine
    343   446   497   653   945   965   979 1181 1270
Mutability: The flower that smiles to-day
    15   50   78   139   149   231   264   377   387   451
    483   498   637   654   829   834   869 1144
Mutability: We are as clouds that veil the midnight
    moon
    201   661
Ode to the west wind: O wild West Wind, thou breath
    of Autumn's being
    45   48   92   268   373   585   667   706 1019 1292
On Fanny Godwin: Her voice did quiver as we parted
    457   551 1009
On a faded violet: The odour (earlier "colour") from
    the flower is gone
    49   140   183   327   336   397   440   452   456   490
    530   589   590   630   778   780   809   840   857   861
    925   939 1007 1079 1162 1178 1197
On death: The pale, the cold, and the moony smile
    (stanza 2)
    1202
Original Poetry by Victor and Cazire (no. 6, Song--Sorrow):
    To me this world's a dreary blank
    383
Ozymandias: I met a traveller from an antique land
    54   74   83   176   221   225   407   475   501   527
    682   958 1020 1133 1194 1254
Prometheus Unbound (opera, cantata, or orchestral
    music for one or more scenes or incidental music)
    91   199   332   631   737   916 1062
Prometheus Unbound: Child of Ocean (II, i, 1.170)
    346   855
Prometheus Unbound: From unremembered ages we (I,
    1.672)
    210 1251
Prometheus Unbound: Here, oh, here (IV, 1.9)
    345
Prometheus Unbound: Life of Life, thy lips enkindle
    (II, v, 48)

To Ianthe: I love thee, Baby! for thine own sake
    415
To Jane (The invitation): Best and brightest, come
    away
    379   472 1018
To Jane (The recollection): Now the last day of many
    days
    41   272   485   712   732   938 1214 1294
To Jane: The keen stars were twinkling
    28   119   130   136   155   192   259   284   372   435
    445   569   622   664   717   755   766   789   839   967
    986 1022 1083 1173 1266 1288
To Mary Shelley: The world is dreary
    491 1011
To Mary: O Mary dear, that you were here
    27   170   233   495   824 1246
To Sophia: Thou art fair, and few are fairer
    8 1277
To ---- (pub. 1839): Yet look on me--take not thine
    eyes away
    629
To ---- (1821): Music, when soft voices die
    4   7   9   21   25   51   64   72   80   97
    112   116   118   127   138   151   153   167   186   187
    197   211   219   223   224   228   236   239   243   247
    248   253   261   266   271   274   275   300   301   303
    304   305   319   326   337   340   359   360   365   371
    388   391   392   401   402   406   463   467   470   478
    503   521   524   528   533   539   540   550   554   555
    558   559   560   561   579   588   594   599   605   614
    619   623   635   641   644   645   648   659   666   673
    677   691   694   695   696   701   705   709   711   714
    722   725   735   739   740   745   748   756   761   770
    777   783   790   796   811   826   837   838   841   846
    848   859   877   904   914   934   935   946   957   968
    974   984 1023 1025 1084 1097 1102 1111 1112 1113
    1114 1120 1137 1147 1161 1164 1170 1176 1180 1183
    1187 1198 1217 1224 1225 1240 1255 1256 1271 1274
    1276 1278 1291 1298 1304
To ----: I fear thy kisses, gentle maiden
    12   58   121   135   147   159   163   190   193   230
    312   439   460   489   547   618   676   683   698   726
    878   886   900   944 1055 1066 1072 1146 1185
To ----: Oh! there are spirits of the air
    960
To ----: When passion's trance is overpast
    107   141   430   476   833   901 1247 1272 1283
To a skylark: Hail to thee, blithe Spirit!

A Hater he came and sat by a ditch
   1258
A Sensitive Plant in a garden grew
   616   827 1006
A widow bird sate mourning
     11   53   57   59   67   76   124   144   165   188
    196   306   361   366   409   431   471   486   488   502
    509   523   525   531   553   571   584   586   621   642
    660   669   690   713   728   729   749   763   785   805
    806   815   816   823   842   856   881   888   907   911
    972   976   978   985   996 1008 1013 1037 1052 1080
   1087 1093 1107 1126 1143 1158 1182 1190 1191 1195
   1196 1227 1239 1243 1248 1264 1273 1282 1295
And earnest to explore within--around
   380
And like a dying lady, lean and pale
   123   252   287   552   596   953 1135
Arethusa arose
    77   177   298   341   505   519   921 1002
Art thou pale for weariness
    19   66   160   171   263   287   375   413   688   718
   719   801   860   876   896 1056 1188 1281
As I lay asleep in Italy (1.147)
   218   680
As one enamoured is upborne in dream (line 367)
   516
Away! the moor is dark beneath the moon
   1296
Behold! Spring sweeps over the world again (IX, xxi,
   3653)
   349
Best and brightest, come away
   379   472 1018
Bright wanderer, fair coquette of heaven
    33   169   784
'Buona notte, buona notte!'--Come mai
   1208
Child of Ocean (II, i, 1.170)
   346   855
Daughters of Jove, whose voice is melody
   1193
Death is here and death is there
   325
False friend, wilt thou smile or weep (Beatrice's
   song)
   314   465   535   626   868   927   973 1155 1199
Follow to the deep wood's weeds

885
From the forests and highlands
    79   216   331   564 1033 1096
From unremembered ages we (I, 1.672)
    210 1251
God prosper, speed, and save
    31
Hail to thee, blithe Spirit!
    26   70   132   217   292   351   604   776   821   983
  1081 1174
Hark! whence that rushing sound? (I, 1.45)
    101
He came like a dream in the dawn of life
    61   202   847 1265
Her voice did quiver as we parted
    457   551 1009
Here, oh, here (IV, 1.9)
    345
How beautiful this night (IV, ii, 1)
    237   418   627   697
How eloquent are eyes!
   1234
How stern are the woes of the desolate mourner (St.
    Irvyne, ch. 9)
    510
How swiftly through Heaven's wide expanse (St. Irvyne,
    ch. 7)
    511
How wonderful is Death
   1267
I am as a spirit who has dwelt
   1069
I am drunk with the honey wine
    87   455   977 1045 1252
I arise from dreams of thee
     1   24   46   71   96   99   103   110   120   128
   133   152   156   161   178   185   209   215   235   240
   242   245   250   267   278   286   289   320   328   367
   381   389   394   419   432   448   454   458   459   461
   464   468   479   494   513   515   518   520   534   548
   565   568   573   582   593   598   600   607   620   632
   634   646   652   655   662   684   685   687   703   715
   716   720   724   750   754   760   764   774   804   808
   810   822   825   828   830   831   835   851   854   858
   862   863   864   871   874   883   890   893   910   920
   926   928   929   930   931   933   941   964   982   989
   997 1000 1005 1012 1014 1015 1024 1039 1058 1060
  1064 1074 1082 1095 1101 1115 1121 1124 1132 1138

That time is dead for ever, child!
      643   819
The cold earth slept below
      207   707   872   987 1152
The fiery mountains answer each other
      1216
The flower that smiles to-day
       15   50   78   139   149   231   264   377   387   451
      483   498   637   654   829   834   869   1144
The fountains mingle with the river
        3   23   55   62   75   90   114   125   137   164
      175   179   191   194   227   234   241   249   265   273
      283   288   293   321   323   329   333   358   368   382
      404   412   424   433   437   449   477   484   496   507
      529   542   557   572   581   587   633   651   681   699
      700   733   736   747   759   767   788   793   794   802
      866   892   894   895   905   906   955   966   975   1026
     1031   1038   1042   1048   1059   1070   1086   1090   1105   1108
     1125   1140   1151   1230   1231   1232   1238   1307   1308
The golden gates of Sleep unbar
      395   436
The keen stars were twinkling
       28   119   130   136   155   192   259   284   372   435
      445   569   622   664   717   755   766   789   839   967
      986   1022   1083   1173   1266   1288
The odour (earlier "colour") from the flower is gone
       49   140   183   327   336   397   440   452   456   490
      530   589   590   630   778   780   809   840   857   861
      925   939   1007   1079   1162   1178   1197
The pale stars are gone (IV, 1.1)
       10   331
The pale, the cold, and the mocny smile (stanza 2)
      1202
The path through which that lovely twain (II, ii,
       1)
      115
The point of one white star is quivering still (II, i)
      1262
The rude wind is singing
      949
The sleepless Hours who watch me as I lie
       60   1029
The sun is set; the swallows are asleep
      426   658
The sun is warm, the sky is clear
      384   845   1017
The warm sun is failing
       13   174   649   675   686   807   993   1099   1127   1149

1168 1279 1289
The waters are flashing
    577   668   988 1076
The world is dreary
    491 1011
There late was One within whose subtle being
    400 1004
There was a little lawny islet
    316   403   420   427   493   820   889   971 1159 1259
    1262 1269 1290
Thou art fair, and few are fairer
      8 1277
Thou wert the morning star among the living
    443
Thy words are sweeter than aught else but his (II,
    v)
    1245
To me this world's a dreary blank
    383
To suffer woes which Hope thinks infinite (IV, 1.570)
    270   474   731 1201 1205 1286
To-whoo! To-whoo! near, nearer now (scene 2)
    421
Tremble, Kings despised of man
    512
Unfathomable Sea! whose waves are years
    111   369   425   473   532   566   721   741   765   772
    773   803   951 1001 1148 1262 1263
Wake the serpent not--lest he
     85   800
We are as clouds that veil the midnight moon
    201   661
Weave the dance on the floor of the breeze (IV)
    276   277   738
When passion's trance is overpast
    107   141   430   476   833   901 1247 1272 1283
When soft winds and sunny skies
     18   32   546 1085
When the lamp is shattered
     34   109   206   212   255   282   296   578   611   702
    942 1189
When winds that move not its calm surface sweep
    1293
Where art thou, beloved To-morrow?
     36   95   353   363   429 1103 1150
Wild, pale, and wonder-stricken, even as one
    909
Wilt thou forget the happy hours

```
1810:    510    511
1811:    512
1819:    874
1822:    715
1830:   1140
1833:    766   1309
1834:    100    101    102    103    104    105    106    107   1139
1835:   1139
1836:    921    924    925    927
1836-1841:      923
1837:    100    143
1839:    377
1839-1841:      922    926
1841:    779
1844:    378    589    750    780    781   1123
1845:     22     99    313    314    315    316    317    318    989
1846:    129    130    131    497
1847:     94     95    157    239    319    816
1848:    780    781    959    960    961   1123
1849:    276    277    931    932
1850:    382    507    516    810    812    814    848   1109
1851:   1037   1038
1852:    514    517    768   1076
1854:    133    782    846
1855:    156    412    515    556    869
1856:    494    997
1857:    156    498    815    834
1858:    435    438    439    440    441    815   1155   1156   1249
1859:     49     52    347    498    542    634    689
1860:    109    146    315    887   1065
1861:    303    341    343    345    346    496    635    903    988
1862:    349   1050
1863:    128    218    344    348    353    495
1864:    342
1865:    350    865
1866:     46    307    513   1058   1059   1153   1209   1236
1867:     63    351    352    423    597    653    815    902    939
        1211
1868:    636    832    982   1058   1153
1869:    186    393   1292
187-:    244
1870:     27     76    541    915   1155   1156
1871:     26    507    508   1285
1872:    740    872    873   1089
1873:    914
1874:    363    508    829    911
1875:    831    875    876
1876:     59    312    313    578    778    810    812    814    973
        1178
```

1877:	6	100	101	102	103	104	105	106	107
	108	570	828	1250					
1878:	50	490	870	1106					
1879:	147	531	570	741	1073				
188-:	894								
1880:	916	933							
1881:	180	181	438	515	1072	1154	1209		
1882:	422	788	1115	1144	1173	1246	1247		
1883:	61	64	442	490	523	655	850	1245	
1884:	539	1197							
1885:	434	435	436	438	439	440	441	776	913
	1177	1284							
1886:	119	134	135	136	137	138	139	140	141
	142	146	443	681	705	868	909	972	1088
	1122								
1887:	179	379	654	700	716	852	908	986	1096
	1145	1146	1147	1148	1149	1150	1151		
1888:	29	31	444	445	446	447	448	449	450
	451	452	453	456	457	458	491	634	636
	680	760	761	762	763	806	853	900	910
	1102	1103	1104	1247	1248				
1889:	264	298	576	584	676	795	856	970	
1890:	557	1029	1033	1090	1091	1092	1212	1253	
1891:	155	167	289	505	579	729	793		
1892:	29	31	262	288	293	328	329	330	432
	519	677	680	763	807	833	1031	1032	1034
1893:	8	90	113	119	245	433	434	502	615
	809	909	1070	1232					
1894:	214	215	216	217	534	806	849	928	1066
	1174	1228	1302						
1895:	120	213	408	409	410	469	485	558	560
	657	747	748	749	808	819	1039		
1896:	336	438	587	730	763	971	1165	1220	1295
1897:	29	31	604	680	914	1071	1179	1297	
1898:	24	231	260	486	563	571	594	774	1042
1899:	284	478	484	528	529	577	642	758	764
	765	857	1026	1030	1080	1095			
1900:	172	173	190	191	271	272	333	334	425
	817	893	1042	1184	1283				
1901:	209	424	890	1110					
1902:	114	116	187	273	437	528	669	733	759
	889	1014	1058	1087					
1903:	71	88	240	247	286	687	830	840	841
	842	843	844	863	895	1040	1117		
1904:	7	117	118	372	468	559	794	883	1256
1905:	40	41	42	43	44	185	210	392	562
	633	835	966	1058	1081	1185	1186	1187	1188
	1189	1190	1239	1265	1288	1294			
1906:	188	459	466	616	627	632	806	867	1184

```
            1218 1244 1307
1906-1909: 1062
1907:   178  261  299  386  387  388  732  854  884
        892  907  955 1008 1009 1010 1011 1132 1196
       1230 1235 1238 1254
1908:    58   81   85   96  124  162  163  164  227
        267  373  424  470  527  593  602  603  637
        638  736  763  827  955 1082 1083 1200 1219
       1291
1909:    82   84   85   87  310  319  334  390  419
        464  592  678  728  775  858  905 1013 1064
       1233
1910:   161  168  169  170  232  233  295  328  329
        330  380  389  477  499  567  605  742  888
       1058 1061 1241
1911:   115  322  340  374  417  420  628  962 1002
       1041 1042 1085 1128 1129 1257 1279 1288
1912:    68   80  193  195  285  339  418  509  537
        538  703  790  880  881  912  938 1004 1005
       1016 1170 1218 1234
1913:    21  297  323  375  404  421  561  569  607
        608  609  701  702  707  708  751  752  755
        756  757  886  913 1237 1257 1264 1291 1293
       1298 1306
1914:   107  256  257  258  308  326  327  365  366
        620  809  822  878 1127 1299 1305
1915:   385  402  472  696 1097
1916:   463  601  724  731 1113 1137 1291
1917:    60  220  461  600  645  725 1194 1195 1221
       1300
1918:   246 1001 1003 1004
1919:    75  127  198  230  248  621  726 1007 1119
       1262
1920:   219  243  362  371  376  460  473  474  671
        915  954 1058 1184
1921:   278  428  554  572  573  667  672  674  683
        787 1078 1079
1921-23 :  92   93
1922:    79  112  153  154  192  427  430  540  657
        667  685  882  885  956  971 1180 1242 1259
       1263 1264 1278
1923:   375  824  913  966 1002 1056 1087 1261 1290
1924:     2   69   83  111  196  234  414  415  416
        426  429  431  686  690  691  709  820  945
        949  950  951  952  953  958  966 1006 1121
       1210 1243 1258 1289
1925:   126  158  182  250  454  455  522  536  590
        611  612  613  658  664  665  666  867 1015
       1036 1199
```

```
1926:     97   177   243   465   724   725   919  1180  1255
        1277
1927:     77   395   396   397   413   546   914   963   968
         974  1023  1051  1107  1217  1269  1271  1273
1928:      9    20   175   222   697   714   799   800   836
         837   998  1017  1018  1019  1020  1021  1022  1180
        1252  1260  1267  1268  1270  1304
1929:     72    73   399   400   545   547   549   550   551
         552   553   675   679   745   797   798   823   979
        1004  1136
193-:    121   698   699
1930:    238   568   651   777   789   929   937  1138  1266
        1272
1931:    152   520   521   536   882   964  1052  1251
1932:     81    86   235   367   588   755   756   826   838
         930  1087  1133  1134  1135  1168  1169
1933:    291   292   394   656   897  1227
1934:    241   477   855  1226
1935:    174   335   475   767  1074  1112  1114  1131  1231
1936:     16    91   148   274   280   281   282   359   564
         565   566   649   650   693   744  1051  1093  1175
1937:     89   132   265   266   479   618   659  1053  1108
1937-44  :     199
1938:     78   296   305   598   599   617   646   660   719
        1054  1126
1939:    236   311   320   467   471   643   899   971   983
        1198
1940:    189   226   275   302   614   792   821   879   901
        1060  1182  1202  1203  1204  1205  1206  1207
1940-55  :     279
1941:     98   489   543   544   946   949  1017  1025  1067
1942:    212   397   596   648   652   737   738   944  1157
        1195
1943:     71   398   403   720   866   940  1012  1141  1164
        1182  1192  1275  1276
1944:    294   337   596
1945:    739   847  1171  1193
1945-1909: 1063
1946:    242   263   338   391   662   713   862   984   985
1947:     25    55    56    57    84   151   243   259   369
         480   481   482   483   586   595   606   644   692
         725   877   898   957   969   971  1159  1160  1161
        1162  1163
1948:    110   125   332   532   533   548   591   695   721
         722   735   965   967  1098  1124
1949:    381   555   934   978  1100  1208
195-:    200
1950:    306   506   839   861   999  1172
1951:     23    32    33    34    35    36    37    38    39
```

```
               47   224   253   504   535   694   704   805   976
              977  1118  1176
1952:         123   361   684   718  1000  1024  1069  1084  1094
             1105  1111  1210
1953:          74   176   360   364   657   710   717   773   796
             1052  1201
1953-54   :    70
1954:          10    11    12    13    14    15    16    17    18
               19    48   160   251   252   269   331   668  1101
             1191
1955:         159   166   241   249   254   255   506   585   629
              941   971  1068
1956:          45   223   325   411   998  1043  1044  1045
1956-60   :   171
1957:         501   630   942   947   948
1958:          74   406   626  1120
1959:         734   896   935
1960:          28   229   270   360   361   488   574   582   583
             1142  1143  1181
1961:         237   725  1046  1291
1962:         268   354   906  1158
1963:         202   208   287   503   706   769   770   771   772
              871  1152
1964:         207   300   647   754   859   981  1086  1286
1965:         723   992   993   994   995   996
1966:         144   228   623   625   641   818
1967:         203   205   225   324   405   407   503   622   624
              661   712  1035
1968:         165   975  1099  1225
1969:          65    66    67   221   328   329   330   358   401
              526   845   860   891  1027  1028  1055  1125  1223
             1224
1970:         204   206   290   357   682  1214
1971:         201   487  1215
```

Danish
   563   580   581   610 1047 1048 1049 1091 1092
Dutch
  1008 1009 1010 1011
Finnish
   851
French
   219   460   602   603   931   932   971 1169 1199 1247
German
    87   146   208   209   328   329   330   413   571   602
   603   670   764   765   773   783   784   785   786   803
   804   851   856   857   922   926   966   971   993   994
   995   996 1002 1006 1029 1032 1033 1076 1091 1092
  1165 1166 1167 1185 1186 1187 1188 1189 1190 1212
  1213 1247 1254 1257
Greek
   692
Italian
   250   399   400   467   476   480   481   482   483   532
   533   822 1001 1002 1003 1004 1005 1006 1007 1208
  1247
Russian
   168   169   170   387   388   493   690   691   727   783
   784   785   786   820   885   889   971 1122 1160 1161
  1162 1163 1165 1166 1167 1308
Spanish
   487
Swedish
   403   737   738 1253
Welsh
   668   835 1141 1175 1176 1275 1276